CW00671193

Discover
Yorkshire's
Wildlife

Your guide to Yorkshire Wildlife Trust's nature reserves

Discover Yorkshire's Wildlife

Designed by Sally Gregory and Sarah Shipley at Yorkshire Wildlife Trust.

This first edition printed 2023.
First paperback edition printed 2023 in the United Kingdom.
A catalogue record for this book is available from the British Library.

ISBN 978-0-9509460-8-5

Published by Yorkshire Wildlife Trust.

For more copies of this book, please email info@ywt.org.uk
or call 01904 659570.

Although every precaution has been taken in the preparation of this book,
the publisher and authors assume no responsibility for errors or omissions.
Neither is any liability assumed for damages resulting from the use of
information contained herein.

The production of this book has been generously supported by
Croda International PLC and the players of the People's Postcode Lottery.

Supported by players of   Awarded funds from

Contents

Wild, Wilder, Wildest Yorkshire

How, where and when to enjoy the best of Yorkshire's wildlife

Now then. If you love wildlife and wild places, you're in the right place – Yorkshire.

Whether it's a close encounter with puffins on spectacular white cliffs, multicolour meadows buzzing with bees and brimful of butterflies, or wondrous wetlands welcoming wintering wildfowl and waders in their thousands, our grand and glorious part of the world is a cracking place to experience nature at its best.

Don't just take our word for it, though. Get out there and discover it for yourself. Wherever you are in Yorkshire, there's a Yorkshire Wildlife Trust nature reserve nearby – usually within 20 miles – just waiting to be explored.

This book is a trusty sidekick on your wild, wilder and wildest Yorkshire wildlife adventures, taking you up hill and down dale, around lakes and lagoons, through woods and fields, and along the coast in search of creatures great and small.

Peruse it with a brew, carry it in your rucksack, skim through it or read every word... it's up to you how you use it, but we've tried to make it as easy as possible for you to find what you're looking for, both within these pages and out there in our wild and wonderful world.

Soak up some seasonal highlights, find out where's best for the creatures and features you're seeking, take inspiration from some of our favourite walks around the region, and get stuck into our A-Z reserve guide.

So off you go – explore the book, explore Yorkshire, and experience the sights, sounds and spectacles of our magnificent wildlife.

Limestone pavement in the Yorkshire Dale

We're all part of something **bigger...**

Yorkshire Wildlife Trust is part of The Wildlife Trusts – a movement of people from a wide range of backgrounds and all walks of life who believe that we need nature and nature needs us.

The **Wildlife** Trusts

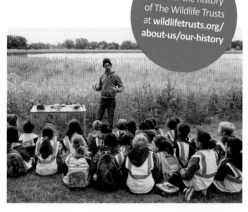

Uncover the history of The Wildlife Trusts at **wildlifetrusts.org/about-us/our-history**

We're one of 46 individual Wildlife Trusts, each a place-based independent charity with its own legal identity. We're formed by groups of people getting together and working with others to make a positive difference to wildlife and future generations, starting where we live and work.

Every Wildlife Trust is part of The Wildlife Trusts federation, a corporate member of the Royal Society of Wildlife Trusts (a registered charity in its own right, founded in 1912) and one of the founding members of IUCN – the International Union for the Conservation of Nature. All together that makes a federation of 47 charities, collectively known as The Wildlife Trusts.

Our purpose is to bring wildlife back, to empower people to take meaningful action for nature, and to create an inclusive society where nature matters.

Our vision is of a thriving natural world, with our wildlife and natural habitats playing a valued role in addressing the climate and ecological emergencies, and everyone inspired to get involved in nature's recovery.

Welcome from Rachael Bice
Chief Executive

Yorkshire is an amazing place. Even the quickest skim through this book reveals an astounding wealth and variety of wild places, and they're all right here, waiting to be discovered throughout the changing seasons.

Yorkshire's scale and diverse landscapes mean we are blessed with an incredible variety of wildlife. We are delighted to own and manage some critical reserves for nature – both resident and passing through on migration – across this wonderful county.

We are one of England's largest Wildlife Trusts, working alongside Sheffield and Rotherham Wildlife Trust. Together we represent a significant group of professional staff and volunteers all dedicated to helping our wildlife survive and thrive through the considerable climate and ecological challenges we all face.

Yorkshire Wildlife Trust was founded in 1946 but our work today is more important than ever. During the many years in which we have been caring for Yorkshire's wildlife, there have been

Skylark

North Cave Wetlands

many successes, but the overall outlook for wildlife has become more perilous.

One of the most visible signs of our changing climate is the spread of some wetland bird species from southern Europe, as they search for suitable habitats. The way we manage our wetlands is crucial, both for these new arrivals and for the species that already depend on them.

Just as our wetlands need restoring, protecting and improving, so do our depleted peatlands and uplands. Find out more about our peat restoration work and ambitious, landscape-scale Wild Ingleborough vision on pages 14 and 18.

There are constant threats to our wonderfully rich coastal waters, which are a vital habitat both for the marvellous maritime creatures that live in them and those that feed on them. Take a dive into our marine and coastal work on page 16.

We manage these incredible wild places and sensitive ecosystems for people as well as for wildlife. After all, we are part of nature, not separate from it. All species need healthy, vibrant living systems to inhabit. We look after some of

Butterflies feeding

our wildest places, but our ambition is for everyone, everywhere to have some way to experience the elements, and remain in tune with our animal senses to enrich our human lives.

Taking time to be still to watch and encounter wildlife, even for just ten minutes, also allows our fellow species to encounter us – that is when the magic happens. One of our members summed this up brilliantly when she took part in one of our nature-surveying activities:

"There is an ebb and a flow about wildlife. There were busy times and quiet times, and I could see how reactive nature is to things in the weather that we don't even notice. Even if you're looking at a flower bed for 15 minutes in your lunch break, it still gives you that little mental pick-me-up if you see something beautiful in a bloom or a butterfly."

We live in a time of big challenges. One of the best ways to find the resilience to face them, is to marvel at the small things that lift our hearts alongside seasonal continuity. And in small things we can trust, as many little actions can make a big difference for wildlife, and for us.

Please enjoy exploring Yorkshire, where we hope our work enhances your experiences.

Welcome from Professor Sir John Lawton CBE FRS President

Wherever we are in Yorkshire and whatever the season, we can always find delight in the abundant and diverse wildlife of God's own country.

By way of introduction, take just two black and white birds.

On the towering white cliffs between Bempton and Flamborough, a seabird city teems with activity. It's a spectacular scene. Above the North Sea and its seals, dolphins and porpoises, thousands of birds are nesting on precarious perches, in a flat-out feeding frenzy as frazzled parents fly back and forth to meet the demands of their squawking chicks. This is the only major sea-bird colony in Europe that you can drive up to! Among the kittiwakes, razorbills and guillemots are one of our best-loved and most instantly recognisable seabirds – puffins. There is nowhere in mainland Britain where you can enjoy better views of these appealing and slightly comical black-and-white birds with their

Flamborough's puffins

bright orange legs and webbed feet, and chunky, colourful blue, red and yellow bills.

At the same time, on a muddy pool in urban Doncaster, surrounded by busy roads, a railway and industrial development, Potteric Carr is hosting the town's most famous fab four since the Beatles played at Gaumont Cinema. Four black-winged stilt chicks have hatched and are teetering around on spindly legs, guarded fiercely by their black-and-white parents, with ridiculously long pink legs. They are the first of their species ever to breed in the north of England, as they spread north from southern Europe (a clear sign of the climate crisis). Around them, dragonflies are darting and the more delicate damselflies flit among the plants on the lagoon fringes. A bittern booms in a nearby reedbed, while the water conceals frogs, toads, newts, and a banquet of invertebrates for the stilts and other wading birds to feast on.

But is this what we mean when we talk about enjoying the 'best' of Yorkshire's wildlife? Well, yes and no.

All of Yorkshire's wildlife is wonderful and vital in its own way, from tiny micro moths known only by their scientific names to

Common darter

specialist entomologists, to the minke (and other) whales that increasingly grace our beautiful coastal waters. Even aphids (greenflies to most of us – and not universally loved!) have a crucial role to play as part of the food chains that support some of our favourite creatures, including ladybirds, blue tits and swifts. And you don't get hedgehogs without beetles and worms for them to feed on.

Beauty of course is in the eye of the beholder, but nature is rarely dull. So, I urge you to get out and enjoy the rich variety that Yorkshire has to offer – species that might be new to you, or familiar friends; paths you've trodden many times before, or those you're yet to find.

The more time we spend in nature and the more we look, the more we find and the more we learn. A springtime ramble in a magnesian limestone valley might reveal a rare purple pasqueflower; a scuttling hermit crab on the bed of a rockpool can enrich summer days by the sea; and the whistling of wigeon on a wetland creates an evocative winter soundtrack.

These experiences are priceless. I hope this book inspires you to seek them out for yourself and discover what the best of Yorkshire's wildlife means for you.

Common frog

Help create a
Wilder Yorkshire.
Join us today!

Our members are wildlife heroes. They help us to bring species back from the brink of extinction, to give wildlife a powerful voice in government and to inspire and enable people all over Yorkshire to enjoy and take action for a wilder future.

Will you join them? Visit ywt.org.uk/membership or call us on **01904 659570** to discover the great benefits of being a member and get your welcome pack on its way!

From tiny acorns...

For more than three quarters of a century, Yorkshire Wildlife Trust has brought together people who wish to see Yorkshire's wildlife and wild places protected and restored.

We began life as the Yorkshire Naturalists' Trust in 1946, formed by the chocolatiers Sir Francis Terry and Arnold Rowntree to receive their gift of Askham Bog, a site much-beloved by York's naturalist community and purchased for preservation with the support of some of the city's most influential figures, including the Lord Mayor J.B. Morrell.

By the following year, we'd set up an office at the Yorkshire Museum, welcomed 94 ordinary members and 76 life members, and resolved to establish and maintain wildlife sanctuaries all over Yorkshire.

Today, we care for well over 100 nature reserves, most of which are in this book, and rely on the generous support of over 45,000 passionate members.

> "The acquisition of this Sanctuary is regarded as a first step only, as it is hoped that other suitable areas in Yorkshire will come into the hands of the Trust"
>
> *Sir Francis Terry, August 1946*

Conservation volunteers at Moorlands in 1964

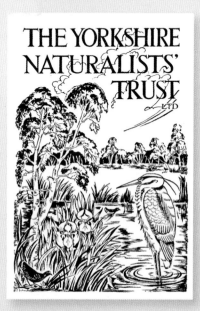

THE YORKSHIRE NATURALISTS' TRUST LTD

70th celebrations at Askham Bog

1955   We acquire our second reserve, Moorlands, for just £500.

1956   Our HQ moves to Coppergate, York.

1959   Despite concerns that the sea would claim the land, we take possession of Spurn. Our gamble paid off – Spurn was designated as a NNR in 1996 and remains one of our most iconic reserves!

1964   We become a charity and acquire our first 'geological' reserve, Rifle Butts Quarry.

1965   We employ our first member of staff – an admin officer to take care of the paperwork and drive membership growth.

1967   With 17 reserves now in our care, we establish a bigger HQ at Clifford Chambers, York. A determined campaign prevents the York outer ring road being put straight through Askham Bog!

1969   We produce our first feature film, *'The Spider's Web'*. You can watch it at yfanefa.com/record/7797

1971   Our Silver Jubilee year. We run a hugely successful appeal and raise £55k to acquire Wheldrake Ings. This also gains us 1,000 new members! Low Ellers (now Potteric Carr) was threatened by the construction of the M18, but our hard-fought campaign averted disaster.

1972   HQ moves to Castlegate, York.

1973   We appoint our first 'field officer' to help with reserve management and campaigning on major conservation issues.

1978   We formed the Yorkshire WATCH Club to engage budding young naturalists.

1980   44 reserves are now in our care. We're supported by over 6,000 members.

1983   Our name changes from the Yorkshire Naturalists' Trust to Yorkshire Wildlife Trust.

1985   We employ our first education officer. HQ moves to Toft Green, York, and we buy our first computer!

1986   The Living Churchyards project is launched, and we prevent damage to the River Derwent in a landmark lawsuit.

1988   Corporate membership is launched. By the following year, we have 70 companies backing us.

1995   Yorkshire Electricity sponsors a TV advert, which helps us attract 1,200 members and 24 corporate supporters.

1996   We celebrated our Golden Jubilee with two big legal victories over quarrying in the Dales and the preservation of a historic hedgerow in Flamborough.

2006   HQ moves to St. George's Place, York.

2016   We celebrate our 70th birthday with a visit from Sir David Attenborough.

2020   We save Askham Bog from development in a high-profile court case.

Yorkshire Peat Partnership

Until a government ban on horticultural peat in 2022, many people only knew of peat because it was in sacks of garden compost. This was a sad end for an incredibly important and terribly depleted natural material that belongs in a bog, not a bag.

Peat forms in wet conditions and is the accumulation of layers and layers of slowly decomposing plants, which gradually turn into a sort of organic soil. Sphagnum moss plays a unique role in forming peat. It grows toward the light and, as it grows, the lower, shaded parts

Sphagnum moss

die. Because of the anaerobic, acidic conditions in a bog, the dead moss doesn't break down fully and becomes peat over thousands of years. This means it doesn't release its carbon (part of the structure of all living things) into the atmosphere – it's trapped within the land and only released if the peatland is disturbed.

Yorkshire Peat Partnership is restoring peatlands in the Yorkshire Dales and North York Moors National Parks and Nidderdale Area of Outstanding Natural Beauty. We work in a peatland habitat called blanket bog, which depends on rain, snow, hail and fog for all of its nutrients. In England, it forms in the uplands above 200 metres.

Yorkshire's blanket bog is a beautiful and

Cottongrass on Fleet Moss

extraordinary habitat: a haven for wildlife; a wild place to unwind; a natural flood defence; a filter for our drinking water; a climate safe locking up millennia of carbon. Sadly, around 80% of it has been dried out – by drainage channels called grips – and damaged through historical management practices. Healthy blanket bog supports breeding waders like curlew and golden plover; short-eared owl quarter the ground with distinctive rowing wingbeats on the hunt for field voles; common lizards scurry through the vegetation; hummocks and carpets of sphagnum mosses form a multi-coloured mosaic dotted with bobbing cottongrass, the carnivorous sundew, and dwarf shrub like crowberry, bilberry and cranberry.

Common lizard

Across our operational area, there are almost 93,000 hectares of blanket bog; and by March 2022, we had brought around 41,500 hectares into restoration management. This is a long-term, step-by-step process:

■ We carry out detailed surveys to assess the

extent of the damage and, crucially, how water is moving across and through the peatland.

■ Once we have an understanding of the site, our first goal is to correct the hydrology. Blocking drainage channels helps to slow the flow of water, helping reduce flood risk downstream, and bringing the water table closer to the surface. This is vital for peat formation and re-establishing bog vegetation.

■ We then address any bare peat, initially by establishing plants to cover and stabilise the peat. We use cut heather stalks, upland grass seed and dwarf shrubs to cover the bare ground. Once this vegetation has taken root, we look to plant sphagnum moss and cottongrass – two blanket bog species vital to peat growth.

Our vision is of a Yorkshire where fully restored peatlands are home to amazing wildlife, and are valued for storing carbon, managing flooding and providing clean water. Our goal is to rewet, replant and restore all of Yorkshire's upland peatlands by March 2035. As partners in the Great North Bog, we're working with other peatland restoration partnerships and universities to pioneer new techniques that will improve restoration across the north of England. **www.yppartnership.org.uk**

Giving Seas a Chance

The wild and beautiful waters of the North Sea provide a hidden home for some of Yorkshire's most extraordinary wildlife.

Most of us experience the sea from the shore or clifftop, enjoying the beautiful views or having a look in the rockpools, but Yorkshire's coastline stretches for 94 miles and our 'territorial' limit extends 12 nautical miles out to sea. Our sea and shoreline are home to wildlife of national and European importance. Here you'll find edible crabs and European lobster, minke whales and harbour porpoise and a mosaic of different habitats like chalk reefs, kelp forests, gravelly seabeds and rocky shores. Yorkshire's coast and sea also host thousands of seabirds each year.

We might be lucky enough to see our brilliant underwater creatures including small fish and sea anemones in rockpools or the head of a curious seal popping up above the waves. However, most of our sea creatures usually go

Sea anemone

Grey seal

about their business out of human sight, which can mean 'out of sight, out of mind.' The same could also be said for the serious threats they face – too easily overlooked and unnoticed until it's too late.

Sadly, human activity and neglect is having a shocking impact on our marine wildlife, and it's a shadow of what it was 75 years ago. Our seas have been exploited, polluted and choked by rubbish, while water temperatures are tipping out of control due to the climate crisis.

But hope is not lost. Protecting and restoring our incredible seascapes for centuries to come isn't easy, but it is possible – and vital. We have the solutions needed to turn the tide on this decline now.

Our vision for Yorkshire's coastline is a connected, protected stretch of land and sea where wildlife can truly thrive. In another 75 years, Yorkshire's waters could once again be filled with giant wonders such as Atlantic bluefin tuna, myriads of colourful creatures covering our chalk reefs and a healthy, thriving marine environment, which plays its part in protecting our climate.

Razorbill

Our dedicated marine officers will keep striving to establish Marine Protected Areas – like nature reserves at sea – along Yorkshire's coast, to ensure a thriving network of marine life, and our Living Seas Centre at Flamborough continues to inspire and educate young people.

Our marine team is working with coastal, urban and rural communities, using cutting-edge science and partnering with other innovative organisations and experts to change the fate of our marine world. Our marine biologists at Spurn are at the forefront of pioneering techniques to replant our seagrass meadows, and release hundreds of thousands of native oysters back into The Humber. These keystone species form part of our ambitious seascape-scale restoration programme and store carbon, acting as nature-based-solutions in response to the climate crisis.

Every year, we have to raise tens of thousands of pounds to fund our vital and effective marine conservation work. It's only with your support that we can carry on championing the conservation of our seas and coastlines. Together we can give our seas a chance.

Native oyster

Wild Ingleborough

The dramatic, stepped peak of Ingleborough, the second-highest mountain in the Yorkshire Dales, towers above rolling hills and hidden valleys.

WILD INGLEBOROUGH

It may seem a wild place but the influence of humans over millennia has tamed this landscape, changing it dramatically. Most woodland was cleared in the Neolithic period and centuries of grazing, agriculture and quarrying have all left their mark. Larger native animals are long gone, and many iconic upland species are now rare.

Our vision of Wild Ingleborough – and that of our project partners at Natural England, the University of Leeds, the United Bank of Carbon, the Woodland Trust and WWF-UK – is to reverse the impact of these activities so nature thrives again. Habitats will be given the chance to recover and natural processes encouraged to return. This will bring massive benefits to both wildlife and the environment, locking up carbon in the restored peatlands and woodlands, and slowing the flow of water down the mountain, reducing flooding downstream.

Yorkshire Wildlife Trust, supported by volunteers from the local community, has

Chimney sweeper moth

Spectacular veiws of Ingleborough

worked in this area for decades. We own several fantastic grassland, meadow and woodland nature reserves around the mountain, and are working to connect them with the Ingleborough National Nature Reserve. By reconnecting the land across the mountainside, we will make it easier for wildlife to move around in the landscape, and better adapt to environmental pressures.

Black grouse

A colourful vision of abundant life

Unlike the green fields of the modern landscape, which have been 'improved' for intensive sheep and cattle rearing, Wild Ingleborough's hues will change throughout the seasons, as carpets of wildflowers come and go, the bright leaves and blossom of trees and shrubs burst forth, before autumnal colours paint a different scene again.

Summer grasslands will buzz with life; northern brown argus and small pearl-bordered fritillary butterflies rub wings with sooty black chimney sweeper moths among swathes of species including common spotted, greater butterfly and chalk fragrant orchids. You might find the inconspicuous frog orchid or even small white orchids in a few corners of the mountain. Come autumn, waxcap fungi lie like coloured jewels, scattered among the grass.

The dawn chorus grows to its melodic best in late May and June, when songs of migrant redstarts, ring ouzels and cuckoos will add to the bubbling of curlews. As the early-morning mist lifts, the strange popping and gurgling of black grouse can sometimes be heard. The dapper males display on a showground, known as a lek, as the demure females calculate who is the season's biggest show-off, while keeping an eye out for hunting peregrines, hen harriers and buzzards.

Discover more about our ambitious vision for this landscape and how you could help us achieve it at wildingleborough.com

Adventure awaits

Much of Ingleborough is open-access, but the terrain is challenging. Our nature reserves are no exception, with only rudimentary visitor facilities in keeping with the wildness of this famous mountain. Way-marked trails and information signs will help you explore, but don't expect car parks, toilets and cafés – please take a break and support local services in a nearby village.

What is a nature reserve?
Professor Alastair Fitter CBE FRS

The answer to this question seems obvious: it's a place that's reserved for nature. One of those places, like the reserves in this book, where you can lose yourself in the natural world.

Every reserve in this book is open for your enjoyment: the wild, the wilder and the wildest, from the big flagship reserves to Yorkshire's most remote hidden gems. 'Reserved for nature' is not (or shouldn't be) a place where things are kept unchanged and where people aren't welcome. Some reserves are quite wild and though people are allowed on them, and encouraged, it's on nature's terms.

At another extreme, urban parks can be important refuges where nature exists on our terms. And then there is everything in between, including my favourite, Askham Bog. It is rarely fully explored but the Trust has created an amazing boardwalk that allows all visitors to experience at least some of its magic.

'Reserved for nature' doesn't mean that

Volunteers help to check our livestock

nature is left alone either; all of the reserves are managed, often to maintain a habitat important for a rare species. Left to nature, most of Yorkshire would turn to woodland; perfect for some creatures, less so for others. It seems contradictory that some species rely on us to maintain the habitats they need, but that's because we have so dramatically altered nature – most large herbivores and all large carnivores have gone. They would have created a mosaic of habitats allowing species to thrive.

We hear a lot nowadays about re-wilding. Properly done, this means letting nature take its course without human intervention. In practice what mostly happens is 'wilding;' reducing our level of management over time to allow natural processes to take the lead. This is what the Trust is now doing on some of its reserves, most recently and notably at Ingleborough.

Could future editions of this book therefore be longer? Yorkshire's nature reserves could have more wildlife to encounter and enjoy; be bigger and support more species including those that cannot survive in small areas. And there could be more reserves too, as we create a network of joined-up habitats that are friendlier to wildlife, to allow plants and animals to meet and mingle. The Trust has also begun to do this in the Lower Aire Valley and around Potteric Carr.

Reserves are what we want – and allow – them to be. You've helped to ensure that crucially, they will also be bigger, better and more joined up.

Alastair and a school group at Askham Bog

Bird's-eye primrose

Spring

As the days grow longer and become gradually warmer, nature bursts joyfully into life.

Buds on trees, ducklings on rivers, frogspawn in ponds, flowers and butterflies emerging... new life is all around us and nature's show is in full swing.

We all have our favourite signs of spring: those moments when we stop, smile and think "Now spring's really here." It could be the first daffodil or swallow; a brimstone or orange-tip butterfly; or the first time we hear a singing chiffchaff. Whatever wild wonders warm your heart at this time of year, you'll find them on a Yorkshire Wildlife Trust nature reserve.

The wildlife around us is waking up and getting busy. It's breeding season and there's no time to waste in finding a mate, establishing a territory, building a nest, laying eggs...

Reptiles emerge from their winter slumbers. You can see grass snakes at a number of our wetland reserves, or try a heathland site like Strensall or Allerthorpe Common if you're looking for lizards or adders.

Everyone loves a bluebell wood, where magical carpets of lilac dress the woodland floor, and we're blessed with many of these

Orange-tip butterfly

special places in our part of the world. We've listed reserves in this book where you can soak up the spellbinding ambience of bluebells in April and May.

The sights and scents of spring flowers aren't the only sensory treat in our woodlands. As migrant songbirds join their resident companions in places like Grass Wood, the dawn chorus reaches its peak and is utterly captivating – definitely worth getting up early for!

Spring also sees a changing of the guard for some of our birds, as winter visitors like redwings and fieldfares depart and summer visitors such as many warbler species, swifts and swallows return. Geese and waders are on the move too, heading back to their breeding grounds further north.

Our wildflower meadows begin to bloom as spring approaches summer, and the stunning array of colours on a sunny day is one of the most magnificent and uplifting sights you'll see anywhere.

Swallow

Summer

Summertime, and the living is easy... or is it? Our wildlife might disagree with the sentiment of the classic song, because for them it's more a case of 'summertime, and we could do with a nice sit down, thanks very much'.

Not long after breeding season, wildlife lurches into feeding season, and parents are run ragged by the demands of their offspring. Not unlike school summer holidays...

From pufflings and ducklings to froglets and hoglets, baby birds and animals are out and about. Which will you see? Perhaps a row of fluffy tawny owlets perched along a branch, foxes with cute cubs in a woodland clearing, or an energetic family of stoats scurrying across a path ahead of you.

On Flamborough Cliffs, the seabird city is mesmerising, with its sensory bombardment of

Buff-tailed bumblebee

sights, sounds and smells. Visit in June to see the puffins and many other seabirds on and around Yorkshire's 'Great White Cape'.

Some summer wildlife experiences are much more tranquil, yet just as busy. In high summer, our meadows are absolutely gorgeous – resplendent with a blaze of colour, studded with orchids and buzzing with bees. This is also the time to look for the greatest variety of butterflies, including the striking marbled white at some reserves, including Ledsham Bank, Brockadale and Wharram Quarry.

While the evocative call of the curlew echoes around our uplands by day, there's a different kind of winged creature in our woodlands at night – bats. Some of our sites host a great variety, such as Owl Wood and Pit Plantation, where you can join a guided walk and use a bat detector to tell the difference between the different species. Still on the subject of wings, dragonflies are zipping back and forth on our wetlands, and young avocets, black-headed gulls and other birds are preparing to test their flying skills, warblers are calling from reedbeds and bushes at reserves like Staveley.

But while we're still in the throes of our summer holiday season, some of our birds are already on the move. The first wading birds pass through in July and August on their return from their Arctic breeding grounds. Puffins have left the cliffs by the time August gets underway, and the sound of screaming swifts disappears from our skies.

Autumn

Back to school. Halloween. Bonfire Night. Harvest. Autumn is an eventful season for people – but even more so for wildlife. In this season of travel and transformation, expect the unexpected.

As summer shifts into autumn, wildlife shifts gear. Our nature reserves are like airports for birds, with winter species arriving, summer species departing, and migrant birds stopping off on their travels. It's the most exciting time of year for birdwatchers, as rare or surprising species occur on migration – passage waders, scarce warblers from Siberia, the chance of an influx of waxwings later in the season, and you never know what else. Birders flock to Spurn, Kilnsea Wetlands, Flamborough and Filey Dams, and our wetlands further inland, to see what turns up.

Early autumn is a time for appreciating our dragonflies and butterflies before the colder weather comes in, and for seeing mammals like badgers and hedgehogs stocking up before heading into hibernation.

On the coast, whales, dolphins and porpoises can be seen from clifftop vantage points following shoals of mackerel and herring. The bobbing heads of seals pop up in the waves. Their pups are born in autumn and winter, and you might spot them on the rocks around Flamborough Head. Offshore, skuas, shearwaters and divers test the identification skills of seawatchers, while short-eared owls appear around coastal marshes.

Autumn is famous for its changing colours, and you can experience the best of the season's foliage with a stroll through woods like Littlebeck, Littleworth Park, North Cliffe, Hollinhurst and Stoneycliffe.

This is also the season to go looking for fungi, in all its many varied and curious forms, particularly – but not exclusively – in our woodlands.

Short-eared owl

Winter

Winter is a season of contrasts for Yorkshire's wildlife and wild places. While badgers, hedgehogs and other mammals are snoozing through the colder, darker days, our wetlands are hosting raucous package holidays for thousands of wintering ducks, geese, swans and waders.

Winter's undoubtedly a time for immense spectacles in Yorkshire. At Potteric Carr and Ripon City Wetlands, huge numbers of starlings form mesmerising murmurations, creating spellbinding patterns across the sky. On the Humber estuary, Spurn and Paull Holme Strays host waders in their thousands, pursued by peregrines and merlins, while inland our wetlands are packed with wildfowl.

Snowdrops

Yet winter is also a time for more intimate encounters. Secretive bird species like bitterns and water rails are more likely to be seen as they step out from their reedbed hideaways in search of food, and there's a greater chance of happening across deer, foxes and some of our smaller mammals that stay awake and active through the chillier months.

With trees having shed their leaves as we enter winter, this is the best time of year to enjoy seeing our woodland birds and small mammals. Roving mixed flocks of finches and tits draw other species like goldcrests, nuthatches, treecreepers and woodpeckers in the hunt for food.

As we move through January and into February, signs of spring start to appear. Look for snowdrops and other early spring flowers at reserves like Askham Bog, and listen for birds singing in our woodlands and grasslands – not least the jumbling tunes of skylarks as they rise up from the ground like helicopters.

Roe deer

Bittern may
be easier to
spot in winter

Best for...
Birdwatching

People travel from all over the UK to go birding in Yorkshire. Why? Because it's brilliant for birds!

Throughout the year, the variety of species and habitats, the scale and spectacle, and sometimes the sheer number of birds, is among the best you'll find anywhere.

We're spoilt for choice up here. We've got woodlands alive with song, uplands echoing to the cry of curlews, and wetlands packed with wildfowl and waders, not to mention the jaw-dropping 'seabird city' at Flamborough. From secretive reedbed-dwellers like bitterns and water rails to the raucous cacophony of a black-headed gull colony or screaming of swifts, from tiny goldcrests to mighty raptors like the marsh harrier, the sights, sounds and sizes of Yorkshire's birdlife are rich and wonderful.

There's just one thing we can guarantee about birding in Yorkshire – you should expect the unexpected! You just never know what will turn up where or when, especially during spring and autumn migration, so grab your binoculars and head out to one of these top spots to see what you can find.

Remember, always watch from a distance to avoid disturbing birds or their nests.

Green woodpecker

NORTH

Grass Wood

Migrant songbirds arrive in spring, joining resident species in a gorgeous dawn chorus. Look for the handsome pied flycatcher, the redstart with its fiery orange tail, and our largest woodpecker species, the green woodpecker.

Bolton-on-Swale

A wetland haven and stop-off for migrating species. Various ducks winter here, including wigeons, goldeneyes, pochards, tufted ducks, teals and shovelers. Arctic and black terns can be seen in spring, while autumn brings green sandpipers, greenshanks and ruffs.

Starling murmuration

SOUTH

Potteric Carr
There's an incredible number and variety of birds: wildfowl, warblers, waders, woodpeckers... and frequent surprises during spring and autumn migration. Visit late in the afternoon on a winter's day to see the incredible starling murmuration.

Sprotbrough Flash
Visit in spring for wetlands bustling with breeding birds; great crested grebe displays are spectacular! Kingfishers are spotted in summer while autumn and winter bring woodpeckers, and the occasional bittern.

EAST

Spurn and Kilnsea Wetlands
Winter visitors including sanderlings and grey plovers join curlews, redshanks and dunlins, not to mention knots, which form mesmerising, swirling flocks. Rarities at this legendary migration hotspot have included two-barred greenish warbler, Marmora's warbler, Pallas's warbler and red-flanked bluetail.

Wheldrake Ings
Winter flooding attracts colossal numbers of ducks, geese, swans, gulls and waders, which could include smew, scaup, or even something rarer. There are three hides where you can watch for elusive species like spotted crake and water rail, and willow tits.

Smew

WEST

Adel Dam
Breeding kingfishers are the star species here, but the lake also hosts exotic-looking mandarin and tufted ducks. Woodland birds include great and lesser spotted woodpeckers, nuthatches, finches and tits, while red kites and sparrowhawks fly over.

Ledston Luck
Keep your eyes peeled for willow tits and green woodpeckers and listen for the distinctive calls of breeding blackcaps and yellowhammers. There are herons, coots and moorhens on the lake, while little egrets sometimes pass overhead.

Grey heron

Best for...
Family Days Out

The great outdoors – so much to see, so much to do, so many experiences to enjoy.

A family outing to one of our reserves offers children the chance to go on adventures, explore amazing places and discover the natural world around them. A spectacular starling murmuration or a memorable close encounter with a frog or butterfly might just spark a lifelong love of wildlife.

Whether you want to take little ones for a buggy ride or a toddle in beautiful surroundings, find space for the kids to run and play, or just to get out of the house for some fresh air, we've got you covered with these recommendations for our top family-friendly reserves.

Wildlife Watch Awards

HEDGEHOG AWARD

Calling all wildlife enthusiasts! Our Hedgehog, Kestrel and Nature Ranger awards are perfect for young wildlife lovers – you earn an award as you complete activities and challenges.

There are many different things to do from exploring the outdoors to creative crafts. There's no better way to sharpen your wildlife skills whilst also helping critters close to home!

Start your adventure at
ywt.org.uk/wildlife-watch-awards

NORTH

Staveley
With accessible paths and four bird hides there are lots of great opportunities to absorb yourself in nature and wonder at the incredible number of birds that Staveley hosts. How many kinds of warbler can you see and hear?

Ripon City Wetlands
This modern wetland reserve has a sensory trail, interactive information hut and an audio station, where you can listen to bird calls and hear about the reserve's wildlife. We recommend taking binoculars for the best views of wildlife across the lagoon.

Close encounters with wildlife

SOUTH

Potteric Carr

This huge, diverse wildlife wonderland has something for everyone. Discover the story trail, try some pond-dipping and finish with a drink and treat at the visitor centre. Potteric Carr also has a brilliant events programme for all ages.

Sprotbrough Flash

Enjoy all year round, but it's at its best in spring and early summer when the wildflowers are blooming, insects are buzzing, and the wetlands are bustling with breeding birds. There's also one of the best views in South Yorkshire!

Pond-dipping for minibeasts

Discover fun activities for kids of all ages at ywt.org.uk/go-wild

EAST

Moorlands

A charming little woodland, with majestic old trees, and colourful spring flowers. Discover a nature trail, pond-dipping, wooden sculptures, and an irresistible tree house. Look carefully for bat boxes hidden in the trees and for autumn fungi.

North Cave Wetlands

Get close to nature with five hides perfectly positioned to look for avocets, sand martins and black-headed gulls. You might spot a grass snake, stoats or even an otter! Enjoy all year round from summer butterflies to winter wildfowl.

WEST

Hetchell Woods

A wild woodland wonderland where childhood memories are made, with adventures to enjoy and wildlife to discover all year round. A circular walk includes towering rocky crags, secret pools and spectacular views. Perfect for a picnic!

Rothwell Country Park

Transformed from a post-industrial wasteland, this family-friendly reserve has woodland, ponds and grassland. Hedgehogs, rabbits and bats, along with red and fallow deer, live in the woods, and you can explore a sculpture trail and pond trail.

Hedgehog

Best for...
Wildflowers and butterflies

Like treasure, these jewels adorn our woodlands and meadows

There's something about seeing wildflowers that enriches our souls and raises our spirits – the emergence of snowdrops early in the year signifying new life, beautiful woodland carpets of bluebells warming our hearts as spring temperatures gradually rise. These are followed by the thrill of finding exotic-looking orchids in flower, the spellbinding summer sight of a meadow in full bloom, the pink and purple hues of heathland heather... The variety of species and colours is vast, and marvellous!

As much as we love wildflowers, butterflies love them even more, and discovering a meadow full of colourful flowers usually means finding a thriving population of insects, not least a variety of delightful butterflies. From the tiny skippers to big, striking butterflies like the peacock and red admiral, these beauties come in a range of shapes, sizes and colours.

You can enjoy gorgeous displays of wildflowers at many of our reserves in spring and summer, but here are a few tips to get you started.

NORTH

Southerscales
Early purple orchids and primroses bring beautiful spring colour to this impressive Ingleborough reserve. In summer, wild thyme and fragrant orchids in the grassland attract butterflies such as the dark green fritillary. In autumn, you might spot a painted lady.

Fen Bog
This upland landscape with stunning views and terrific wildlife is home to chickweed wintergreen, also known as Arctic starflower, in the upper areas. In early summer, butterflies include small pearl-bordered fritillary, dark green fritillary and large heath.

Primrose

Small pearl-bordered fritillary

SOUTH

Maltby Low Common

With three types of grassland close together, early summer at Maltby Low Common is paradise for insects and botanists. Over 400 insect species have been recorded, including dark green fritillaries, brimstones and orange-tips, while plants range from grass-of-Parnassus to meadow thistle.

Carlton Marsh

On warm summer days, look out for the delightful little purple hairstreak butterfly. Small skipper and small heath are just two of the other species found here and wildflowers include field scabious, devil's-bit scabious, weld, yellow archangel and oxeye daisy.

Harebell

EAST

Kiplingcotes

Late spring and early summer bring a dazzling array of colour: pyramidal, twayblade and common spotted-orchids, common and greater knapweed, field scabious, harebell and lady's bedstraw. Marbled whites, dingy skippers, gatekeepers and brimstones flutter through this blaze of colour.

Wharram Quarry

The glorious wildflower display includes the yellows of cowslip, rough hawkbit, mouse-ear hawkweed and bird's-foot trefoil; purple wild thyme and clustered bellflower; pink restharrow and blue common milkwort. These entice marbled whites, dingy skippers and small heaths.

WEST

Brockadale

Discover the treasures of this rare grassland habitat, such as bee orchids, clustered bellflowers and hellibores, along with daphne, purple milk vetch and spring cinquefoil. The abundant wildflowers attract marbled whites, dark green fritillaries and silver-washed fritillaries.

Townclose Hills

The magnesian limestone becomes a sea of wildflower colours in the summer: bluebells give way to wild anemones, yellow archangels, orchids and others. This encourages huge numbers of butterflies, including marbled whites, dark green fritillaries and gatekeepers.

Marbled white

Best for...
Fungi

Curiously weird and wonderful, fungi are the stars of autumn

Autumn is the best season for finding fungi, in all their varied, curious and fascinating forms, and with some of the most interesting names in nature, often rooted in countryside folklore.

Fungi play a vital role in our ecosystems. The fruit bodies – the parts you can see - emerge above the surface of the woodland floor, grassland or tree bark. Hidden below, there's a vast network of root-like mycelium that breaks down organic matter like decaying wood and dung, releasing essential nutrients. It also helps form a 'wood wide web', linking trees and, we think, allowing them to communicate with each other. Here are some of our best reserves for discovering fungi:

Shaggy inkcap

NORTH

Grass Wood

Grass Wood is home to some unusual fungi like the white saddle, vinegar cup and shaggy inkcap. The white saddle and vinegar cup fungi are spore shooters (as opposed to spore droppers like most toadstool-shaped mushrooms). When the spores are mature, they are catapulted into the air in puffs of white dust!

Littlebeck Wood

Search the heath and woods for fungi like the tawny grisette, birch polypore and fly agaric – the classic 'fairytale' red toadstool with white spots. The birch polypore is renowned for its antiseptic qualities and it's flesh was often used to make wound dressings in years gone by. Also known as razor strop fungus, it can be used to sharpen knives too!

Some fungi are highly poisonous! Make sure you wash your hands after touching fungi and please do not eat them unless you are 100% sure of identification.

Fly agaric

SOUTH

Potteric Carr

Potteric's woodlands are enchanted with witch's hats, woolly milkcaps, earth stars, bird's nest fungi, shaggy parasols and poison pies.

Potteric is also home to a very rare fungus, known only as *allopsalliota geesterani*, which is recorded in just one other UK location, in Norfolk, and may have arrived here via the East Coast railway line!

Barnsley Main

Colliery spoil sites are a great place to see nature reclaiming land from industry, including some really interesting fungi. At Barnsley Main you can find earthtongues, which look like little black tongues appearing from the earth.

Earthtongue

EAST

North Cliffe Wood

Take a walk in these woods and you'll be rewarded with some quirkily magnificent fungi: the delicate lilac wood blewit; the shaggy inkcap with its cap that looks like a lawyer's wig; and the tiny candlesnuff fungus, which resembles a snuffed-out candle wick and releases whisps of smokey spores when disturbed.

Allerthorpe Common

The mix of lowland heath, acid grassland and woodland here creates great conditions for fungi to thrive. Along with fly agaric, there are brown birch bolete and ochre brittlegill. Look for the striking witch's butter on fallen or dying branches of hardwood trees – it's black with a jelly-like texture and frilly shape.

WEST

Stoneycliffe Wood

Step into Stoneycliffe Wood to find a fantastic display of fly agaric, false death caps and old man of the woods – a rare find, perfectly camouflaged as rotting pine cones or leaf litter with its shaggy textured cap.

Broadhead Clough

Broadhead Clough is home to a variety of specialist fungi, from waxcaps like the ballerina and pinkgills in the nationally important grasslands to boletes, jelly ears and bog beacons in the wood. Please note that the grasslands are accessed through private land.

Best for...
Accessibility

We're wild about inclusion! We want all our visitors to enjoy the best possible experience at our reserves.

We've picked out some of the best sites in each region for wildlife lovers with disabilities to connect with nature. Here you'll find mostly flat paths, slopes are gradual and suitable for standard wheelchairs, as well as short walks with nearby parking. At some, there are also designed disabled parking spaces, accessible toilets and hides with wheelchair access.

Remember:

■ Please use your own judgement about what is safe and suitable for you

■ Bring your Radar key to make use of accessible gates

■ Look at 'the lowdown' on each reserve page in this book for an accessibility overview

■ Visit **ywt.org.uk/nature-reserves** for more detailed and up-to-date information about accessibility at each site

You'll also find more information about our reserves at **accessiblenatureuk.com**

NORTH

Staveley

This gorgeous wetland reserve is mostly flat with a network of accessible paths. Three of the five hides are fully accessible. Sand martins, commons terns and even otters are seen here. Disabled parking (Radar key access) is available off Main Street, from the track by the church.

Filey Dams

As the last remaining freshwater marsh in the area, Filey Dams is a magnet for migratory birds. There's wheelchair access to the main hide and the pond dipping platform.

Ripon City Wetlands

This modern wetland reserve attracts swathes of wildfowl and waders. There's a designated disabled parking area accessed through a Radar key gate. This is by the Riverside Lagoon screen, which has a viewing space for wheelchairs. Bring binoculars to get the best view of birds across the lake.

SOUTH

Potteric Carr
You'll find an accessible route signposted on this spectacular wetland reserve. Most hides are accessible, giving excellent views of the lakes. There's a café and accessible toilets in our visitor centre, as well as disabled parking.

Dearne Valley Country Park
There's something for everyone here with a mixture of woodland, grassland, and river. The river Dearne at the centre is fantastic for seeing kingfishers. Most paths are flat and tarmacked or surfaced. Use the main car park for accessible access.

Sprotbrough Flash
The riverside towpath along the Don is flat and level. It passes through the picturesque Don Gorge and you can get close views of wetland wildlife from two accessible hides – perhaps a bittern if you're lucky.

Marsh hide at Adel Dam

EAST

North Cave Wetlands
A surfaced, accessible footpath goes around part of this wetland bird paradise and all the hides except Turret are accessible, giving excellent views of spring waders and winter wildfowl. The car park on Dryham Lane has two accessible spaces and there are accessible toilets at the entrance.

Askham Bog
A boardwalk loops around this beautiful ancient fenland creating a half-mile circuit, although this can be slippery in wet weather. The large car park has a compacted gravel surface, and a short, slightly sloped dirt path leads to the boardwalk.

WEST

Adel Dam
This woodland-wetland reserve has a level path up to the first hide, which is accessible and gives an excellent view of the feeding station. Park at Golden Acre car park (tarmac with disabled parking).

Rothwell Country Park
A peaceful, family-friendly reserve with a good network of accessible tracks, but there are long gradual slopes so best tackled with a mobility scooter or powered wheelchair. Take extra care in wet weather. Roadside parking is limited on Bullough Lane.

May Beck to Little Beck Wood (autumn)

This makes a gorgeous autumnal walk, full of fallen leaves and mossy trees. It's quite hilly in places but has well-worn paths and spectacular views – you can even see the sea on a clear day!

1 Starting in the car park, exit over the cattle grid and turn left to follow the 'Coast to Coast' footpath along the stream, which winds its way downwards with occasional paddling-sized pools through the bronzed woodland.

2 Once you reach Foss Lane, cross the bridge (ideal for playing 'pooh sticks') and take the right fork (marked 'Coast to Coast'). This crosses the river again, bringing you to Falling Foss waterfall. Carved into a hollow inamongst the trees and cascading an impressive 30 feet into a plunge pool, the waterfall is well-worth a pause to enjoy - particularly sat with a hot drink at the nearby tea rooms.

3 Taking the left fork and being mindful of the steep drop to one side, continue along the path beside the beck. Here, wide carpets of rusty orange leaves are

offset by silvery tree trunks and a green-gold canopy. Explore 'The Hermitage' en-route – a hollowed-out boulder said to have been inhabited by an 18th-century hermit.

4 A dry-stone wall and Yorkshire Wildlife Trust sign marks Little Beck Wood reserve. A mixture of oak, ash, alder, and cherry arch over the boardwalk and gives the path a more secluded feel. Treasures abound around every corner, including a 17th century alum mine, a lazily winding stream perfect for dippers, clusters of fungi and a cacophony of birdsong from tits and nuthatches overhead.

5 Exit through the gate, turn left and follow the road down and around the bend. Cross the small stream on your left just before the bench to re-enter the reserve.

6 The path slopes back upwards, through a gate at the top and along a bridleway through the farmland. Take in the wide open space, occasional drystone wall, and the autumnal crowns of the reserve woodland on your left.

7 Just after you pass the farm at the end of Foss Lane, take the middle path without a gate offroad and uphill. Enjoy the panoramic views towards Whitby as you go, and the woodland laid out below.

Nuthatch

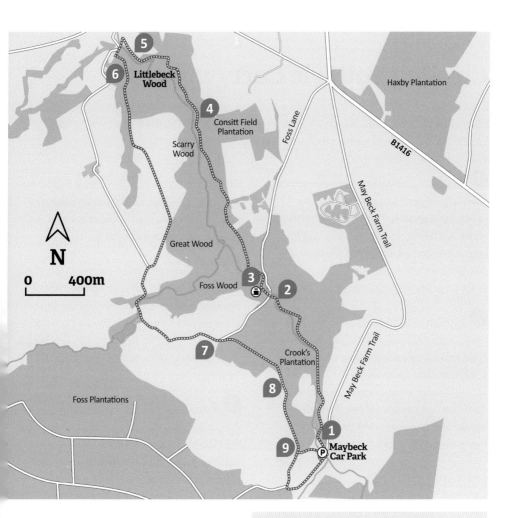

8 Follow the path across a few stiles and through some fields, gradually dipping back down into the woodland and onto a well-worn path.

9 Finally, there is a junction with a gate on the left and stile on the right. The path through the gate leads back to the carpark. Going over the stile creates a slightly a longer route, coming out on the road further along from the car park.

Suggested start point – May Beck Car Park
Parking – May Beck Car Park
Length – 4.3 miles/7km

Other useful info: The Falling Foss Tea Garden is only open in summer, but you can find several pubs and cafés in Goathland and Sleights. The closest public toilets are in Ruswarp and Goathland.

Circling Potteric Carr (winter)

Explore our wealth of wildlife corridors and urban green spaces in the area around Potteric Carr nature reserve. Winter is an ideal time to try this walk, as you're likely to catch some breath-taking starling murmurations as dusk approaches.

1 Turn left out of Manor Farm car park onto Cammidge Way, then take the left-hand tarmacked footpath. The woodland on the left is home to a wealth of wildlife; listen out for nuthatches and great spotted woodpeckers calling from the canopy, and fungi such as shaggy inkcaps fringe the floor into November.

2 Turn left onto Stayers Road, then turn right onto Sceptre Avenue and follow the track as it turns into a bridleway winding through scrubland dotted with trees. The bridleway passes through an underpass, then turn left at Carr Lane and continue along the path signposted 'Doncaster Greenway.' Either follow the main path or explore the meadow paths on your left - in spring these are absolutely stunning and bursting with colour.

3 Continue along the path until you reach a residential area on both sides. At Short Lane, turn left and then at the end turn right along the tarmac path under the bridge. There are several lakes and ponds nearby, so look out for distinctive groups of pink-footed geese or winter flocks of redwings and fieldfares flying overhead in search of food.

4 When you reach the lakeside, go left and follow the tarmac path as far as Carolina Way. Turn left and follow the road round, and then left again at White Rose Way. You'll find Potteric Carr nature reserve after the bridge over the railway, where you can refuel at our café and enjoy views over the reedbeds.

5 Nicely warmed, head back to White Rose Way. Cross over to the path via the pelican crossings and turn left, following the downward slope parallel to the road. The wet grasslands of Carr Lodge lie to the right. Flocks of redwings, thrushes and ducks may be seen from the viewing screen accessible by a woodland path.

6 Follow the main path skirting the edge of Carr Lodge until the track junction, then go left over the M18 flyover. Look out for overwintering wildfowl in the lakes as you pass; great crested grebes, tufted ducks, little grebes and more are often spotted here. Take a right just after Annabel's, following the tarmac path around the long lake and over the bridge by the warehouses.

You can take a detour to Parson's Carr by turning right just before the railway bridge and following the path past Mombrick Wood.

7 Follow the hardcore path to the left as it curves towards the roads, passing under the Great Yorkshire Way and then under the M18 onto the bridleway. Huxterwell Marsh first on

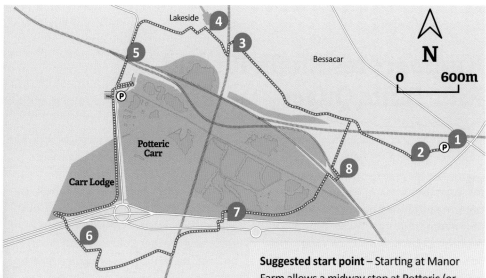

Lakeside

Bessacar

N

0 600m

Potteric Carr

Carr Lodge

your left and then Rossington Carr Fields on the right are both fantastic spaces for wetland wildlife, with the chance to see a marsh harrier wheeling overhead or hear the boom of a bittern.

8 Go over a small green bridge and through a wooded area to cross a much larger green bridge. Continue along the path until you have safely crossed the railway. Turn right onto Carr Lane, then right again to reach the underpass from the beginning of the route. Retrace your steps from here along the bridleway to return to the car park.

Tufted duck

Suggested start point – Starting at Manor Farm allows a midway stop at Potteric (or you can start at Potteric Carr.)

Parking – Cammidge Way (Manor Farm) car park (24 hour) or Potteric Carr car park. The main car park locked at 5pm, use overflow if staying later.

Public transport – Buses run from Doncaster Station to the bus stop at Bawtry Road/ Plumpton Park, just a few minutes' walk from Manor Farm.

Length – 7.5 miles/12 km

Dogs allowed although they can't be brought into Potteric Carr's visitor centre, café or reserve.

Other useful info: You'll find a great café and accessible toilets at Potteric Carr Nature Reserve. The top stretch from Manor Farm to Potteric is accessible to standard wheelchairs and pushchairs. The bottom section is bumpier in places and large puddles may form after heavy rain so be prepared!

Kiplingcotes Chalk Pit and Rifle Butts Quarry (summer)

Summertime heralds an abundance of chalk grassland flowers in this historic area of Yorkshire which hosts one of the best places to see striking, monochrome marbled white butterflies.

1 From the car park in Goodmanham Dale, take the path heading north-eastwards. This was once a railway line from Market Weighton to Beverley but is now the Hudson Way rail trail open to walkers, cyclists and horse riders. After a few hundred metres you'll reach Kiplingcotes Chalk Pit.

2 As the reserve opens out before you, pause for a moment to look across the valley floor. The distinctive mounds of tufted grass harbour gloriously scented wild thyme and basil. Listen carefully for linnets, yellowhammers, and busy bees.

> **Did you know?** These mounds are made by yellow meadow ants and attract green woodpeckers who probe them with their long tongues.

Yellow meadow ant

3 If you're sure-footed and able to make the short, steep climb up the embankment on the left, you'll be rewarded with fine views, a welcoming bench and often a wonderful breeze on a hot day. There is only one access point up onto the bank, so you can do a loop before heading back into the valley bottom. Watch your step as there are steep drops in places.

4 Once you've soaked in the sights, sounds and smells of this wildflower paradise, retrace your steps back to the carpark and then follow the Hudson Way towards Market Weighton until you emerge onto a small road. Turn right along the road to reach Rifle Butts Quarry.

5 The reserve sits on the right at the end of the first field, through a kissing gate. Here, the exposed rock face showcases a unique geological timeline starting in the Jurassic period. The reserve is awash with wild colours through the spring and summer including lady's bedstraw, and clustered bellflower. From here, continue along the minor road for around 1km, keeping your eyes peeled for brown hares and whitethroats, and listening out for skylarks.

6 At Goodmanham, turn left along Main Street and you'll pass All Hallows, a delightful 12th-century church. Keep following the road a

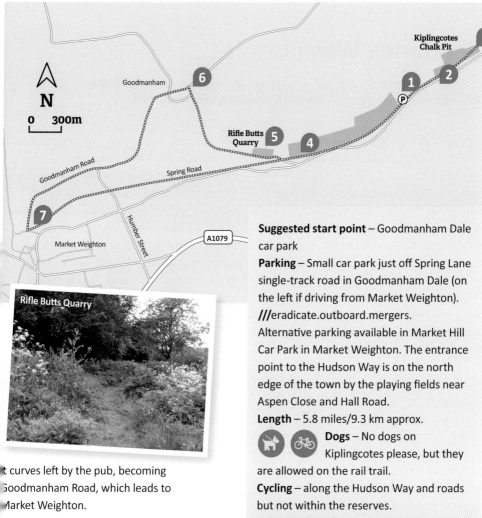

Goodmanham

Kiplingcotes
Chalk Pit

3

1 **2**

6

N

0   300m

Rifle Butts
Quarry **5**

4

Goodmanham Road

Spring Road

7

Market Weighton

Humber Street

A1079

Rifle Butts Quarry

t curves left by the pub, becoming
Goodmanham Road, which leads to
Market Weighton.

7 Just to the left of the sign for Market
Weighton, take the path through the kissing
gate. When you emerge onto Hall Road by the
playing fields, take a sharp left back onto the
Hudson Way in the direction of Beverley and
enjoy a shaded walk back to the car park under
the canopy of trees, past the natural spring of St
Helen's Well on your right.

Suggested start point – Goodmanham Dale
car park
Parking – Small car park just off Spring Lane
single-track road in Goodmanham Dale (on
the left if driving from Market Weighton).
///eradicate.outboard.mergers.
Alternative parking available in Market Hill
Car Park in Market Weighton. The entrance
point to the Hudson Way is on the north
edge of the town by the playing fields near
Aspen Close and Hall Road.
Length – 5.8 miles/9.3 km approx.

Dogs – No dogs on
Kiplingcotes please, but they
are allowed on the rail trail.
Cycling – along the Hudson Way and roads
but not within the reserves.
Other useful info: There are a few pubs and
other places to get food in Market
Weighton, as well as a public toilet on
Londesborough Road. You'll also find a pub
(the Goodmanham Arms) and café (the
Fiddle Drill Tearooms) in Goodmanham.
Access: Kiplingcotes is a short walk from the
car park, flat easy walking, can be uneven
underfoot. Steep bank on reserve is
unsuitable for pushchairs or wheelchairs.

The Lines Way (spring)

The Lines Way provides an attractive and accessible wildlife corridor for about three and a half miles along the disused Garforth-Castleford railway line.

The main trail is bordered by a variety of habitats from hedgerows to wet woodland. In springtime, listen for cuckoos calling from the trees and glimpse smooth and great-crested newts in the ditches. Wildflowers flourish on the embankments, with common spotted-orchids and clustered bellflowers, and you may even spot glow-worms at dusk.

The main path goes from Park Lane in Allerton Bywater to Ninelands Lane in Garforth and is accessible for wheelchair users and pushchairs, as well as horses and cyclists. Cyclists can join the National Route 67 heading east from Allerton Bywater or continue out of Garforth on Route 66.

Walkers can easily meander on and off the main trail to visit one or more of our nearby reserves. With lots of opportunities for extension, pick and choose the route that suits you best!

1 Why not begin with a stroll around Letchmire Pastures? As spring turns to summer, flowers including marsh orchids, meadow vetchling and cranes-bill bring bursts of colour to the grasslands here. From the reserve, take a left along Station Road and then a right onto Park Lane where you'll spot the black metal sign for Lines Way on your left.

2 For another adventure, Owl Wood and Pit Plantation lie half a mile further north-east – turn right onto Doctors Lane and the reserve will be about five minutes' walk. The mixture of sycamore, oak, silver birch and beech in the two connected woodlands make this reserve a fantastic home for bats: common and soprano pipistrelle, noctule and myotis can all be spotted by the patient visitor. In the daytime spring brings a fabulously scented carpet of bluebells.

3 A little further up Doctors Lane, a bridleway intersects the road. A left turn here will take you back to the Lines Way, or if you head right along the bridleway for a little over half a mile you'll find Kippax Meadows, where you can hear bullfinches, yellowhammers and linnets calling. Exiting onto Cromwell Rise and then walking straight down Brigshaw Lane will take you back to the Lines Way.

4 For an evening spectacle, head for Townclose Hills (known locally as Billy Wood) by crossing the road from Kippax Meadows and heading down Station Road. The entrance lies just behind Kippax Leisure Centre. A steep-sided grassland plateau gives a beautiful view of the surrounding countryside and comes alive with clustered bellflower, field scabious and orchids in the summer. Even more excitingly, once night falls the reserve is also a fantastic place to see glow-worms, which are active for only a few

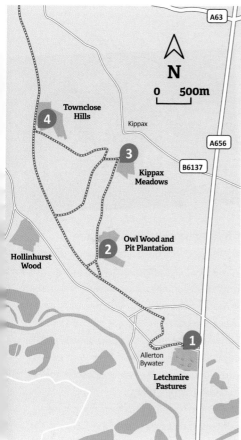

Suggested start point – Station Road Allerton Bywater

Parking – On-road Station Road in Allerton Bywater; car park Station Road Kippax (midway)

Length – 9 miles/14.5 km (Letchmire Pastures to Garforth route) allow 4 hours or longer if you want to explore the reserves; 5.8 miles/9.4 km (Letchmire Pastures to Townclose Hills route) allow around 2.5 hours or more if you'd like time to explore the reserves.

Other useful info: You can find the occasional bench along The Lines Way where you can stop for a picnic; there's also a pub called The Boat next to Letchmire Pastures and Samuel Valentine Urban Food Hall in Allerton Bywater.

■ Letchmire Pastures to Garforth route (14.5km approx)

■ Letchmire Pastures to Townclose Hills route (9.4km approx)

veeks in the summer and a wildlife wonder not o be missed! From here, you can rejoin the nain path directly and continue to Garforth or llerton Bywater.

Hollinhurst Wood sits about half a mile to the west of the path. It's named for the holly that grows there alongside oak, wych elm and hazel. Although it's small, walking through the reserve gives a lovely feeling of enclosure, while a sea of bluebells in spring followed by summer wildflowers in the meadow make this a treat for the senses.

Meadow cranes-bill

Get Ready to **Go Wild**

Here are a few tips to help you explore, experience, and enjoy the wonderful wildlife all around us:

Wild, Wilder or Wildest?

We've grouped our reserves by their different levels of wilderness to suit your interests and skills:

Wild: Relaxed and welcoming all year round, our wild reserves offer an introduction to Yorkshire's wild places for all ages, complete with creature comforts – but still with plenty for more experienced naturalists to enjoy.

Wilder: Places where you can step off the beaten track, explore, and nurture your budding passion for Yorkshire's wildlife.

Wildest: Our remotest reserves, ideal for adventurous wildlife lovers who are experienced in navigating the great outdoors.

The adventure starts at home

■ Always check the weather conditions before you set out and dress accordingly. Wear suitable clothes and sturdy shoes, a hat and suncream!

■ Make sure you know where you're heading; check the route and bring a map with you. Consider if recent events (like heavy rainfall) might cause you to divert from your path. If you're bound for the beach or shore, remember to check the tide times.

■ If you're heading into long grass, wear full-length trousers tucked into socks to prevent tick bites. Always carry a tick removal kit.

■ Pack at least one bottle of water and some snacks. Very few of our reserves have refreshments available.

■ Don't head out without a basic first aid kit – they're lifesavers!

■ If you're striking out alone, always tell someone where you're going and when you expect to be back. If something doesn't feel right, it probably isn't – listen to your intuition and turn around if needed.

■ Reception isn't guaranteed but take a charged mobile, especially for photos!

■ If you're going wilder, binoculars, and notebooks may come in handy.

Leave only footprints, take only photos...

Please help us to keep Yorkshire's wild places special:

- Use bins where provided, or take your litter home
- Follow our instruction signs
- Keep to marked paths
- Leave gates and property as you find them
- Be considerate of other visitors, especially in viewing hides
- Never light fires or BBQs
- Never remove plants or animals from our reserves.
- Follow the Countryside Code - respect, protect and enjoy.

Access & facilities

Some of our sites can be challenging to access by their very nature. When we say that somewhere is 'accessible' we mean that it has a good level of standard wheelchair access. Only a few of our reserves have toilets - please check before visiting and plan ahead.

Getting there safely

We'd love to see more people reaching our reserves using public transport or pedal power. If you need to drive, please respect local residents and park responsibly – never block gates, passing places or access for others.

Always walk on the right-hand side of roads without pavements, unless approaching a sharp right-hand bend.

Take great care at railways crossings and follow all signs. Look both ways and listen. Cross sensibly and close gates behind you.

Dogs

We love our four-legged friends, but they can disturb wildlife and grazing animals, especially in spring and summer when birds nest on the ground or are fledging. If dogs are permitted on the reserve you're visiting, please always keep them on a lead and pick up their mess – it can cause real harm to other animals and visitors. Please contact us before you visit if you want to visit a resticted reserve with an assistance dog.

Amazing grazing

You're likely to meet some of our conservation grazing colleagues on our great grasslands, nibbling away to create species-rich meadows! Please give our cows, sheep and ponies plenty of space and don't feed them. If an animal approaches you, walk away calmly. Avoid passing between adults and their young as this can appear threatening. If you are chased by livestock whilst walking a dog, let go of the lead. It'll help you both get to safety.

Expect the unexpected

We can't guarantee what you'll see, because wildlife does its own thing in its own time – but this means you might see something you never expected! Think carefully about the season, weather and time of day before you head out to try and find that special something – it'll really could boost your chances of success.

Visit **ywt.org.uk/nature-reserves** or call us on **01904 659570** for fuller, up-to-date information about our reserves before you set off!

How going wild works wonders for our wellbeing

Kat Woolley, Inspiring People Officer and Forest School Leader

Being outside, surrounded by nature, brings enormous benefit to our physical and mental wellbeing. Researchers have found in multiple studies that there's a link between access to green space and a reduced risk of mental health problems. Regular walkers know that spending time in nature improves our mood, increases our physical activity, helps us to de-stress and develop a stronger connection to nature – and where better to spend this time than at one of Yorkshire Wildlife Trust's reserves?

We all have different ways of interacting with nature and the outdoors, but here are our top tips for making a deeper connection.

Moving mindfully

'Mindfulness' simply means being present in your thoughts and being more aware of your surroundings and other people. You don't need any special training to become more mindful – it's actually very easy to get started.

If you'd like to give it a try, we recommend that you start by simply engaging your senses – it's a neat trick to ease your body and mind into a more 'present' state.

Try this activity, noting how you are feeling at the start.

Look. Spend time looking at five different things you can see around you. Really look. You might see patterns in nature, spot shapes in the clouds, or watch a bee pollinate.

Touch. Now, touch four things you can see around you. Feel the textures in nature. The rough bark of a tree, the slippery mud, a furry leaf.

Listen. Listen to three different sounds. Home in on the natural sounds around you like the wind rushing between the leaves of a tree, a blackbird singing, or a grasshopper chirping.

Smell. Sniff out two different smells. Engage your sense of smell to discover the scent of the wild roses, or mayflower when it's in bloom. If you're feeling more adventurous, give the whiff of otter spraint (that's droppings) a try!

Taste. Lastly, taste one thing in nature. B careful here and only taste something if you are confident that it's safe to do so! If not, tr and imagine what it might taste like.

Now ask yourself how you are feeling compared to the start. Do you feel calmer? Less stressed o worried? More connected to the nature around you? Maybe more alive?

Five ways to wellbeing

We can also harness the power of 'five ways to wellbeing' while out in nature.

1 Connect with people while enjoying the nature around you. Meeting friends can be even more special with some wildlife spotting thrown in! You could also foster new friendships by joining a local outdoors group.

2 Being out in nature helps us to be active. It's easy to be more active in the great outdoors, especially if you can tackle something new. Challenge yourself to complete a longer or steeper walk now and again – you'll soon start to feel the benefits.

3 Ever wondered what a beautiful bloom is called or which bird is singing? Try and find out! Learning a new fact about nature can be a great way to boost your wellbeing – there are now apps, online resources and books to help.

4 Take notice of what is going on in nature. Spend time watching wildlife doing its thing. Sit quietly and see what happens. Take a sketchbook and capture what you see. Don't forget the detail!

5 Give back time to help nature. Make space for wildlife at home – from feeding birds and hedgehogs to planting a container garden or creating a pond. Come and volunteer with us! 100% of our volunteers have said their volunteering has improved their mental health.

Find more ways to give back to nature at
ywt.org.uk/get-involved

North

With a boot in two national parks – the Yorkshire Dales and
the North York Moors – our northern region includes some
of our wildest reserves, from the mountain pastures around
Ingleborough to the wetlands of the Vale of York, through lush
woodland and over towards the northern stretch of our coastline.

Ashberry

This ancient woodland nestles in a steep-sided valley carved out by glacial meltwater, flanked by flower-rich limestone grassland and marshes, and home to many specialised species.

The lowdown

Nearest town: Helmsley (3.9m/6.3km)
Nearest postcode: YO62 5LE
Grid ref: SE 5680 8470
///thick.constants.tips
Parking: Limited parking at roadside near to where public bridleway enters the reserve off Clavery Lea Lane
Size: 52ha

  Dogs welcome on lead on public right of way only. Cycling on bridleway only (can be wet and muddy)

A great place for:

☑ Bird watchers
☐ Cyclists
☑ Wildflower enthusiasts
☑ Families
☐ Leisurely stroll
☑ Peace and tranquility
☑ Walkers

Recommended time to make the most of your visit:

☐ Full day
☑ Half day
☐ Just an hour

ℹ Before you go...

This is a fragile and sensitive habitat so please stick to the paths. It can be very wet, even in summer, so it's best to wear wellies.

Peace in the valley

This timelessly tranquil valley owes its mosaic of rare habitats to the site's underlying geology. A beautifully clear stream – in which freshwater shrimps and white-clawed crayfish live – and calcium-rich springs flow through the site. The marshy valley bottom hosts rare plants including bird's-eye primrose, globeflower, marsh hawk's-beard and grass-of-Parnassus. In the woods, search for birds including nuthatch, treecreeper, great spotted woodpecker and redstart. You might see fallow and roe deer on the valley sides.

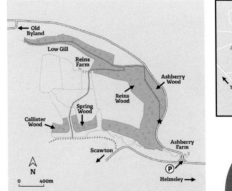

Tranquil grassland and woods

For a longer trip, visit nearby Rievaulx Abbey and Rievaulx Terrace and Temples.

✻ Magic ★ moment
Glimpsing the day-flying black chimney sweeper moth restlessly dancing around the grassland.

Ashes Pasture

WILD INGLEBOROUGH

The largest of our cluster of reserves at the north-eastern tip of Ingleborough, this diverse grassland is home to nationally rare flower species, including ten species of orchid.

Orchid paradise

When the blanket of beautiful wildflowers is buzzing with bees, and the calls of cuckoos, curlews and skylarks drift on the breeze, there are few finer places to be than idyllic Ashes Pasture in late spring. It's a joy for orchid lovers, supporting ten species including the scarce small white orchid and heath spotted-orchid. Other colourful flowers to enjoy include devil's-bit scabious, globeflower and bird's-eye primrose. In autumn, look for goldfinches feeding on the seeds of meadowsweet and the common carder bee nectaring on late blooms

The lowdown...

Nearest town: Horton-in-Ribblesdale (3.9m/6.3km)
Nearest postcode: LA6 3AS
Grid ref: SD 77627 78357
///ribcage.apples.cure
Parking: Informal roadside parking
Site designation: SSSI, Special Area of Conservation
Size: 26ha

A great place for:

- ☑ Bird watchers
- ☐ Cyclists
- ☑ Wildflower enthusiasts
- ☐ Families
- ☐ Leisurely stroll
- ☑ Peace and tranquility
- ☑ Walkers

Recommended time to make the most of your visit:

- ☐ Full day
- ☑ Half day
- ☐ Just an hour

ℹ Before you go...

Follow the informal nature trail on site. While access is uneven and steep, you can still get excellent views of the flowers near the entrance without going down the slope.

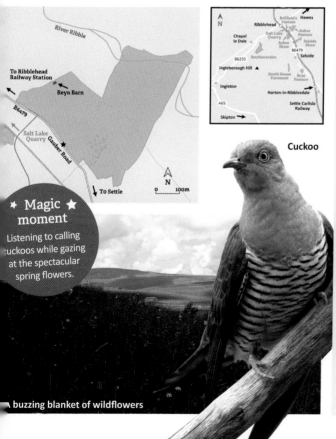

Cuckoo

★ **Magic moment** ★
Listening to calling cuckoos while gazing at the spectacular spring flowers.

buzzing blanket of wildflowers

Map labels: River Ribble, To Ribblehead Railway Station, Reyn Barn, B6479, Salt Lake Quarry, Gauber Road, To Settle, N, 0 100m

Inset map labels: N, Ribblehead, Bellfield's Pasture, Hawes, Chapel le Dale, Salt Lake Quarry, Ashes Pasture, Ashes Shaw, Selside Shaw, B6479, Selside, B6255, Southerscales, Ingleborough Hill, South House Pavement, Braw Pasture, Ingleton, Horton-in-Ribblesdale, A65, Settle Carlisle Railway, Skipton

VISITED ✓

Ashes Shaw

WILD INGLEBOROUGH

Grassland borders beautiful ash woodland between Colt Park and the Settle-Carlisle railway. Here you'll find a Scheduled Ancient Monument and other archaeological features.

The lowdown...

Nearest town: Horton-in-Ribblesdale (5m/8km)
Nearest postcode: LA6 3JF
Grid ref: SD 77343 78037
///battle.correctly.plots
Parking: No parking on site. You can walk to the reserve from Ribblehead Station or Ribblehead Quarry via Gauber High Pasture.
Size: 18ha

A great place for:

- ☑ Bird watchers
- ☐ Cyclists
- ☑ Wildflower enthusiasts
- ☐ Families
- ☐ Leisurely stroll
- ☑ Peace and tranquility
- ☑ Walkers

Recommended time to make the most of your visit:

- ☐ Full day
- ☐ Half day
- ☑ Just an hour

ⓘ Before you go...
Follow the marked trail to explore the features of Ashes Shaw, learn about the archaeology and limestone pavement and enjoy stunning views. Be aware of cattle grazing and please don't stand on the limestone pavement.

A tale of two grazers

Sheep grazing is 'out' and light cattle grazing is 'in' as we improve Ashes Shaw for wildlife. A nature reserve since 2022, it's a vital connection between Ingleborough National Nature Reserve and Ashes Pasture. With time, bushes and trees may colonise the limestone pavement and elsewhere, providing habitats for insects, in turn supporting birds and small mammals. Look for orchids in June, and listen for the springtime songs of redstarts, cuckoos and blackcaps, which all breed in the area.

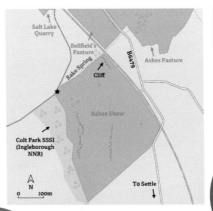

★ Magic moment ★
Common blue butterflies laying their eggs on the yellow and red flowers of bird's-foot trefoil.

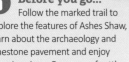
Combine your visit with a walk at one of the nearby Wild Ingleborough reserves.

Limestone pavement

WILD INGLEBOROUGH

Bellfield's Pasture

This small pasture is being restored after years of sheep grazing. It is an important wild link between neighbouring Ashes Pasture and Ingleborough National Nature Reserve.

A vital stepping stone for wildlife

Bees, butterflies and other insects are drawn to the colourful wildflowers at Bellfield's Pasture during the summer – and the developing grassland and wood pasture should attract more and more species in the future. The native tree and shrub species that have been planted will help link nearby wooded areas to make it easier for species like red squirrels, birds and bats to move around.

Yorkshire Wildlife Trust purchased this site, which has fine views of Pen-y-Ghent, in 2021 with generous support from Mr and Mrs Bellfield.

The lowdown...

Nearest town: Horton-in-Ribblesdale (4.8m/7.7km)
Nearest postcode: LA6 3JF
Grid ref: SD 77448 78516
///conceals.command.tests
Parking: No parking on site. You can walk to the reserve from Ribblehead Station or Ribblehead Quarry via Gauber High Pasture.
Size: 3.2ha

A great place for:

- [ ] Bird watchers
- [ ] Cyclists
- [x] Wildflower enthusiasts
- [ ] Families
- [ ] Leisurely stroll
- [ ] Peace and tranquility
- [x] Walkers

Recommended time to make the most of your visit:

- [ ] Full day
- [x] Half day
- [x] Just an hour

ℹ️ Before you go...
There's a marked trail on site but the path is grassy and uneven. Take care if you're using nearby footpaths, as the road is fast and busy. Visit in spring to hear cuckoos calling.

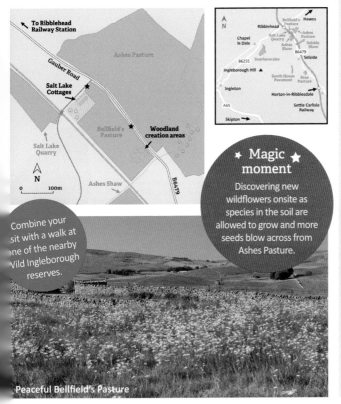

Combine your visit with a walk at one of the nearby Wild Ingleborough reserves.

★ Magic moment ★
Discovering new wildflowers onsite as species in the soil are allowed to grow and more seeds blow across from Ashes Pasture.

Peaceful Bellfield's Pasture

Birch Wood

This beautiful and relatively undisturbed semi-ancient woodland in the western North York Moors is full of wildlife and has spectacular views across the picturesque valley.

The lowdown...

Nearest town: Helmsley (7m/11.3km)
Nearest postcode: YO62 5NA
Grid ref: SE 569 919
///taxpayers.owned.requires
Parking: In large layby just past north of the reserve entrance (if heading north, it's on the right of the road)
Size: 16ha

  Dogs welcome on leads and on public rights of way only.

A great place for:

☑ Bird watchers
☐ Cyclists
☑ Wildflower enthusiasts
☐ Families
☐ Leisurely stroll
☑ Peace and tranquility
☐ Walkers

Recommended time to make the most of your visit:

☐ Full day
☑ Half day
☐ Just an hour

ⓘ Before you go...
Take care walking from the layby to the reserve entrance as there is no footpath. Access via the linear public rights of way through the reserve. The paths are unsurfaced, sloping and uneven.

A woodland wander to savour

Tread quietly to see the deer before they see you; both roe and fallow are common here. Listen to the chorus of woodland birds. Seek out the gnarled veteran oaks and giant holly trees that give this woodland a distinctive character. Birch Wood is an enchanting hideaway where it's worth savouring every step.

In spring the reserve is at its charming best: redstarts, pied flycatchers, blackcaps and chiffchaffs join the dawn chorus, and bluebells decorate the woodland floor. In summer, keep an eye out for common spotted-orchids.

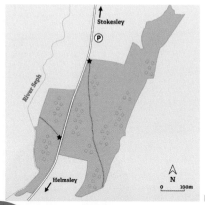

Redstart

You can combine with a trip to nearby Garbutt Wood or Ashberry.

Bluebells carpet the ground in May

★ Magic ★ moment
A redstart perched in the open in spring, flicking its bright orange tail.

Bishop Monkton Railway Cutting

This sheltered stretch of a former railway line is a hidden haven for butterflies, moths and other insects. It reveals its simple splendour only to those who go looking for it.

The lowdown...

Nearest town: Ripon (4m/6.5km)
Nearest postcode: HG3 3QD
Grid ref: SE 31420 66268
///decorator.turkey.blocks
Parking: Limited roadside parking nearby
Size: 2ha

A great place for:

☐ Bird watchers
☐ Cyclists
☑ Wildflower enthusiasts
☐ Families
☐ Leisurely stroll
☑ Peace and tranquility
☐ Walkers

Recommended time to make the most of your visit:

☐ Full day
☐ Half day
☑ Just an hour

ⓘ Before you go...
Visit in spring and summer for the wildflowers and insects, or try an early morning visit in spring, to listen to the dawn chorus of whitethroats, blackcaps and yellowhammers.

Make a day of it with a visit to nearby Burton Leonard Lime Quarries, Staveley and Ripon City Wetlands.

Enter the lost kingdom

It's easy to miss Bishop Monkton Railway Cutting from the road – look for the gateway to the reserve just before the humpback bridge – but once you've found it, you'll quickly become immersed in a tranquil haven.

In an area dominated by large arable fields, this strip of grassland, flower-rich meadow and dense scrub is an oasis for wildlife. The cutting, originally carved out of the magnesian limestone landscape to make way for the now-disused London and Northeast Railway, is rich in insect life. Bees and butterflies can refuel along a corridor of wildflowers, while tussocky grasses provide homes and feeding grounds for small mammals, beetles and other insects, and thickets of brambles and scrub offer great nesting sites for birds.

The walk through the reserve is a short and straightforward there-and-back stroll along the old railway cutting. It's the perfect place to get away for some peace, quiet and solace in nature, even if you don't have much time.

Nature has reclaimed this former railway line

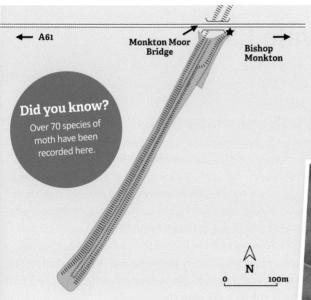

← A61

Monkton Moor Bridge

Bishop Monkton →

Ripon ↑

Bishop Monkton

Bishop Monkton Railway Cutting

Wormald Green

A61

Burton Leonard

↓ Harrogate

N

Did you know?

Over 70 species of moth have been recorded here.

N

0   100m

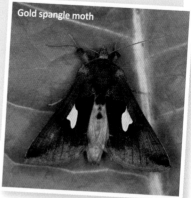

Gold spangle moth

Moth magic and butterfly bonanzas

You don't have to be an expert, specialist or even own a pair of binoculars to enjoy your visit here, but it's a fantastic place for those lovers of wildflowers and insects who are looking for something a bit special. The natural limestone grassland supports a wealth of plants that create a delightful carpet of summer colour, including cowslip, wild marjoram, oxeye daisy, bird's-foot trefoil, lady's mantle, salad burnet and St John's-wort.

Insects are drawn to this treasure trove of flowers, and you'll find some brilliant butterflies basking in the cutting's inviting sun traps, including small and large skippers, gatekeeper, ringlet, comma, and small copper. The roll call of moths includes marbled beauty, July highflyer, gold spangle and flounced rustic.

Barn owl

⭐ **Magic moment** ⭐

Glimpse a barn owl hunting for voles along the cutting.

Seasonal highlights

✿ Spring
Cowslip
Bird's-foot trefoil
Hawthorn blossom

❀ Summer
Bee orchid
Ringlet
Gatekeeper
Salad burnet

❧ Autumn
Roe deer
Fieldfare
Redwing
Bullfinch

❄ Winter
Barn owl
Stoat
Kestrel

Bolton-on-Swale Lake

Of the many former sand and gravel quarries along the river Swale, Bolton-on-Swale Lake is one of the few that has been looked after for wildlife.

The lowdown...

Nearest town: Catterick (4m/6.5km)
Nearest postcode: DL10 6AH
Grid ref: SE 24869 98735
///epidemics.routine.olive
Parking: Car park at entrance to reserve
Site designation: SSSI
Size: 35 ha

A great place for:

☑ Bird watchers
☐ Cyclists
☐ Wildflower enthusiasts
☑ Families
☐ Leisurely stroll
☑ Peace and tranquility
☐ Walkers

Recommended time to make the most of your visit:

☐ Full day
☑ Half day
☐ Just an hour

 Before you go...
Take binoculars to enjoy birds on the far side of the lake and on the islands.

Did you know?
We have erected a platform with an artificial nest to encourage ospreys to stay and breed.

A welcome winter retreat

Despite its proximity to the A1, this ever-improving reserve is a peaceful place where you can often spend time alone in nature. A little outside the north-eastern corner of the Yorkshire Dales, it's one of our most northerly reserves. The lake was created as a result of sand and gravel quarrying and has been landscaped and flooded to create a suitable habitat for many wetland bird species. Trees and bushes around the northern end of the lake have increased the diversity of birdlife, and several islands in the lake have been cleared to create more breeding spaces for birds like oystercatchers and little ringed plovers.

Two hides give great views over the lake. Wading birds and wildfowl are the stars of the show, with huge numbers of ducks wintering here, including nationally important numbers of wigeon, along with goldeneye, pochard, tufted duck, teal and shoveler. Large numbers of curlews winter in the area, and can often be seen feeding on the grassland around the lake.

Lakeside views

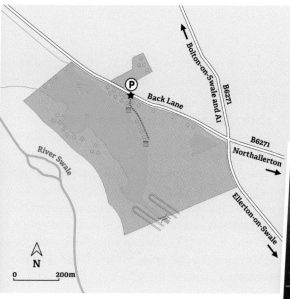

Osprey

A valuable migration station

While winter's the time for soaking up the spectacle of the wildfowl and summer has its breeding birds and dragonflies, spring and autumn see the lake serving as a welcome stop-off for some species. The reserve is on a migration route; ospreys are seen most years and the wetland attracts passage migrants such as Arctic and black terns in spring, and green sandpipers, greenshank and ruff in later summer and autumn. Watch for dazzling yellow wagtails on the lake edge in spring too.

★ **Magic** ★
moment
The headshaking and 'dancing' of displaying great crested grebes.

Great crested grebes

Seasonal highlights

✲ Spring
Oystercatcher
Sand martin
Yellow wagtail
Common sandpiper
Sedge warbler

☀ Summer
Lapwing
Greenshank
Ruff
Common darter

☘ Autumn
Great crested grebe
Osprey
Green sandpiper

❄ Winter
Wigeon
Pochard
Goldeneye
Curlew

Brae Pasture

Visit Brae Pasture on a still, warm summer's day and you'll be enchanted by the colours of its wildflowers and butterflies. The views across the Ribble Valley to Pen-y-Ghent aren't bad either!

The lowdown...

Nearest town: Horton in Ribblesdale (1.4m/2.2km)
Nearest postcode: BD24 0HY
Grid ref: SD 78996 74317
///blaring.bind.routs
Parking: Unsurfaced layby near main entrance
Site designation: SSSI, adjacent to Ingleborough National Nature Reserve
Size: 9ha

  Dogs on public footpath only please

A great place for:

☑ Bird watchers
☐ Cyclists
☑ Wildflower enthusiasts
☐ Families
☐ Leisurely stroll
☑ Peace and tranquility
☑ Walkers

Recommended time to make the most of your visit:

☐ Full day
☐ Half day
☑ Just an hour

ℹ️ **Before you go...**
There's a public footpath across the reserve leading to Ingleborough National Nature Reserve. Wheelchair access only in dry weather on a short linear grassy track from Eastern gate.

A rich abundance of limestone species

It may only cover two fields, but Brae Pasture is home to 150 plant species. This is thanks to a variety of habitats including limestone pavement, grasslands and a wooded ravine. The rare Alpine bistort grows here, along with Oeder's apple moss, so called because its capsules look like miniature apples. Other notable species include rock-rose, blue moor grass, bird's-eye primrose and frog orchid. The numerous butterflies include northern brown argus and dark green fritillary. Breeding birds include meadow pipit, redstart and skylark.

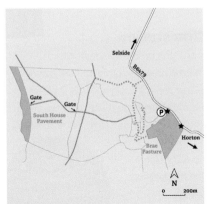

★ Magic ★ moment
Sitting for a while up in the limestone crags and watching the butterflies.

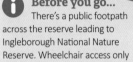
You can combine with a trip to South House Pavement.

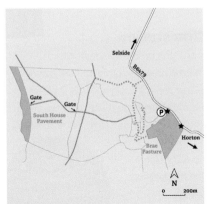
The meadows looking towards Pen-y-Ghent

Burton Leonard Lime Quarries

At this former quarry, there's now peace and quiet where there was once dust and noise. Disused lime kilns can still be found amidst grassland, broadleaved woodland, and scrub.

A place to gaze on sunny days

As you take in the peaceful air and wonderful views from the hilltop and pause to watch a buzzard or red kite soaring over, it's hard to imagine that Burton Leonard was a hive of industrial activity from the late 1700s until 1941, when the quarry was closed due to concerns about the kiln fires being visible to enemy planes.

Spring and summer are the best times to visit. There's rare spring sedge in the magnesian limestone grassland, as well as bee and common spotted-orchids, squinancywort, wild thyme, eyebright and fairy flax. In sheltered spots, butterflies such as dingy skipper, brimstone and speckled wood bask in the sun.

The lowdown...

Nearest town: Ripon/ Boroughbridge (6.5 mi/10.5km)
Nearest postcode: HG3 3TE
Grid ref: SE 32440 63193
///proves.searcher.remotest
Parking: Park considerately in Burton Leonard village and walk along Lime Kiln Lane to reach the reserve.
Site designation: SSSI
Size: 3ha

A great place for:

- ☑ Bird watchers
- ☐ Cyclists
- ☑ Wildflower enthusiasts
- ☑ Families
- ☐ Leisurely stroll
- ☑ Peace and tranquility
- ☑ Walkers

Recommended time to make the most of your visit:

- ☐ Full day
- ☐ Half day
- ☑ Just an hour

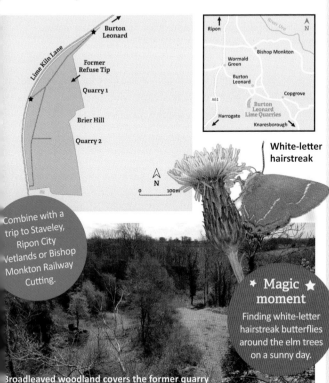

White-letter hairstreak

Combine with a trip to Staveley, Ripon City Wetlands or Bishop Monkton Railway Cutting.

★ **Magic moment** ★

Finding white-letter hairstreak butterflies around the elm trees on a sunny day.

ℹ **Before you go...**
To explore the reserve, take the public right of way through the woodlands, and then skirt the edge of the limestone grass banks, but please stay on the path: this is a sensitive and historical site.

Broadleaved woodland covers the former quarry

Burton Riggs

Burton Riggs is a valuable and popular green space, offering easy access to nature and a spot of serenity bounded by industrial units and the railway line on the edge of Scarborough.

The lowdown...

Nearest town: Seamer (2m/3.2km)
Nearest postcode: YO11 3ZB
Grid ref: TA 0303 8351
///recorders.wiping.polite
Parking: Car park with space for six cars at the north entrance, or on side of road on Lake View (easy access entrance with no gates).
Size: 14ha

A great place for:

☑ Bird watchers
☐ Cyclists
☑ Wildflower enthusiasts
☑ Families
☐ Leisurely stroll
☑ Peace and tranquility
☐ Walkers

Recommended time to make the most of your visit:

☐ Full day
☐ Half day
☑ Just an hour

ℹ **Before you go...**
Paths circle the site, including a route around the smaller lake for wheelchair access, and a track around the larger lake, with steps and boardwalks over boggy and undulating parts. Strictly no swimming.

From gravel to greenery

Despite it's urban surroundings, Burton Riggs has a rich mix of habitats and species. It owes its existence to the A64, having been created by gravel quarrying in the 1970s to help build the nearby road.

With two large, open lakes, several ponds, woodland, scrub and grassland, the site is an oasis that provides space to breathe and appreciate the birds, amphibians, mammals and flowers. The expanses of freshwater make this a great place to watch wildfowl and waders, especially during autumn migration and over the winter. Ducks including pochard, goldeneye and tufted duck gather here with swans and geese, while oystercatchers use the islands, grey herons hunt for fish, and little egrets sometimes visit.

Take an early morning walk in spring and look for migrant birds in the scrub, such as common and lesser whitethroats, blackcaps, chiffchaffs and occasionally garden warblers.

Can you help?
With some extra funding and resources we could improve the habitat here for both wildlife and visitors.

Views across the water

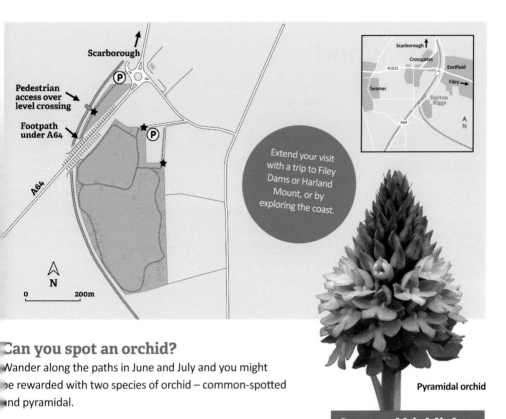

Extend your visit with a trip to Filey Dams or Harland Mount, or by exploring the coast.

Can you spot an orchid?

Wander along the paths in June and July and you might be rewarded with two species of orchid – common-spotted and pyramidal.

Some of the work we do to give wildlife a helping hand includes keeping the ponds clear by coppicing willows and caring for the young woodland. We retain as much scrub as possible, as it's vital for smaller birds and mammals, and only cut it back along the footpaths.

Pyramidal orchid

Seasonal highlights

✿ Spring
Cowslip
Willow warbler
Sedge warbler
Great crested newt

✹ Summer
Common darter
Gatekeeper
Pyramidal orchid

◉ Autumn
Green sandpiper
Grey heron

❄ Winter
Pochard
Goldeneye
Tufted duck
Little egret

★ **Magic moment** ★
Watching dragonflies zipping over the lake on a lazy summer afternoon.

Emperor dragonfly

Chafer Wood

Enjoy an uplifting and invigorating walk through this idyllic broadleaved woodland and take in the breathtaking views across the Vale of Pickering.

The lowdown...

Nearest town: Pickering (7m/11.3km)
Nearest postcode: YO13 9NX
Grid ref: SE899832
///rejoins.elated.pouch
Parking: Limited roadside parking at southern main entrance and northern end of reserve
Size: 28ha

  Dogs welcome on lead on public and permissive footpaths.

A great place for:

☑ Bird watchers
☐ Cyclists
☑ Wildflower enthusiasts
☑ Families
☐ Leisurely stroll
☑ Peace and tranquility
☑ Walkers

Recommended time to make the most of your visit:

☐ Full day
☑ Half day
☐ Just an hour

ⓘ Before you go...

There are steep, uneven and unsurfaced waymarked paths through the woodland. Enjoy views from King Alfred's Cairn which commemorates the battle of Ebberston. The ancient pinfold pasture was restored by the Trust.

The sights, sounds and scents of spring

Climb the valley sides of young woodland and scrub, where small open glades contain limestone grassland. The shaded lower parts of the valley, which have been wooded for longer, are covered in delicate ferns and mosses, and rare species of cranefly thrive. Look for baneberry, goldilocks buttercup and leopard's-bane by the stream. Resident birds include green and great spotted woodpeckers and nuthatch, with redstart and blackcap arriving in spring.

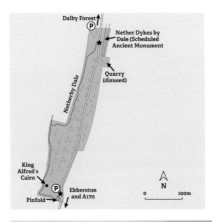

Combine with a visit to Ellerburn Bank, Fen Bog or Robinson's Field.

★ Magic ★ moment

Spring scents of wild garlic, with carpets of wood anemone and lesser celandine.

King Alfred's Cairn built in 1770

Ellerburn Bank

A small, sloping limestone grassland on the edge of Dalby Forest, Ellerburn Bank is crammed full of wildflowers, and is at its best on sunny days in June and July.

Picture the scene...

The sun is out, and so are the vibrantly coloured meadow flowers – several species of orchid, rock-rose, cowslip and quaking grass. Bright orange small copper and small skipper butterflies, and black-and-red, day-flying six-spot burnet moths flutter between them. Adders bask by the drystone walls, and stoats cavort around the flower stems. Willow tits are occasionally seen, while willow warblers and yellowhammers sing from coppiced scrub and trees around the site. Keep a close eye on the sky, as goshawks are regularly seen in the area, and common buzzards nest nearby.

The lowdown...

Nearest town: Pickering (5m/8km)
Nearest postcode: YO18 7LU
Grid ref: SE 8532 8503
///jumbo.welcome.president
Parking: Park at Haygate car park on the Dalby Forest Drive (charge applies), then walk 750 metres (1/2 mile) south on the footpath.
Site designation: SSSI
Size: 3ha

A great place for:

☑ Bird watchers
☐ Cyclists
☑ Wildflower enthusiasts
☐ Families
☐ Leisurely stroll
☑ Peace and tranquility
☐ Walkers

Recommended time to make the most of your visit:

☐ Full day
☐ Half day
☑ Just an hour

ⓘ Before you go...
Stick to the worn path around this sensitive site between May and July to appreciate the variety of species – and maybe spot a rarity!

★ **Magic moment** ★
A wildlife walk enriched by a crossbill or goshawk flying over.

Explore more of Dalby Forest for a longer visit.

Wildflowers flourish at Ellerburn Bank

Fen Bog

A unique reserve in the North York Moors, bounded by moorland streams at both ends, Fen Bog offers a winning combination of stunning views and some of Yorkshire's best wildlife.

The lowdown...

Nearest town: Pickering (11m/17.7km)
Nearest postcode: YO18 7NT
Grid ref: SE 857982
///aviation.behalf.envy
Parking: Small car park at reserve entrance off the A169 at Ellerbeck.
Size: 19ha

  Dogs on leads on public footpaths, but not on the reserve

A great place for:

☑ Bird watchers

☐ Cyclists

☑ Wildflower enthusiasts

☐ Families

☐ Leisurely stroll

☑ Peace and tranquility

☐ Walkers

Recommended time to make the most of your visit:

☐ Full day

☑ Half day

☐ Just an hour

ℹ **Before you go...**
Please stick to the permissive footpaths and stay off the bog to avoid damage to the fragile habitat. Parts of the bog are very deep. One bonus highlight of your trip could be a passing steam train!

Visit for regional rarities

In this upland landscape of basking adders, calling curlews, passing merlins and breeding whinchats, stonechats and willow warblers, there are also fascinating and unusual plants and butterflies to discover. The mire bottom has some of the region's most unusual species of sphagnum moss, and interesting plants including slender sedge, round-leaved sundew, cranberry, common butterwort, marsh violet and bog asphodel. Look for chickweed wintergreen, also known as Arctic starflower, in the drier heathland areas. In early summer, butterflies include dark green and small pearl-bordered fritillaries and the rare large heath.

You can combine with a visit to Little Beck Wood or Ellerburn Bank.

Small pearl-bordered fritillary

⭐ **Magic moment** ⭐
The heady scent of bog myrtle fills the air on warm summer days.

Peaceful views across the bog

Round-leaved sundew

Filey Dams

Holidaymakers and birdwatchers alike head to Filey for its long expanse of sand, seaside charm and seabirds, but birders in the know also seek out the hidden wetland haven of Filey Dams.

The lowdown...

Nearest town: Filey (1m/1.6km)
Nearest postcode: YO14 0DP
Grid ref: TA 1065 8070
///unlocking.swims.doped
Parking: Small reserve car park at the end of Wharfedale, off Muston Road (A1039)
Size: 6ha

Accessible by bike but no cycling onsite

A great place for:

☑ Bird watchers

☐ Cyclists

☐ Wildflower enthusiasts

☑ Families

☐ Leisurely stroll

☑ Peace and tranquility

☐ Walkers

Recommended time to make the most of your visit:

☐ Full day

☐ Half day

☑ Just an hour

ℹ️ **Before you go...**
Filey Dams is a level nature reserve. It has three hides and a flat, accessible path, with wheelchair access to the main hide and pond-dipping platform. It's just a ten-minute walk from the bus and train stations.

Somewhere beyond the sea

Set back from the town centre on the edge of a housing estate, Filey Dams is the last remaining freshwater marsh of any size in the area, making it a magnet for migratory birds. Not just that: it's home to a variety of insects, amphibians, small mammals and plants, and with three viewing hides along a short path it's one of our easiest reserves to get around. The hides provide excellent views across the reserve and often close views of the birds. It's worth checking the pool edges for water rails and snipe.

The Dams is a pit-stop where migrating birds can refuel. Alongside regular migrants, which include greenshank and dunlin plus common, green and wood sandpipers, every year something surprising turns up. Spoonbills and little egrets are increasingly seen, and yellow-browed warblers are among the smaller autumn visitors.

Look for tree sparrows on your short walk through the copse to the boardwalk, and on to a pond-dipping platform, where dragonflies skim the water and water voles hide. All three British species of newt can be found here – smooth, palmate and great crested.

Did you know?
Filey Dams was almost lost to development in the 1980s, but FBOG campaigned to save the site and it became a nature reserve.

Filey Dams freshwater marsh

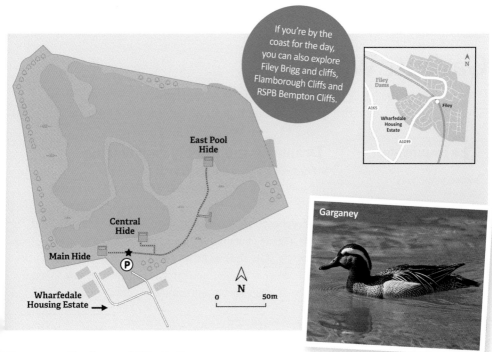

If you're by the coast for the day, you can also explore Filey Brigg and cliffs, Flamborough Cliffs and RSPB Bempton Cliffs.

East Pool Hide

Central Hide

Main Hide

Wharfedale Housing Estate →

N

0   50m

Garganey

Filey Dams

A165
Wharfedale Housing Estate
A1039
Filey

N

Can you find an old lady?

The reserve, managed in partnership with Filey Bird Observatory and Group (FBOG), consists of freshwater lagoons surrounded by marsh and grassland. The dominant plant is soft rush, with toad rush, bottle sedge, branched bur-reed and yellow flag iris in the shallows. Looking across the pools from the East Pool hide, you'll spot the barn owl box and possibly one or more owls – the male often perches in nearby cover.

Filey Dams is also great for moths, including small rufous and old lady, which provide food for bats, such as Nathusius' pipistrelle and Daubenton's bat.

★ **Magic** ★
moment
Being in the right place at the right time when a rare migrant wader drops in.

Seasonal highlights

✤ Spring
Water vole
Sedge warbler
Broad-bodied chaser

❀ Summer
Green sandpiper
Wood sandpiper
Barn owl
Great crested newt
Nathusius' pipistrelle and Daubenton's bats

◉ Autumn
Ruff
Greenshank
Common darter
Curlew sandpiper
Snipe

❄ Winter
Tree sparrow
Great spotted woodpecker
Water rail

Litte egret

Garbutt Wood

If you've ever marvelled at the stunning view from Sutton Bank, you'll have seen Lake Gormire below, and an enticing wood that's crying out to be explored. That's Garbutt Wood.

The lowdown...

Nearest town: Thirsk (6.5m/10.5km)
Nearest postcode: YO7 2EH
Grid ref: SE507833
///tailors.intrigued.topmost
Parking: Large car park, cafe and toilets at National Park Centre off the A170 (charge applies).
Site designation: SSSI
Size: 24ha

  Dogs welcome on leads on public and permissive footpaths.

A great place for:

- ☑ Bird watchers
- ☐ Cyclists
- ☑ Wildflower enthusiasts
- ☑ Families
- ☑ Leisurely stroll
- ☑ Peace and tranquility
- ☑ Walkers

Recommended time to make the most of your visit:

- ☐ Full day
- ☑ Half day
- ☐ Just an hour

ℹ️ **Before you go...**
Paths can be muddy, steep and uneven, with flights of steps and boardwalks. Wheelchair/buggy access is limited to the Cleveland Way from the National Park Centre to clifftop edge of the reserve.

Dramatic and utterly captivating

This spellbinding woodland is at its most magical when the flowers are out in May and June, and the songs of redstarts, blackcaps and other breeding birds create an enchanting atmosphere. Whitestone Cliff, towering above the woodland, adds a sense of drama, while on a smaller scale there are micro-habitats ideal for lichens, mosses and ferns. In the north-west corner of the site, you can find plants including common fleabane, ragged robin and common spotted-orchid.

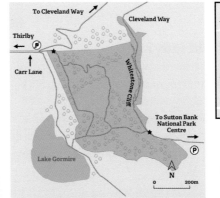

Common spotted-orchid

Combine with walks around Sutton Bank, listen out for the purr of turtle doves and nightjars on summer evenings.

★ **Magic moment** ★
The 'orchid ride' is peppered with spikes of common spotted-orchids in June.

Whitestone Cliff

Globeflower Wood

High in the Yorkshire Dales on Malham Moor, close to Malham Tarn, is one of our smallest and oldest reserves. It's named after its brightest and best-known attraction – the globeflower.

Mellow yellow

The nature reserve is tiny, fragile and isolated but is well worth a look if you are in the area. This triangular reserve of ungrazed damp meadow, fringed by willows, shines golden yellow in late May and early June when the globeflowers are in bloom. Just look over the wall to enjoy this stunning display.

The Trust took over the site in 1963 from a farmer who wanted to ensure that the globeflowers were protected. Alongside them, you can see great burnet, water avens, meadowsweet and melancholy thistle, with early purple orchids in spring.

The lowdown...

Nearest town: Settle (3.9m/6.3km)
Nearest postcode: BD24 9PR
Grid ref: SD 87253 66670
///welfare.knees.poorly
Parking: In small layby by cattle grid next to reserve
Size: 0.08ha

A great place for:

- [ ] Bird watchers
- [ ] Cyclists
- [x] Wildflower enthusiasts
- [ ] Families
- [ ] Leisurely stroll
- [x] Peace and tranquility
- [ ] Walkers

Recommended time to make the most of your visit:

- [ ] Full day
- [ ] Half day
- [x] Just an hour

ⓘ Before you go...
Although you might see a stile onsite, there's no public access into the reserve. If able, you can view the flowers from the boundary wall. This is so we can protect this especially delicate habitat.

A meadow of globeflowers

★ **Magic moment** ★
The stunning display of golden yellow globeflowers.

Grass Wood

Discover delightful Grass Wood, a woodland full of character and wildlife in beautiful Wharfedale.

The lowdown...

Nearest town: Grassington (1.25m/2km)
Nearest postcode: BD23 5FA
Grid ref: Roadside parking: SD 98555 65102
///fitter.offstage.could
Parking: In small quarry car park, or on roadside in several places
Site designation: SSSI
Size: 78ha

  Dogs welcome on leads.

A great place for:

☑ Bird watchers
☐ Cyclists
☑ Wildflower enthusiasts
☑ Families
☐ Leisurely stroll
☑ Peace and tranquility
☑ Walkers

Recommended time to make the most of your visit:

☐ Full day
☑ Half day
☐ Just an hour

ℹ Before you go...

There are public footpaths in the wood, and a well-surfaced access track. Paths are very steep in places, and conditions underfoot can be rocky and difficult when it is wet or icy.

It is worth a longer visit to do the five-mile circular walk from Grassington.

Woodland wildlife by the Wharfe

A short walk up the valley from the popular village of Grassington, Grass Wood is one of the largest areas of broadleaved woodland in the Dales. It's chiefly an ash woodland, growing on a series of limestone terraces, with open glades and exposed rock.

Yorkshire Wildlife Trust has been involved in Grass Wood since the 1960s and took ownership from the Forestry Commission in 1983. We work with a very active group of volunteers to manage the reserve, removing non-native trees and initially replanting these areas, which we now leave to regenerate naturally.

Some of the plant species you might find include bird's-nest orchid, horseshoe vetch, wild basil, spring sandwort and green spleenwort, along with commoner species like lily-of-the-valley, lady's-mantle and rock rose. Autumn is the season for a fascinating array of fungi, including the distinctive common puffball.

With a discerning eye for butterflies, you might be lucky enough to spot the northern brown argus, (a small, chocolate-brown butterfly at the southern edge of its British range), among the speckled woods and ringlets.

Bluebells on the woodland floor

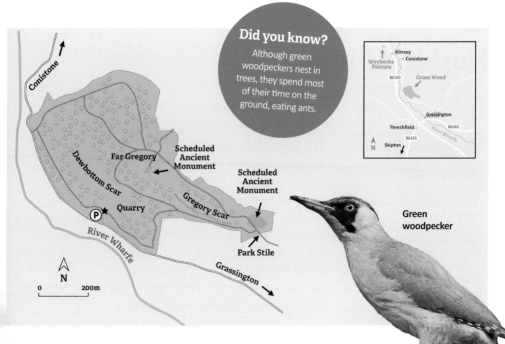

Did you know?
Although green woodpeckers nest in trees, they spend most of their time on the ground, eating ants.

Conistone

Far Gregory

Scheduled Ancient Monument

Scheduled Ancient Monument

Dewbottom Scar

Gregory Scar

Quarry

River Wharfe

Park Stile

Grassington

N

0   200m

Kilnsey
Weybecks Pasture
Conistone
B6160
Grass Wood
Grassington
Threshfield
B6265
B6265
River Wharfe
Skipton
N

Green woodpecker

Singing in the spring

When spring arrives in the woodland, so too do migrant songbirds, joining resident species in a gorgeous dawn chorus. The birds you might see on your visit include some of our most colourful and striking species – the handsome pied flycatcher, the lovely redstart with its fiery orange tail, and our largest woodpecker species, the green woodpecker. Sadly, wood warblers are rare now, but listen for their spinning-coin song in May, just in case one calls in.

Seasonal highlights

✿ Spring
Bluebell
Primrose
Lily-of-the-valley
Pied flycatcher
Spotted flycatcher

✿ Summer
Northern brown argus
Dropwort
Bloody cranesbill

✿ Autumn
Common puffball
Milkcap
Brittlegills
Clouded funnel cap
Roe deer

✿ Winter
Tawny owl
Nuthatch
Treecreeper

★ **Magic moment** ★
Watching pied and spotted flycatchers catching insects from a favourite perch.

Spotted flycatcher

Harland Mount

Along with the better-known Oliver's Mount, Harland Mount has been referred to as one of Scarborough's 'twin peaks', offering magnificent views across the town and over the sea.

The lowdown...

Nearest town: Scarborough (3.6m/5.8km)
Nearest postcode: YO12 5NL
Grid ref: TA019875
///sleeps.pulse.soccer
Parking: Informal parking for one car on grassy track off A170 (between 2 houses) leading to reserve entrance
Size: 8ha

  Dogs welcome on leads

A great place for:

- ☑ Bird watchers
- ☐ Cyclists
- ☐ Wildflower enthusiasts
- ☑ Families
- ☐ Leisurely stroll
- ☑ Peace and tranquility
- ☑ Walkers

Recommended time to make the most of your visit:

- ☐ Full day
- ☐ Half day
- ☑ Just an hour

ⓘ Before you go...

There's a public footpath and permissive route through the reserve, but the uphill path is steep and can get slippery, so it's best to go in dry weather.

An unspoilt spot

'Rough acid pasture' might not be the most appealing description of a nature reserve you'll ever hear, but by managing the pastures of this unspoilt reserve through traditional methods we're restoring it to the species-rich grassland it once was. Oxeye daisy and common knapweed flourish here, and bluebell, primrose and dog violet grow on the heaths that occur on the steep banks below. Common lizards are frequent and there may be adders here. Look and listen for whitethroats and willow warblers in the spring, and grasshoppers in the summer.

Make it part of a day by the coast.

Blackca[p]

The view towards Scarborough

★ **Magic** ★
moment
Enjoy spectacular view over Scarborough and the North Sea serenad[e] by blackcaps, nuthatch and marsh tits.

Can you make a **bigger commitment** to a **wilder future?**

Become a Wildlife Guardian!

Our Wildlife Guardians are a special group of people who make a bigger commitment to supporting Yorkshire's wildlife and enjoy a deeper connection with the Trust's work. You can join these like-minded individuals, who care passionately about protecting Yorkshire's wildlife, by contacting us to increase your monthly membership donation.

As a Wildlife Guardian, you'll enjoy:

■ Exclusive behind-the-scenes visits to our nature reserves, led by our wildlife experts
■ Reports which bring you closer to the cutting edge of conservation in Yorkshire
■ Invitations to exclusive events, hosted by our Chief Executive and Trustees
■ Detailed insights into the impact you are making for wildlife and wild places
■ All the usual benefits of Yorkshire Wildlife Trust membership, including copies of our quarterly *Wildlife Yorkshire* magazine and complimentary admission to over 100 nature reserves across Yorkshire.

Find out more at **ywt.org.uk/ wildlife-guardians**

Leyburn Old Glebe

A traditional hay meadow, with an eye-popping display of flowers between May and mid-July, this is a glorious example of the species-rich meadows that were once common in the Dales.

The lowdown...

Nearest town: Leyburn (3.4m/5.5km)
Nearest postcode: DL8 4HU
Grid ref: SE 10017 89547
///helm.manicured.stormed
Parking: Layby across the road
Size: 16ha
Site designation: SSSI

A great place for:

☐ Bird watchers

☐ Cyclists

☑ Wildflower enthusiasts

☐ Families

☐ Leisurely stroll

☑ Peace and tranquility

☐ Walkers

Recommended time to make the most of your visit:

☐ Full day

☐ Half day

☑ Just an hour

ℹ **Before you go...**
This is a small, fragile site, so please take care not to flatten plants, especially if photographing orchids. There's a footpath around the edge of the reserve, which connects with a public footpath running through the top of the field.

An hour with the flowers

If you love wildflowers, you need to visit Leyburn Old Glebe. Simple as that. In fact, you'll probably want to visit more than once. At the springtime height of its botanical bounty, the colours seem to change every couple of weeks, as plants come into flower, then fade to be replaced by equally beautiful species. It's the richest remaining fragment of Ellershaw, a district well-known to naturalists since the 19th century.

The reserve is at its most charming in spring: redstarts, pied flycatchers, blackcaps and chiffchaffs join the dawn chorus, and bluebells decorate the woodland floor. In summer, keep an eye out for common spotted orchids.

More than 80 plant species have been recorded here, including salad burnet, wild thyme, fairy flax, cowslips and agrimony. And if you enjoy seeking out orchids, see if you can find green winged, common-spotted, early purple, bee, and the nationally scarce burnt.

As you might expect, this decadent carpet of flowers attracts plentiful butterflies, including masses of orange-tips, along with small skipper, common blue and dark green fritillary. Redstarts sing from the large trees along the hedgerows, and ospreys are frequently seen hunting along the river.

Did you know?
The burnt orchid gets its name from the unopened dark purple flowers at the top, which appear burnt compared to the paler, open flowers below it.

Burnt orchid

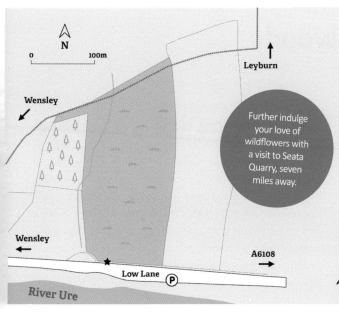

Further indulge your love of wildflowers with a visit to Seata Quarry, seven miles away.

Common blue

Ure going to love the view

Leyburn Old Glebe is on a south-facing, sloping bank above the River Ure, giving visitors an excellent vantage point for views over the Yorkshire Dales to Penhill and to the ridge above Coverdale.

Yorkshire Wildlife Trust took on care of the meadow from a local church in 1983. It has never been ploughed or re-seeded and has been managed as a traditional hay meadow to retain its rich botanical diversity. The hay is cut in late summer then grazed by sheep. Although there's less to see in winter, you might happen across a stoat running past or yellowhammers in the hedgerows.

Seasonal highlights

✿ Spring
Osprey
Redstart
Cowslip
Green-winged orchid
Burnt orchid

✺ Summer
Eyebright
Fairy flax
Bee orchid
Common blue
Small skipper

◑ Autumn
Yellowhammer
Redwing
Bullfinch

✺ Winter
Stoat
Fieldfare

★ **Magic** ★
moment
The carpet of green-winged orchids in spring.

Orchids are dotted across the meadow

Little Beck Wood

In a sheltered, secluded valley in the North York Moors lies lovely Little Beck Wood, close to the beauty spot of the Falling Foss waterfall and home to a wealth of wildlife.

The lowdown...

Nearest town: Whitby
(6.2m/10km)
Nearest postcode: YO22 5HA
Grid ref: NZ 8789 0490 - west side.
NZ 87951 04929 - east side.
///hillsides.detection.responded
(west)unveils.jobs.commuted (east)
Parking: Surfaced car park at Littlebeck village hall (suggested donation) then short walk down steep hill to reserve entrance.
Site designation: SSSI
Size: 26ha

  No cycling except on bridleway.

A great place for:

☑ Bird watchers
☐ Cyclists
☑ Wildflower enthusiasts
☑ Families
☐ Leisurely stroll
☑ Peace and tranquility
☑ Walkers

Recommended time to make the most of your visit:

☐ Full day
☑ Half day
☐ Just an hour

For a full day visit Fen Bog, Falling Foss or Whitby.

ℹ **Before you go...**
There are public paths throughout the woodland, but they can be steep, muddy and uneven.

Ideal for dipping, wagging and bobbing!

A lush, characterful woodland of oak, ash, alder and cherry, Little Beck Wood is split into two by Little Beck – the perfect place to see dippers and grey wagtails. Look out for woodland birds including great spotted woodpecker, marsh tit, nuthatch and treecreeper, and spotted flycatchers in summer. In spring and early summer, the woodland floor bursts into life, with wood anemone, bluebell, primrose, moschatel and early purple orchids. Can you spot badger scrapes, deer tracks and rodent holes around the site?

There's a beautiful circular route taking in Falling Foss waterfall, where there's a tearoom.

★ **Magic moment** ★
Watching a dipper bobbing on a rock in the beck.

Dipper

A little beck with a lot to see

Newbiggin Pastures

Just down the road from Aysgarth Falls, picturesque Newbiggin Pastures feels remote and undiscovered, and has stunning views over Bishopdale.

More than just a pretty place

Newbiggin Pastures is managed as a patchwork of flower-rich traditional hay meadows, developing open woodland, and upland grassland. In time, we hope the six hectares of sparse juniper woodland that volunteers helped us plant will attract black grouse – it's a part of their favoured habitat.

Watch and listen for lapwings, curlews and wheatears in spring, spotted flycatchers in summer, ravens in autumn and barn owls in winter. Visit in summer to admire the wildflowers, including lady's-mantle, eyebright, yellow rattle and agrimony.

The lowdown...

Nearest town: Aysgarth (2.2m/3.6km)
Nearest postcode: DL8 3TF
Grid ref: SD 98799 85093
///september.scars.foster
Parking: Informal roadside parking
Size: 28ha

A great place for:

- ☑ Bird watchers
- ☐ Cyclists
- ☑ Wildflower enthusiasts
- ☐ Families
- ☐ Leisurely stroll
- ☑ Peace and tranquillity
- ☑ Walkers

Recommended time to make the most of your visit:

- ☐ Full day
- ☑ Half day
- ☐ Just an hour

Magic moment

The flash of a wheatear's white rump as it flies up to perch on a drystone wall.

Before you go...

The reserve is on a steep slope with no formal routes, so be prepared for a steep hill hike and take care in wet or hot conditions.

Please keep to the field edges and avoid disturbing livestock.

Enjoy delightful views at this remote reserve

Wheatear

Ripon City Wetlands

Within the footprint of a former quarry and located on a natural floodplain between the river Ure and Ripon Canal, this modern wetland was designed as a year-round haven for wildlife.

The lowdown...

Nearest town: Ripon (1 m/1.5km)
Nearest postcode: HG4 1UG
Grid ref: SE 33137 69950
///scripted.pampering.joystick
Parking: Car park at entrance, open 9am to 5pm except on race days. Please use the furthest end of the car park (furthest from the road). For disabled visitors, a metal gate is accessible with a Radar key. You can then drive along the entrance track before turning left at the end and into the disabled parking area.
Size: 41ha

  No cycling on site, but bike racks in car park

A great place for:

☑ Bird watchers
☐ Cyclists
☑ Wildflower enthusiasts
☑ Families
☐ Leisurely stroll
☑ Peace and tranquility
☑ Walkers

Recommended time to make the most of your visit:

☐ Full day
☑ Half day
☐ Just an hour

ℹ **Before you go...** Keep to the footpaths which are mainly flat, the reserve is a short walk from the car park.

Backing a winner!

Ripon City Wetlands, next to Ripon Racecourse, is one of the newest reserves in our stable, opening in 2019.

You can bet on discovering many wild delights around the reserve as you follow the trail – perhaps while watched by an inquisitive stoat – to the Riverside Lagoon viewing screen, then along the towpath to the Canal Reedbed hide. Look for the wild bird crop adjacent to the canal which provides food for linnets, yellowhammers and reed buntings during the winter.

★ **Magic moment** The jaw-dropping winter spectacle of a starling murmuration swirling through the sky.

Starling murmuration

Discover and do

This is a family-friendly reserve, with a sensory trail, interactive information hut and audio station, where you can listen to bird calls and find out about the reserve and its wildlife.

There are excellent views of the wetlands from the many paths and viewing areas but bring binoculars to watch wildfowl at the end of the lagoon, and maybe bitterns, avocets, little ringed plovers, kingfishers and otters among the extensive reedbeds and in the water.

Lagoon view

Did you know?
The Cetti's warbler is one of the few warblers to spend the winter in the UK. They even give the occasional burst of distinctive and loud song in the colder months.

Cetti's warbler

Sights and sounds for all seasons

Pause to appreciate the sounds of the wetlands: the rustling of reeds, or the pattering feet and beating wings of a mute swan taking off. The expanses of water fill with ducks, geese, and swans in winter, and attract waders including lapwings, curlews, snipe, and migrating species like green sandpipers, little ringed plovers and greenshanks. In spring, the purpose-built reedbeds are alive with the songs of reed, sedge and Cetti's warblers. In summer and early autumn, dragonflies and damselflies hover around the lakeside paths, sometimes pursued by a hobby. As autumn sets in, redwings drop down to feast on hawthorn berries.

Seasonal highlights

✿ Spring
Willow warbler
Sedge warbler
Sand martin
Little ringed plover
Brimstone butterfly

❋ Summer
Common blue damselfly
Emperor dragonfly
Ragged robin
Green sandpiper
Hobby

◐ Autumn
Snipe
Curlew
Teal
Redwing

❋ Winter
Starling murmurations
Brown hare
Fox

Broad-bodied chaser

Brown hare

To carpark
Nursery Pond
Northern Reedbeds
Sand martin bank
Riverside Lagoon Screen
To Ripon
Central Reedbeds
Riverside Lagoon
River Ure
Canal Reedbeds
Littlethorpe Meadows
Southern Reedbeds
Canal Reedbed Hide
To Littlethorpe
Renton's Bridge
Adam's Pond
Littlethorpe Meadows
Canal towpath
N
0   100m

Extend your visit with a walk by the canal, or a trip to our nearby reserves at Staveley or Burton Leonard Lime Quarries.

Ripon
B6265
A61
Ripon Racecourse
River Ure
Ripon Canal
Littlethorpe
Ripon City Wetlands

For a wild day...

Bring the family, stop for a picnic and explore the sensory nature trail, pond dipping platform, and wood carvings. How many different creatures can you spot?

Go a little wilder...

At dusk on a late autumn or winter afternoon, get a grandstand view of a starling murmuration for a wild 'wow' moment.

Experience Ripon City Wetlands' wildest side...

Visit in spring or autumn for a chance of finding migrant birds, some of which may have travelled from eastern Europe or southern Africa.

And there's more...

Join one of our events! Visitors of all ages can enjoy taking part in a nature hunt or craft activities.

Green sandpiper

Designed with wildlife in mind

Ripon City Wetlands' transformation from quarry to thriving wetland happened thanks to a partnership between Aggregate Industries, Yorkshire Wildlife Trust and Middlemarch Environmental.

It was designed to create valuable habitat for species like bitterns, marsh harriers and reed warblers. Birds that have been seen breeding at Staveley, five miles away, have been seen feeding at Ripon, showing the importance of creating and linking up these habitats.

The reserve also helps to reduce flood risk. When the Ure bursts its banks, the water pours onto the wetland, where it's held before slowly flowing back when the river levels have dropped.

Marsh harrier

Robinson's Field

With magnificent views over the Levisham valley, and close to the pretty villages of Lockton and Levisham, this reserve is a summer sanctuary for some very special birds.

The lowdown...

Nearest town: Pickering (6.4m/10.3km)
Nearest postcode: YO18 7NJ
Grid ref: SE839901
///poster.shaves.lawns
Parking: Park considerately in Lockton village and walk down Mill Bank Road to reserve entrance.
Size: 3.75ha

 Dogs allowed at viewpoint but not on reserve

A great place for:

☑ Bird watchers
☐ Cyclists
☐ Wildflower enthusiasts
☐ Families
☐ Leisurely stroll
☑ Peace and tranquility
☐ Walkers

Recommended time to make the most of your visit:

☐ Full day
☐ Half day
☑ Just an hour

ℹ️ **Before you go...**
Terrain is extremely steep and there are no marked paths. Please take care as you explore.

You can combine with a trip to nearby Garbutt Wood or Ashberry.

A purr-fect beauty spot

Named after the late George Robinson, who lived in Lockton village and kindly gifted this land to Yorkshire Wildlife Trust in 2018, Robinson's Field and its surrounding mix of farmland, woodland and scrub supports a small population of the rapidly declining turtle dove. Listen for their purring call from the viewpoint, and see what other birds you can spot in the valley below. At the bottom of this steep (!) wooded valley you'll find some remarkable woodland flowers, including the early purple orchid.

Magic moment
The gentle purring call of the turtle dove.

A wooded valley is central to the reserve

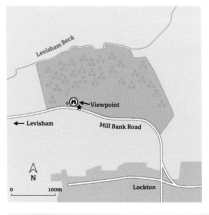

Turtle dove

Salt Lake Quarry

This tranquil former limestone quarry is a veritable Aladdin's Cave of botanists' treasures. Its gems include several nationally scarce plants.

Off the beaten track

Tucked away amidst Yorkshire's famous Three Peaks, Salt Lake Quarry is a calming, secluded place where you can see a surprising variety of habitats: species-rich limestone grassland, marshy grassland, a pond, bare limestone and willow scrub. The shady areas are a tangle of bryophyte-covered scrub and fern-rich rock faces.

The grasslands sport a wonderful palette of colours, starring oxeye daisy, water avens, bird's-foot trefoil, marsh valerian, common spotted-orchid, frog orchid, crane's-bill, blue moor grass, common twayblade, *Daphne mezereum* and marsh marigold. Moonwort, believed by some to have magical properties, has also been found here and it was the last known Yorkshire site for coralroot orchid.

The lowdown...

Nearest town: Horton in Ribblesdale (4m/6.5km)
Nearest postcode: LA6 3AS
Grid ref: SD 77355 78432
///dummy.canines.display
Parking: None onsite, but you can park in the large lay-by 0.5 miles along the B6479 (Gauber Road) towards Ribblehead, on the right-hand side.
Site designation: SSSI
Size: 2 ha

A great place for:

- [ ] Bird watchers
- [ ] Cyclists
- [x] Wildflower enthusiasts
- [ ] Families
- [ ] Leisurely stroll
- [x] Peace and tranquility
- [ ] Walkers

Recommended time to make the most of your visit:

- [ ] Full day
- [ ] Half day
- [x] Just an hour

Before you go...

Visit in spring and early summer to see stunning swathes of bird's-eye primroses, and in June and July for the grassland colours. The reserve has uneven ground, is on different levels and has steep steps.

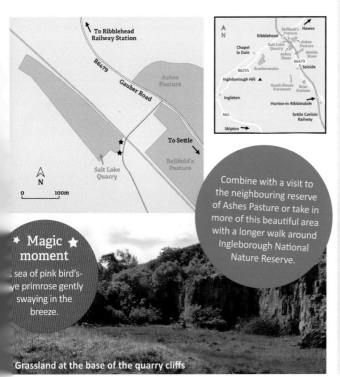

Combine with a visit to the neighbouring reserve of Ashes Pasture or take in more of this beautiful area with a longer walk around Ingleborough National Nature Reserve.

★ Magic ★ moment
sea of pink bird's-eye primrose gently swaying in the breeze.

Grassland at the base of the quarry cliffs

Seata Quarry

With over 100 plant species flowering in this small former stone quarry in the Dales, including four species of orchid, a spring or summer visit is a must for wildflower enthusiasts.

The lowdown...

Nearest town: Aysgarth (0.6m/1km)
Nearest postcode: DL8 3AL
Grid ref: SD 99224 88442
///picturing.chap.chip
Parking: Informal roadside parking
Size: 0.6ha

  Dogs welcome on a lead

A great place for:

☐ Bird watchers
☐ Cyclists
☑ Wildflower enthusiasts
☐ Families
☐ Leisurely stroll
☑ Peace and tranquility
☑ Walkers

Recommended time to make the most of your visit:

☐ Full day
☐ Half day
☑ Just an hour

ℹ Before you go...
This small site is accessed down a rough, grassy farm track from the road. Once on site, take care as the terrain is uneven. Please keep away from cliff edges and don't visit in wet conditions. Keep children under close supervision at all times.

Visit our other local reserves: Newbiggin Pastures, Semer Water and Leyburn Old Glebe.

First-class grasses

Seata Quarry is packed with grasses; blue moor-grass is the most abundant, but the grass at the top of the class is the rare spiky fescue, a native of the Pyrenees. Look for two other non-native Pyrenean plants: round-leaved St John's-wort and fairy foxglove. Other plants include bird's-foot trefoil, purging flax, harebell, small scabious, field madder and biting stonecrop. The flowers attract six-spot burnet moths, and butterflies including common blue and ringlet. Curlews and grey partridges have nested in the surrounding fields.

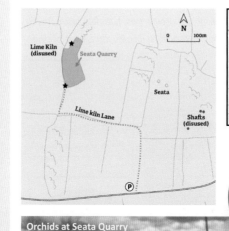

Orchids at Seata Quarry

★ Magic ★ moment
Autumn gentians grow 20cms high in damp autumn.

Yorkshire
Wildlife Trust

For your loved one
For Yorkshire's wildlife

Tom was a committed supporter and tireless volunteer at Grass Wood – the place he called his second home.

His family knew the best way to honour his life was to ask for donations for the Trust, and reserve he loved so well.

Tom is missed by all who knew him, but his memory lives on in the wild place he cared for.

We're here to help – please do get in touch and speak to someone to find out more, or to arrange a dedication or gift in memory. Call us on **01904 659570** or email **info@ywt.org.uk**

Semer Water

A glacial lake formed at the end of the last Ice Age, Semer Water is the second-largest natural lake in North Yorkshire, and provides valuable habitat for breeding and wintering birds.

The lowdown...

Nearest town: Hawes (2.9m/4.6km)
Nearest postcode: DL8 3DG (Marsett village)
Grid ref: Marsett village: SD 90396 86194
///Marsett village: publisher.valve.funnels
Parking: Parking (managed by landowner – charges apply) at end of Semer Water, or informal parking at Marsett or Stalling Busk
Size: 37ha

  Dogs welcome on a lead

A great place for:

☑ Bird watchers
☐ Cyclists
☐ Wildflower enthusiasts
☐ Families
☐ Leisurely stroll
☑ Peace and tranquility
☑ Walkers

Recommended time to make the most of your visit:

☐ Full day
☑ Half day
☐ Just an hour

ⓘ **Before you go...**
For safety, you must keep to the public footpaths. Take care on the track from Marsett, especially if you have limited mobility or in wet conditions; it's uneven and rocky.

Discover life on the lakeside

The reserve is a mix of habitats, including fen, marsh, species-rich meadows, willow carr and developing mixed woodland. Wading birds feed on the lake's sandy shore, which supports needle spike-rush and sedge species. Much of the site is an old lake bed, which still floods regularly, attracting overwintering birds including wigeon, teal and snipe. In winter, you might also hear the musical echo of ice breaking up. Birds to spot (bring binoculars!) in spring and summer include curlew, oystercatcher, lapwing, redshank and sand martin. Keep an eye on the sky for a visiting osprey; Yorkshire's first breeding pair in centuries nested in Wensleydale recently.

Lapwing

Include in a day out in the Dales. Nearby Hawes, Bainbridge and Askrigg are worth a visit.

View down towards the lake

★ **Magic moment** ★
The aerial acrobatics and loud 'peewit' call of lapwings in spring.

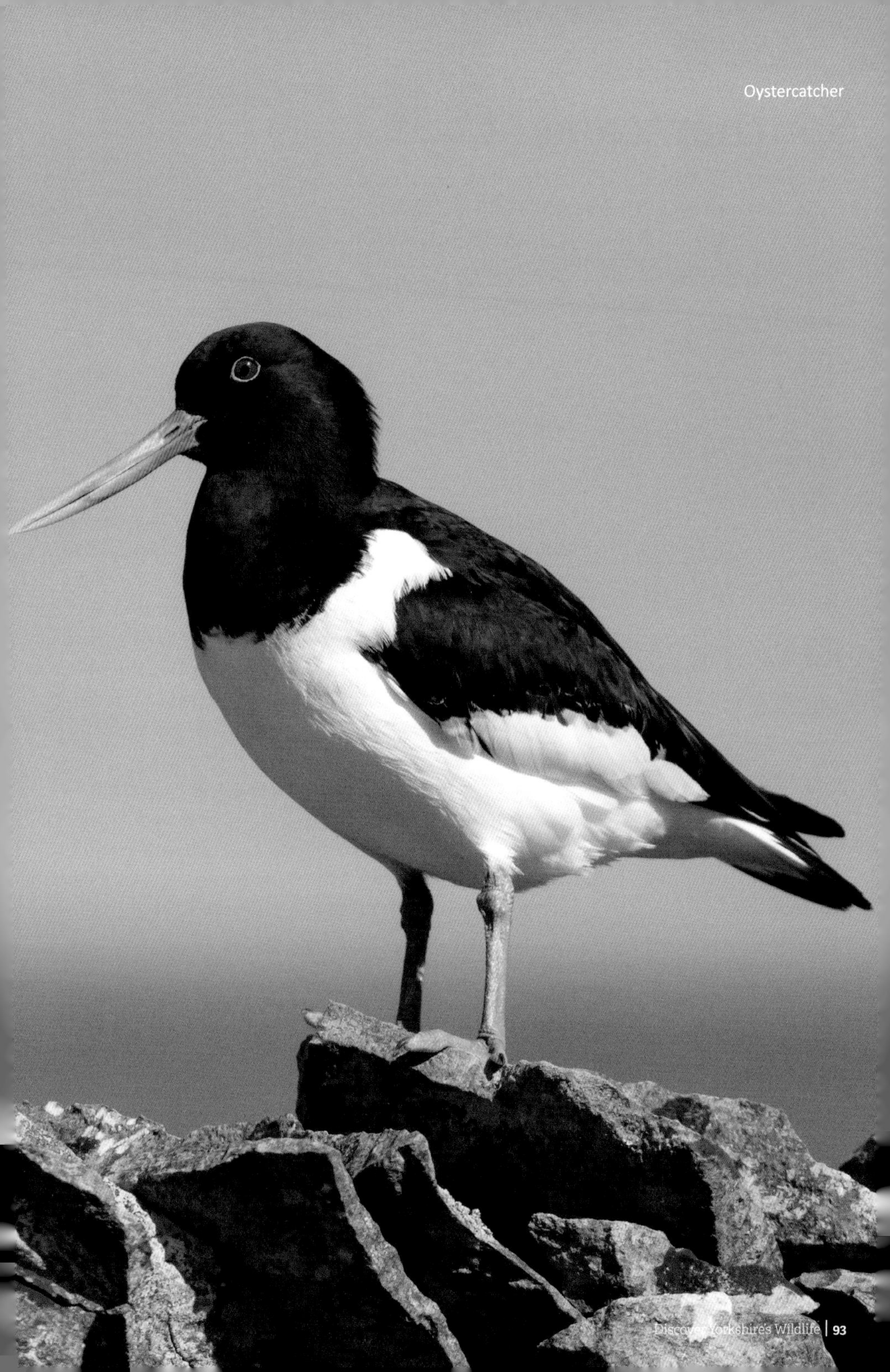

Oystercatcher

Southerscales

WILD INGLEBOROUGH

'Impressive' and 'dramatic' are two words you could use to describe this reserve on the western slopes of Ingleborough, but 'WOW!' should do the trick.

The lowdown...

Nearest town: Ingleton 4.2m/6.7km
Nearest postcode: LA6 3FH
Grid ref: Roadside parking: SD 74537 77790. Site entrance: SD 74377 76995
///presented.cute.tolls (roadside parking). large.metals.appoints (site entrance).
Parking: Informal roadside parking
Site designation: Part of Ingleborough National Nature Reserve
Size: 42ha

 Dogs on leads on public footpath only

A great place for:

☑ Bird watchers
☐ Cyclists
☑ Wildflower enthusiasts
☑ Families
☐ Leisurely stroll
☑ Peace and tranquility
☑ Walkers

Recommended time to make the most of your visit:

☐ Full day
☑ Half day
☐ Just an hour

ℹ **Before you go...**
Yorkshire's Three Peaks route runs through the reserve. The limestone pavement can be very slippy in wet or frosty weather.

Amazing paving

The spectacular moonscape-like limestone pavement of Southerscales will take your breath away, as will the views on a clear day, revealing the tallest two of Yorkshire's Three Peaks – Ingleborough and Whernside – and the majestic Ribblehead Viaduct.

Look closer and you'll find diverse and rare plant species, both in the pavement itself and in the surrounding grassland, blanket bog and heath, including blue moor-grass, frog orchid and bird's-eye primrose. The spring colours are beyond beautiful, as early purple orchids and primrose come into flower. You might be lucky enough to find the striking emperor moth amongst the flowers, and there are classic upland birds to watch for, including breeding wheatears and meadow pipits. Listen out for singing skylarks and redstarts; ring ouzels sometimes breed in the wooded ghylls nearby.

Pink is the colour of summer in the grassland around the pavement, with wild thyme and fragrant orchids attracting butterflies such as northern brown argus and small pearl-bordered fritillary. As the flowers fade in autumn, you might spot a black darter or painted lady.

Limestone pavement in the winter

Make a full day of it as part of a longer walk around Wild Ingleborough.

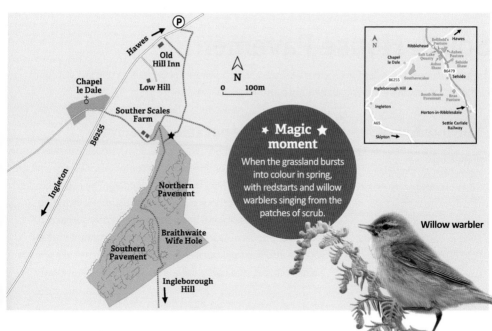

Willow warbler

A world of clints and grykes

Limestone pavement is made up of clints (the blocks) and grykes (the fissures or cracks in between). If you peer into the grykes, you'll discover a rich, hidden world of plants, such as baneberry, green spleenwort, lesser meadow-rue, wood sorrel and herb Robert. The site is rich in ferns, including rigid buckler and hart's-tongue.

There are different plants to find in each habitat on the reserve. The limestone grassland contains small scabious, early purple orchid and mountain everlasting; the acid grassland has heather; and the blanket bog boasts cross-leaved heath, cranberry, round-leaved sundew and bog asphodel.

Seasonal highlights

☼ Spring
Early purple orchid
Emperor moth
Wheatear
Primrose

☀ Summer
Frog orchid
Fragrant orchid
Small pearl-bordered fritillary
Redstart
Mouse-ear hawkweed

◑ Autumn
Redwing
Hen harrier
Waxcap fungi

❄ Winter
Rigid buckler fern
Merlin

Thank you

By volunteering and getting involved in citizen science, you're helping us to understand, manage and improve Ingleborough's precious landscape. Donations help us to keep traditional conservation grazing with cattle.

Herb Robert

South House Pavement

An adventure to this fantastic strip of limestone pavement promises to reward you with glimpses of treasure amongst the clints and grykes.

The lowdown...

Nearest town: Horton-in-Ribblesdale (2m/3.2km)
Nearest postcode: BD25 0HX
Grid ref: Site entrance: SD 77569 74414. Roadside parking: SD 78791 74642
///recall.slippers.agreeable (site entrance), exacted.premature. fetches (roadside parking).
Parking: Informal roadside parking on Horton Road
Size: 5ha

A great place for:

☐ Bird watchers

☐ Cyclists

☑ Wildflower enthusiasts

☐ Families

☐ Leisurely stroll

☑ Peace and tranquility

☐ Walkers

Recommended time to make the most of your visit:

☐ Full day

☑ Half day

☑ Just an hour

ⓘ Before you go...

Access is by permissive path from South House. Beware of unstable and slippery pavement. The route to the entrance is a 20-minute walk up a steady slope of mixed road, track and open field.

Discover the pavement's secrets

Spectacular (but slippery when wet!) South House Pavement is an exciting destination for intrepid, sure-footed plant lovers who are happiest when searching for hidden wonders. The clints (blocks) and grykes (gaps) harbour highly diverse plant life, including meadowsweet and broad buckler fern. Pink hairy stonecrop grows near pools of water on the bare rock in summer, when you can also see rigid buckler fern. Rowan and harebells provide autumn colour, and hart's-tongue fern stands out in winter.

★ Magic ★ moment

Enjoying the nationally scarce blue moor-grass flowers in spring, as wheatear and meadow pipits sing.

People and dogs should proceed with caution – the terrain here can be dangerous, especially when it's wet or icy!

Extend your trip with a visit to our other Ingleborough reserves. Brae Pasture is just one mile away.

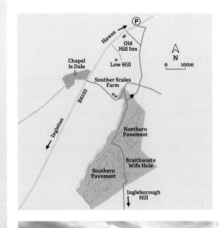

Limestone pavement

Go **wild** online...

Our website is bursting with ideas and inspiration to keep the whole family entertained and help you live a wilder life wherever you are.

Discover free activities, from nature treasure hunts to wildlife-inspired yoga poses, how-to guides and so much more at **ywt.org.uk/go-wild**

Discover Yorkshire's Wildlife

Staveley

Staveley is a superb wetland reserve with something for everyone, from experienced birders to people who just fancy a leisurely stroll on its network of paths.

The lowdown...

Nearest town: Boroughbridge (3 m/5 km)
Nearest postcode: HG5 9LQ
Grid ref: Roadside parking: SE 36991 63039
///spoons.dose.bogus
Parking: Car park just outside Staveley village on Minskip Road, holding 12 cars. Please park considerately and safely.
Size: 79ha

  No cycling on site, but bike racks in car park

A great place for:

☑ Bird watchers
☐ Cyclists
☑ Wildflower enthusiasts
☑ Families
☐ Leisurely stroll
☑ Peace and tranquility
☑ Walkers

Recommended time to make the most of your visit:

☑ Full day
☐ Half day
☐ Just an hour

ⓘ Before you go...
The reserve has good accessibility for wheelchairs and buggies. Disabled parking is available off Main Street, up the track by the village church, and you can access this with a Radar key.

Space for wildlife and for people

A year-round wild refuge with an industrial past, Staveley offers wildlife a large space and variety of habitats to move around. With accessible paths and five bird hides – three fully accessible – there are lots of great opportunities to absorb yourself in nature, and wonder at the incredible number of birds that it plays host to, including enormous numbers of geese and lapwings. It's easy to get to – just ten minutes' drive from the A1M.

Did you know?
On a clear day, you can see a different kind of animal from the top of the reserve's central hill – the famous White Horse of Kilburn!

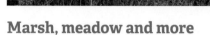
Staveley's lakes are a great place for birdwatching

Marsh, meadow and more

This lush, wet landscape by the river Tutt has several lakes and ponds which, alongside an 11-hectare hay meadow and a matrix of grasslands and scrub, form a rare and intricate mosaic of fen and marsh habitats. Much of the reserve has been sculpted from the remains of quarrying activities, and the species-rich meadow has been slowly converted back from arable land, with wildflowers blooming again in a place that's been renowned for rare plants for centuries.

Starling murmuration at Staveley

A haven and a highway

Staveley is a great place for seeing otters, sometimes in the middle of the day. You might also see roe deer, foxes and, if you sit very still in a quiet spot, you might glimpse two much smaller mammals – the water shrew and harvest mouse – particularly around dusk and dawn.

Common breeding birds include several warbler species, with common terns on the rafts created for them and barn owls in nest boxes. Little ringed plovers, avocets and oystercatchers sometimes breed, while in winter the lagoons are home to pintails, wigeons, goldeneyes, snipe and shovelers. Rarer visitors include bitterns.

Seasonal highlights

✷ Spring
Large red damselfly
Orange-tip
Common tern
Sand martin
Otter

✷ Summer
Marsh helleborine
Common spotted-orchid
Bee orchid
Peacock butterfly
Barn owl

✷ Autumn
Greenshank
Migrant hawker
Common pipistrelle

✷ Winter
Red kite
Reed bunting
Tree sparrow

Otter

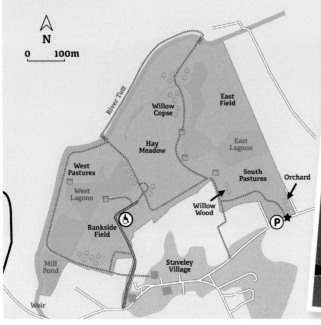

N

0   100m

River Tutt

Willow Copse

East Field

Hay Meadow

East Lagoon

West Pastures

West Lagoon

South Pastures

Orchard

Bankside Field

Willow Wood

P ★

Mill Pond

Staveley Village

Weir

If you're in the area for longer, try Bishop Monkton Railway Cutting, Burton Leonard Lime Quarries and Ripon City Wetlands.

Grasshopper warbler

Boroughbridge

Minskip

Staveley

Copgrove

A1M

Staveley

A168

Arkendale

Farnham

Ferrensby

A6055

Wetherby

Knaresborough

N

For a wild day...

Pop into each of the hides, savour the views and wildlife spectacles, and soak up the atmosphere.

Go a little wilder...

Brush up on your knowledge of warblers in spring by looking and listening for our top ten: grasshopper, garden, Cetti's, willow, sedge and reed warblers, blackcap, chiffchaff, whitethroat and lesser whitethroat.

Experience Staveley's wildest side...

22 species of damselflies and dragonflies have been recorded on the main lagoons, small ponds and along the ditches, including the willow emerald. How many can you find?

And there's more...

Staveley is also home to a community orchard, which you'll walk through when you enter the reserve. Did somebody say apple crumble?

Willow emerald

Discover Yorkshire's Wildlife

The hard work that makes life easier for wildlife

Staveley is a precious sanctuary for visitors and wildlife. That's thanks in no small part to the hard work of the local community, our loyal volunteers, and Trust staff. They're regularly out on the reserve carrying out Himalayan balsam-bashing, meadow-mowing and raking, cattle-herding, scrub-clearing, coppicing, reed-cutting and traditional haymaking.

There are two main parts to the reserve. The East Lagoon's edges feature vegetation that was allowed to develop naturally when quarrying finished, made up of fen, reed swamp, scrub and flower-rich grassland. The West Lagoons area was landscaped and returned to agricultural use after quarrying, with arable and intensively grazed areas. We've done a lot of work to create more interesting wildlife habitats since we bought the land in 2010.

Volunteering on the reserve

Upper Dunsforth Carrs

If you're feeling adventurous and looking for an exciting wilder experience, pull on your wellies and discover an oasis that's alive with wildlife all year round.

The lowdown...

Nearest town: Boroughbridge (4.5m/7km)
Nearest postcode: YO26 9RU
Grid ref: SE 44379 62965
///cowering.finishers.worthy
Parking: Limited roadside parking
Site designation: SSSI
Size: 10 ha

A great place for:

☑ Bird watchers
☐ Cyclists
☑ Wildflower enthusiasts
☑ Families
☐ Leisurely stroll
☑ Peace and tranquility
☑ Walkers

Recommended time to make the most of your visit:

☐ Full day
☑ Half day
☐ Just an hour

ℹ Before you go...
The reserve can be boggy all year round, so bring your boots. You might also want to use insect repellent in the summer.

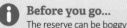
For a longer day out, combine with other nearby reserves – Bishop Monkton Railway Cutting, Burton Leonard Lime Quarries, Staveley and Ripon City Wetlands.

Welcome to the jungle!

Tucked away on the outskirts of a small village and surrounded by farmland, Upper Dunsforth Carrs packs a lot of wild habitat into a small space: rush-pasture, swamp, wet woodland, and fen meadows. In summer, the fen meadows are splashed with the pinks and purples of marsh orchids, purple loosestrife and ragged robin. You can enjoy the company of woodland and farmland birds like green woodpeckers and yellowhammers. Insects also abound – 120 beetle species have been recorded, including a nationally scarce diving beetle and a large click beetle.

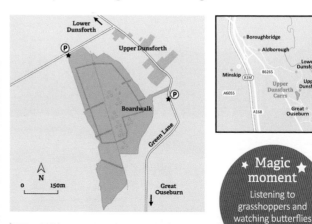

★ Magic ★ moment
Listening to grasshoppers and watching butterflies dance in the meadow.

Fen meadows with ragged robin

Weybeck's Pasture

A summer visit to Weybeck's Pasture reveals a rich, rectangular field full of flowers and butterflies sloping down to the River Skirfare in the midst of glorious upper Dales countryside.

Botanical heaven awaits

In midsummer, walk through the meadow and down the slope towards the little River Skirfare, close to where it meets the Wharfe at the foot of Littondale, and discover wildflowers, mosses and grasses galore.

Chalk fragrant-orchid, marsh helleborine and bogbean are among the standout species, along with early marsh-orchid, common butterwort, fairy flax, mouse-ear hawkweed, lesser clubmoss and brittle bladder-fern, to name just a few. Butterflies including orange-tip and dark green fritillary, and birds include little owl, dipper, curlew and sand martin.

The lowdown...

Nearest town: Grassington (4.5m/7.2km)
Nearest postcode: BD23 5PT
Grid ref: SD 96838 69230
///refuse.factoring.sampling
Parking: Informal roadside parking for three vehicles
Size: 3ha

A great place for:

- ☑ Bird watchers
- ☐ Cyclists
- ☑ Wildflower enthusiasts
- ☑ Families
- ☐ Leisurely stroll
- ☑ Peace and tranquility
- ☑ Walkers

Recommended time to make the most of your visit:

- ☐ Full day
- ☑ Half day
- ☐ Just an hour

ℹ **Before you go...**
The site is on a grassy bank and the ground is uneven in places.

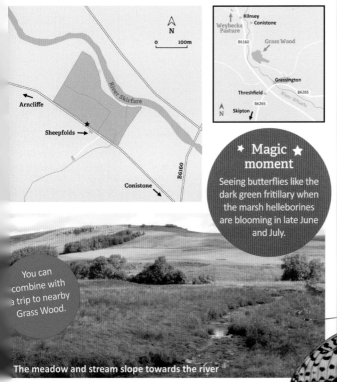

You can combine with a trip to nearby Grass Wood.

★ Magic moment ★
Seeing butterflies like the dark green fritillary when the marsh helleborines are blooming in late June and July.

The meadow and stream slope towards the river

Dark green fritillary

Yellands Meadow

Up here in the hills of ruggedly beautiful Swaledale, the climate can be harsh, but this traditionally managed meadow by the river provides a sanctuary for flowers and insects.

The lowdown...

Nearest town: Muker (0.5m/0.8km)
Nearest postcode: DL11 6QQ
Grid ref: SD 91892 97704
///riverboat.leaves.mailbox
Parking: Informal roadside parking for three vehicles
Site designation: SSSI
Size: 1ha

A great place for:

☑ Bird watchers

☐ Cyclists

☑ Wildflower enthusiasts

☐ Families

☐ Leisurely stroll

☑ Peace and tranquility

☑ Walkers

Recommended time to make the most of your visit:

☐ Full day

☐ Half day

☑ Just an hour

ℹ **Before you go...**
The site has even ground, with an informal track round the edge and two easy footbridges.

Mellow Yellands

Yellands is a small meadow next to the Swale, with an alder-lined stream running across it. In June and July, it's alive with grasshoppers, bees and butterflies, and resplendent with radiant colour, thanks to flowers including cuckooflower, yellow rattle, pignut, lady's-mantle, meadow vetchling, bugle, eyebright, bird's-foot trefoil and common spotted-orchid. You might also find melancholy thistle, meadowsweet and marsh marigold on the riverbanks. In winter, you may be lucky enough to spot otters in the water.

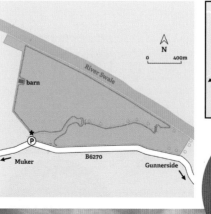

★ **Magic moment** ★
Patiently watching the barn on the reserve's western boundary to be rewarded with views of barn owls.

A wealth of wildflowers fill the meadow

Potteric Carr

South

Nature is returning with abundance to restored
wetlands and woodland around Doncaster
and Barnsley, with an astonishing wealth of
wildlife to discover, right on the urban fringe.

Barnsley Main

On the edge of urban Barnsley, and well connected to other wildlife havens in the Dearne Valley, Barnsley Main is part of a green landscape with an industrial past.

The lowdown...

Nearest town: Barnsley (1.9m/3.1km)
Nearest postcode: S70 3ET
Grid ref: SE 36412 06349
///violin.those.edit
Parking: Informal street parking only on Oaks Lane. Entry across from the old mine shaft building.
Size: 21ha

  Dogs on leads

A great place for:

- ☐ Bird watchers
- ☐ Cyclists
- ☐ Wildflower enthusiasts
- ☐ Families
- ☐ Leisurely stroll
- ☑ Peace and tranquility
- ☑ Walkers

Recommended time to make the most of your visit:

- ☐ Full day
- ☐ Half day
- ☑ Just an hour

ⓘ Before you go...
The lower area is fairly flat with a wide footpath, but the walk up to the top is very steep, with a one in five gradient. The hilltop is very exposed, so not one for a windy or rainy day!

The green, green grass of Barnsley

A walk along Barnsley Main will put you on top of the world – or at least on top of the Dearne Valley. The hilltop offers the best panoramic view of Barnsley and the river Dearne corridor than anywhere else in the area. For somewhere so close to the centre of a large town, you'll be amazed at how green this landscape is.

The reserve's rolling grassland is surrounded by a fringe of broadleaved woodland and scrub, which hasn't always looked this green and pleasant. It was once the black spoil heap of the Oaks Colliery pit head that still stands on Oaks Lane. We care for the restored grassland with seasonal cutting for a hay crop. In spring and summer, it's a good place to watch butterflies on the wing, including some rarer populations of small heath.

We are also encouraging more amphibians, insects and birds to the surrounding ditches with better habitat.

Barnsley Main

Did you know?
Buzzards are our most common birds of prey, but always an impressive sight when they soar overhead, with a wingspan of up to four feet.

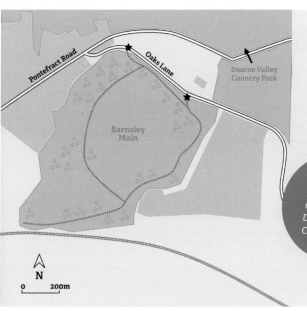

Combine with a visit to neighbouring Dearne Valley Country Park.

N
0   200m

Linking up sites for wildlife and people

Barnsley Main is more than just one nature reserve in isolation – it's part of an important network of wildlife sites in the area, connected by the Trans-Pennine Trail. Dearne Valley Country Park is only a short walk away, with Littleworth Park just a mile away.

These links allow both people and wildlife to move more freely around the area and between habitats.

Small heath

★ **Magic** ★
moment

Swifts and swallows flying overhead as you enjoy a summer view over the Dearne Valley.

Seasonal highlights

❀ Spring
Red clover
Bird's-foot trefoil
Speedwells
Small copper
Small heath

❀ Summer
Swallow
Swift
Knapweed
Lady's bedstraw

◉ Autumn
Black earth tongue

❀ Winter
Buzzard
Kestrel

Swift

Carlton Marsh

With a mixture of open wetland, woodland, grassland and scrub, Carlton Marsh hosts an amazing variety of wildlife – a remarkable transformation from a polluted past.

The lowdown...

Nearest town: Cudworth (1.1m/1.8km)
Nearest postcode: S71 3HL
Grid ref: SE 37935 10349
///chin.albums.weeps
Parking: Small, free car park for around 10 cars on Shaw Lane from dawn until dusk (locked in between)
Site designation: SSSI
Size: 25ha

  Dogs on leads

A great place for:

☑ Bird watchers
☐ Cyclists
☑ Wildflower enthusiasts
☑ Families
☐ Leisurely stroll
☐ Peace and tranquility
☑ Walkers

Recommended time to make the most of your visit:

☐ Full day
☐ Half day
☑ Just an hour

ℹ **Before you go...**
The walk is fairly flat, but unsurfaced and can be muddy. There are some steps up to the embankment footpath and short but steep slopes connecting to other paths to join the Trans Pennine Trail.

Marvellous marshland

Carlton Marsh is part of a network of important wildlife refuges in the Dearne Valley, now a Site of Special Scientific Interest (SSSI), but formerly a major part of the country's coal mining industry.

Cudworth Dyke, which supplies the marsh, was once one of South Yorkshire's most polluted water bodies, but the tireless work of volunteers and local partnerships including the Friends of Carlton Marsh and the Dearne Valley Green Heart Partnership has changed all that. The Marsh also benefited from significant habitat improvements in 2015, restoring its ecology and hydrology and rejuvenating the reedbed.

The footpath along the old railway line gives excellent views across the wetland and it's worth bringing binoculars to appreciate the variety of birds. One of the star attractions is the nationally endangered willow tit, which has made a home in the wet-woodland fringe and scrub. In late spring and summer, listen for the distinctive reeling sound of grasshopper warblers in the brambles. You can find lapwings, redshanks and green sandpipers on the open grassland and wader scrape, and if you visit at dusk in the winter you might spot a bittern or barn owl.

Did you know?
Well over 110 species of bird are recorded annually at Carlton Marsh.

Wetlands provide more homes for wildlife

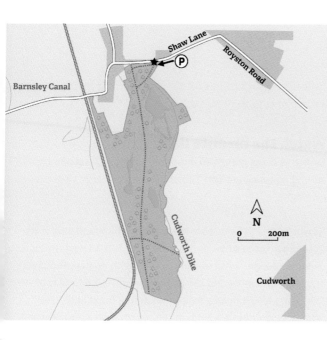

Shaw Lane

Royston Road

Barnsley Canal

P

Cudworth Dike

N

0   200m

Cudworth

Footpaths connect the reserve to other green spaces in the area if you want to explore further. There is a picnic area with benches and tables.

Purple patch

Carlton Marsh is brilliant for butterflies. On warm summer days, the delightful purple hairstreak can be seen flying around the tops of tall oak trees, and might sometimes venture down to seek nectar from brambles and other flowers. Small skipper and small heath are just two of the other species you might find.

There's plenty for wildflower lovers to enjoy throughout the seasons too, including field scabious, devil's-bit scabious, weld, yellow archangel and ox-eye daisy.

Seasonal highlights

✿ Spring
Willow tit
Kingfisher
Cuckoo
Bird's-foot trefoil

❋ Summer
Field scabious
Purple loosestrife
Purple hairstreak
Small heath

◉ Autumn
Green sandpiper
Gadwall
Shoveler
Bullfinch

❋ Winter
Bittern
Buzzard
Fieldfare
Redwing

★ **Magic** ★
moment
A grass snake swimming in the marsh as a kingfisher flies down to perch.

Grass snake

Carr Lodge

Carr Lodge is like Potteric Carr's little sibling and shares family features, it's a highly valuable habitat for a variety of wetland birds, plants and creatures.

The lowdown...

Nearest town: Balby, Doncaster (1.5m/2.4km)
Nearest postcode: DN11 9DG
Grid ref: SK 57898 99698
///refills.handfuls.covenants
Parking: Limited parking on Pegasus Way, or in small layby on Hall Balk Lane, or walk from Potteric Carr car park
Site designation: none
Size: 35ha

  Dogs on a lead. Cycling permitted around perimeter, to Potteric Carr, or over the M18 to Parson's Carr, Wadworth, Rossington or Bessacarr

A great place for:

- ☑ Bird watchers
- ☐ Cyclists
- ☐ Wildflower enthusiasts
- ☐ Families
- ☐ Leisurely stroll
- ☐ Peace and tranquility
- ☐ Walkers

Recommended time to make the most of your visit:

- ☐ Full day
- ☑ Half day
- ☐ Just an hour

ℹ️ **Before you go...**
A circular uneven walk around the reserve, but no access to the fields, which can be wet.

Watch the birdlife flooding in

As well as being part of an important network of satellite reserves around Potteric Carr, Carr Lodge has plenty to offer visitors in its own right.

Its wet grassland fields hold many nesting birds and host visits from other species that pop in from next door to feed. This is a dynamic reserve, which begins to flood with very shallow water between November and January, which can last into May or June. This is an excellent place for overwintering ducks and geese, and for ground-nesting birds in the spring, such as lapwing and sometimes redshank, so access is mostly around the perimeter. Find the viewing screen in the small wood by junction 3 of the M18 and scan the floodwater in winter and spring to pick out different species.

There are high numbers of great crested newts in the ponds, and if you're very lucky you might catch a glimpse of a grass snake. Around the ponds, grazing cattle help to provide varied conditions for different plants including stoneworts, fen pondweed, and whorled water-milfoil. There's also a great variety of dragonflies.

Wet grassland fields

Easy to combine with Potteric Carr, Parson's Carr or as part of our walk on page 42.

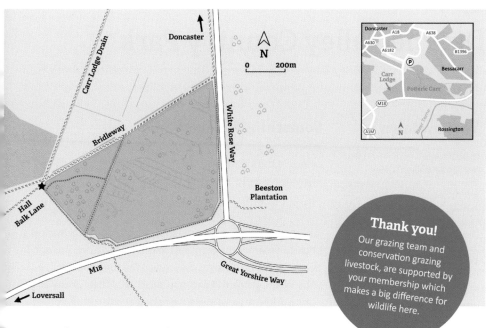

Expect the unexpected

Carr Lodge is a relatively new Yorkshire Wildlife Trust site, managed as a nature reserve following mitigation for a housing estate development. Many of the species that are found at Potteric Carr will also appear here, which means you can expect a great diversity of bird and insect life, especially dragonflies and damselflies – you never know exactly what might turn up.

This is one of only three places in Yorkshire where the nocturnal and very rare crucifix ground beetle has been recorded. It's around 8mm in length, black with red spots, and rather bristly.

Redshank

★ Magic ★ moment
Enjoy the huge number of overwintering birds on the flooded fields – how many kinds can you spot?

Thank you!
Our grazing team and conservation grazing livestock, are supported by your membership which makes a big difference for wildlife here.

Seasonal highlights

✿ Spring
Lapwing
Redshank
Great crested newt
Grass snake

☀ Summer
Common darter dragonfly
Meadow brown butterfly
Essex skipper
Speckled wood

✦ Autumn
Flocks of starlings
Common sandpiper
Green sandpiper

❄ Winter
Redwing
Fieldfare
Pink-footed goose
Wintering ducks

Dearne Valley Country Park

Right in the heart of Barnsley, Dearne Valley Country Park is criss-crossed by inviting paths, taking you through woodland and grassland, with riverside wildlife to enjoy along the way.

The lowdown...

Nearest town: Barnsley (1m/1.6km)
Nearest postcode: S71 1HS
Grid ref: SE 36285 06591 (car park)
///title.jumps.origin
Parking: Car park on Pontefract Road. Additional parking is just off Eaming View at the western end of the site.
Site designation: Cliffe Wood in the park is a Local Wildlife Site (LWS)
Size: 80ha

A great place for:

- ☐ Bird watchers
- ☐ Cyclists
- ☐ Wildflower enthusiasts
- ☑ Families
- ☐ Leisurely stroll
- ☑ Peace and tranquility
- ☑ Walkers

Recommended time to make the most of your visit:

- ☐ Full day
- ☑ Half day
- ☐ Just an hour

ℹ **Before you go...**
The Trans Pennine Trail connects Dearne Valley Country Park to the regional cycling and walking network. The site is flat and most paths are tarmacked or surfaced. In the woods, some paths are unsurfaced and there are some steep steps.

Something for everyone

Whether you're looking for a leisurely stroll, somewhere to entertain the kids or walk the dog, or to spend some down-time enjoying a variety of wildlife, Dearne Valley Country Park offers something for everyone all year round.

It hasn't always been this way though - the site of the park was once dominated by mining infrastructure; the roads and spoil heaps, canals and bridges that served the coal industry. Cliffe Wood, inside the park, pre-dates all of that. Gnarly and otherworldly, it's an ancient woodland of oak and silver birch, filled with bluebells in spring and fungi in autumn, with roaming flocks of siskins and other woodland birds in winter. Keep your eyes peeled for some more unusual varieties of mushrooms as you walk through - amethyst deceivers have been spotted here. As you might expect from the name, they're violet in colour, like amethyst crystals.

The park's a great place for a family outing, with picnic benches, a skatepark and play area, as well as space to explore.

Did you know?
Feeding the ducks has always been a popular activity for families – but bread isn't very good for them. Instead, give them seeds or oats, which are more nutritious and less messy.

View across the lake to the woodland

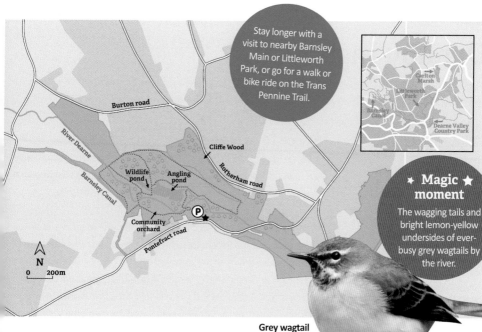

Stay longer with a visit to nearby Barnsley Main or Littleworth Park, or go for a walk or bike ride on the Trans Pennine Trail.

Burton road

River Dearne

Cliffe Wood

Barnsley Canal

Wildlife pond

Angling pond

Rotherham road

Community orchard

Pontefract road

P

N

0   200m

Carlton Marsh

Littleworth Park

Barnsley Canal

Dearne Valley Country Park

★ Magic ★ moment

The wagging tails and bright lemon-yellow undersides of ever-busy grey wagtails by the river.

Grey wagtail

Wildlife on – and in – the water

The river Dearne, full of life and with grey wagtails flitting from bank to bank, flows through the park, supplying the large fishing lake that's the focal point of the reserve. The water attracts ducks aplenty, and kingfishers are a regular sight on the river and on Barnsley Canal at the west end of the park. Upstream of the fishing lake, a wildlife lake emerges from the wet woodland.

There are frogs and toads galore, and you might even see the odd pike basking in the summer. These large fish can grow to more than a metre long!

Seasonal highlights

✿ Spring
Bluebells
Wild garlic
Willow tit
Great spotted woodpecker
Frogs and toads

✵ Summer
Brown hawker
Kingfisher
Grey wagtail
Pike

◉ Autumn
Scarlet elfcup
Amethyst deceiver
Teal

✲ Winter
Tawny owl
Goldcrest
Treecreeper
Bullfinch

Pike

Denaby Ings

In an area shaped by mining and farming, you can still see evidence of this reserve's past as you enjoy its diverse range of present-day wild wonders.

The lowdown...

Nearest town: Mexborough (1.9m/3.1km)
Nearest postcode: S64 0JJ
Grid ref: SE 49831 00843 (car park) or SE 50636 00691 (lay-by parking)
///sprinter.enjoy.crouch
Parking: Car park off Pastures Road. Limited parking in lay-by on Pastures Lane
Site designation: SSSI
Size: 23ha

A great place for:

☑ Bird watchers
☐ Cyclists
☐ Wildflower enthusiasts
☐ Families
☐ Leisurely stroll
☑ Peace and tranquility
☐ Walkers

Recommended time to make the most of your visit:

☐ Full day
☑ Half day
☐ Just an hour

ℹ **Before you go...**
There are steep steps, grassy fields with uneven surfaces, gates, slopes, and narrow paths, so this site isn't suitable for wheelchairs or buggies.

Thank you
Your donations help us to maintain the permissive pathways on the site and to look after the hides.

Space to breathe

A green lung close to South Yorkshire's urban heart, Denaby Ings is a haven for wetland and woodland wildlife, in a landscape that's been chopped and changed many times over its history.

Even the river Dearne has changed course – the reserve sits on its old course and next to its straightened new route. The lake was formed when the river was blocked off by tipping coal spoil from a nearby mine. Trees where herons, little egrets, great white egrets and even the odd spoonbill occasionally roost show the Dearne's historical route. Areas of open water have formed where the river used to flow and these are now rich in aquatic life.

The raised embankment that takes you to the two hides was previously the Dearne Valley Railway, which transported coal from the local mines. The hides offer excellent views out over the main marsh and open water across to wooded crags in the distance, and great vantage points for seeing goosanders, kingfishers and other birds.

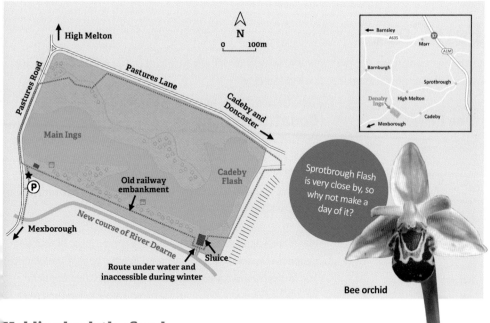

High Melton

Pastures Road

Pastures Lane

Cadeby and Doncaster →

N
0   100m

Barnsley
A635
Marr
A1M
Barnburgh
Sprotbrough
Denaby Ings
High Melton
Cadeby
Mexborough

Main Ings

Old railway embankment

Cadeby Flash

P

New course of River Dearne

Mexborough

Sluice

Route under water and inaccessible during winter

Sprotbrough Flash is very close by, so why not make a day of it?

Bee orchid

Holding back the floods

In spring and summer, the reserve fills with the sound of birdsong, and flowers, including several species of orchid, bloom in the meadows, visited by abundant butterflies.

Denaby Ings also plays an important role in flood relief. When there's severe flooding, the river can be diverted so that water escapes into the meadows, and can be slowly released after the flood's peak, providing a mix of reedbeds and muddy shoreline that attracts several species of wading birds, including avocets, bitterns and green sandpipers.

Spoonbill

★ Magic ★ moment

An exotic-looking spoonbill, whooper swan or great white egret joining grey herons and little egrets to roost.

Seasonal highlights

✲ Spring
Avocet
Sand martin
Sedge warbler
Grasshopper warbler

✲ Summer
Bee orchid
Pyramidal orchid
Common spotted-orchid
Grass snake

✲ Autumn
Common, green and wood sandpipers
Greenshank
Redshank
Black-tailed godwit
Little egret

✲ Winter
Bittern
Goosander
Siskin

Fen Carr

With over 70 species of plant, many of which are locally rare and nationally declining, this botanically important reserve is a hidden gem.

The lowdown...

Nearest town: Fishlake (1.1m/1.7km)
Nearest postcode: Corner of DN7 5LU and DN7 5LQ
Grid ref: Entrance gate SE 65740 15492, parking at SE 65957 15442
///unfolds.formless.racks
Parking: Limited parking in layby at corner of Geeseness Lane and Black Skye Lane
Size: 4ha

A great place for:

☐ Bird watchers

☐ Cyclists

☑ Wildflower enthusiasts

☐ Families

☐ Leisurely stroll

☑ Peace and tranquility

☐ Walkers

Recommended time to make the most of your visit:

☐ Full day

☐ Half day

☑ Just an hour

ⓘ **Before you go...**
The reserve is at its best in spring and summer, and the team hold regular guided walks. There is no footpath, so please keep to the edge of the fields and avoid trampling the hay crop.

Bountiful botany

Fen Carr is a floodplain meadow packed with plants. Comprising two traditional hay meadows, it was previously owned by the Church of England, which protected it from intensive farming. The land is grazed following a late haycut, and the hedgerows are protected and maintained.

Plants such as sneezewort, sweet vernal grass, great burnet and pepper saxifrage thrive, supporting a healthy population of moths and butterflies, including hairstreaks, browns, blues, coppers, whites and skippers. Look out for green woodpeckers and hear their yaffling call or that of a burbling curlew.

★ **Magic moment** ★
Finding butterflies among the wildflowers in summer.

Fen Carr's floodplain meadow

Sheffield & Rotherham Wildlife Trust

Sheffield & Rotherham
Wildlife Trust

In addition to Yorkshire Wildlife Trust's reserves across Yorkshire, our friends and neighbours at Sheffield & Rotherham Wildlife Trust take care of 15 nature reserves (almost 600 hectares) in South Yorkshire, ranging from large moorland areas of international importance to small city centre nature parks.

1 Agden Bog: a classic example of a type of bog that has now mostly disappeared from our landscape

2 Blacka Moor: a massive and magnificent moorland, where you're likely to see red deer

3 Carbrook Ravine: a small but varied reserve nestled amongst the urban landscape, where the skylarks sing

4 Carr House Meadows: a patchwork of flower-rich meadows, perched above the Ewden Valley

5 Centenary Riverside: a former steel works turned wetland wildlife haven

6 Crabtree Ponds: Burngreave's hidden gem! A green oasis in the urban sprawl

7 Fox Hagg: a remarkable heathland and woodland, with magnificent views

8 Greno Woods: an ancient woodland, rich in wildlife and full of historic interest

9 Hammond's Field: one of the few remaining areas of unimproved farmland (not seeded, ploughed or heavily fertilised) on the moorland fringes

10 Kilnhurst Ings: a post-industrial washland on the River Don

11 Moss Valley Woodlands: bluebells bloom and majestic beech trees tower overhead in these beautiful ancient woodlands

12 Salmon Pastures: a vital green corridor, transformed from a post-industrial wasteland

13 Sunnybank: a scenic short-cut, for people and wildlife

14 Woodhouse Washlands: a marvellous mosaic of wet and dry grasslands, swamps, ponds and scrub

15 Wyming Brook: babbling streams, mossy crags and sweet-smelling pines await in this ancient hunting ground

Discover more at
wildsheffield.com

Littleworth Park

In this park on the edge of Barnsley, nature is reclaiming the land from an old colliery spoil heap and landfill site, and it's full of surprises.

The lowdown...

Nearest town: Barnsley (2.5m/4km)
Nearest postcode: S71 5RG
Grid ref: Roadside parking: SE 36895 07292
///this.organ.this
Parking: Two small lay-bys on Littleworth Lane
Site designation: Local Wildlife Site
Size: 38ha

A great place for:

- ☐ Bird watchers
- ☐ Cyclists
- ☑ Wildflower enthusiasts
- ☐ Families
- ☑ Leisurely stroll
- ☐ Peace and tranquility
- ☐ Walkers

Recommended time to make the most of your visit:

- ☐ Full day
- ☐ Half day
- ☑ Just an hour

ⓘ Before you go...
The site has good paths, including tarmac routes. It's a great place for a stroll and walking the dog.

Thank you
Your support means we can give nature a helping hand at reserves like Littleworth, managing and improving the habitat for wildlife and people.

Scrubbing up nicely

Plants, insects and amphibians are flourishing in the extensive grassland, lowland heath and pockets of woodland at Littleworth Park – not bad for an out-of-town spot that once had a railway and canal running through it.

Birdlife is increasing too, with willow warblers, lesser redpolls and others benefiting from the scrub habitat.

Smooth newts, common frogs and toads have made themselves at home in the drainage ditches around the edge of the park, along with dragonflies and other wetland insects. We're creating new ponds to attract more amphibians and insects, as well as birds.

In place of the old towpath and railway line, there's a perfect wildlife corridor and path to the south of the site, connecting Littleworth Park to Dearne Valley Country Park – ideal if you want to extend your outing and discover more of the local wildlife.

Lowland heath at Littleworth Park

Combine with a visit to Dearne Valley Country Park.

Goldcrest

Summer lovin'

The largest colony of heather is at the northern end of the site, although new colonies are also springing up around the reserve. Its flowers create a luscious spread of purple in summer, and on warm days it can be buzzing with bumblebees and other insects. Many other plants are thriving here, in a grassland rich in wildflowers, such as bird's-foot trefoil, various clovers, and knapweed. This makes it an excellent place for butterflies, with 24 species recorded, including occasional appearances from dingy skippers. The six-spot burnet is one of the moth species you might find.

★ Magic ★ moment
Purple heather buzzing with bumblebees on a warm August day.

Seasonal highlights

❁ Spring
Dingy skipper
Smooth newt
Willow warbler
Lesser redpoll

❁ Summer
Bird's-foot trefoil
Bee orchid
Common centaury
Heather

❁ Autumn
Six-spot burnet
Bullfinch
Fox
Fungi

❁ Winter
Fieldfare
Redwing
Goldcrest
Goldfinch

Bumblebee on heather

Maltby Low Common

With three types of grassland close together, sporting a profusion of plants, early summer at Maltby Low Common is a paradise for insects and botanists.

The lowdown...

Nearest town: Maltby (1.1m/1.8km)
Nearest postcode: S66 7JX
Grid ref: SK 53992 91271
///soggy.preoccupied.future
Parking: Small car park on Lansbury Avenue, 40 metres from the railway bridge on Outgang Lane, or at the Far Common on Stoneywell lane.
Site designation: SSSI, LNR
Size: 7ha

A great place for:

☐ Bird watchers
☐ Cyclists
☑ Wildflower enthusiasts
☐ Families
☐ Leisurely stroll
☐ Peace and tranquility
☑ Walkers

Recommended time to make the most of your visit:

☐ Full day
☑ Half day
☐ Just an hour

ℹ️ **Before you go...**
The paths are fairly flat but can be wet and muddy at times.

Buzzing and bustling with insect life

If you know your calcareous grassland species from your acid and neutral grassland species, or you're keen to learn, there's no finer place to compare these side by side. And if you don't really care what all that means but like seeing how different plants grow in different places, and enjoy seeing an array of beautiful flowers, then look no further than the steep limestone bank, flat grassland, and wetter and drier areas of Maltby Low Common.

It's part of a network of commons on the south-east side of Maltby, and you can enjoy a circular walk of around two miles to Maltby Far Common. Both are great for grassland flowers in later spring and summer and host a wide variety of insects – well over 400 species have been recorded, including many species of butterfly and moth, such as dark green fritillaries, brimstones, orange-tips, small coppers, walls, heaths, cinnabars and silver Ys. Just over the railway line, Maltby Wood is full of woodland flowers in the spring, and can be incorporated as part of a longer walk.

Woodland flowers in Maltby Wood

Did you know?
Grass-of-parnassus isn't actually a grass! Its name comes from the translucent green stripes on the white petals of its cup-shaped flower. It's also known as bog star.

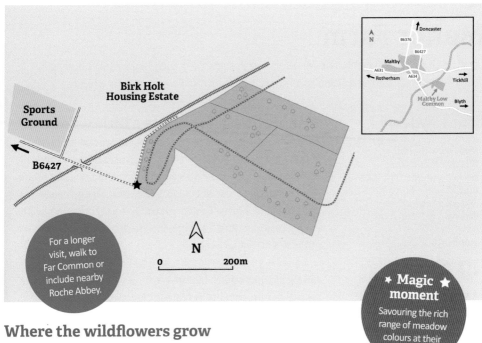

Where the wildflowers grow

On the south-west part of the common, typical limestone grassland species grow, including the declining grass-of-Parnassus, field scabious and small scabious. The flat area below the bank includes species more typical of fen meadow.

Other plants to find on the reserve include marsh valerian, mat grass, tufted hair-grass, heather, pepper saxifrage, meadow thistle, sneezewort, lousewort and aspen, along with glaucous, oval and carnation sedges. From June, look for common spotted-orchids flowering in abundance.

In spring, cuckoos, whitethroats and garden warblers join resident species including buzzards, kestrels and barn owls, with parties of foraging tits and thrushes in the winter.

Grass-of-Parnassus

★ **Magic ★ moment**

Savouring the rich range of meadow colours at their peak.

Seasonal highlights

✿ **Spring**
Whitethroat
Garden warbler
Orange-tip
Wood anemone

✿ **Summer**
Grass-of-Parnassus
Tufted hair-grass
Pepper saxifrage
Meadow thistle
Sneezewort
Meadowsweet
Devil's-bit scabious

🍂 **Autumn**
Fungi in the woods

❄ **Winter**
Long-tailed tit

Manor Farm

Located next to our flagship nature reserve at Potteric Carr, the Manor Farm housing development is a 'stepping stone' to a larger, interconnected landscape for wildlife.

The lowdown...

Nearest town: Bessacarr, Doncaster (1m/1.6km)
Nearest postcode: DN4 7BX
Grid ref: SE 61936 00078 (car park)
///nods.intent.evaporate
Parking: Small car park off Cammidge Way
Size: 35ha

A great place for:
☐ Bird watchers
☐ Cyclists
☐ Wildflower enthusiasts
☑ Families
☐ Leisurely stroll
☐ Peace and tranquility
☐ Walkers

Recommended time to make the most of your visit:
☐ Full day
☐ Half day
☑ Just an hour

ⓘ Before you go...
There's a mix of path types: grit surfaced, bare ground, and mown grass. It's mainly flat with slight hills (one steep). Take care during wet weather.

Making South Yorkshire a little wilder

As part of a planning agreement between Doncaster Council and the developer at Warren Park, the Trust now owns and manages the open green space surrounding the housing estate. A combination of oak woodland, heathland, a reed-fringed pond, and grassland, Manor Farm provides the local community with easy access to nature – a connection shown to improve our physical and mental health.

Talking of connections, the site is part of a network of reserves around our flagship site at Potteric Carr which form a wilder landscape where wildlife can move from one place to another. At Manor Farm, we also demonstrate how green spaces can be havens for pollinators, from bees and butterflies to birds and bats, and corridors for amphibians and mammals to move and migrate.

Early risers can enjoy watching the morning sun through the mist and trees, and seeing spider webs outlined in dew. This is also a great place to look for different fungi in the autumn, including the shaggy inkcap.

Did you know? The shaggy inkcap mushroom is also known as 'lawyer's wig' and 'shaggy mane' thanks to its tall, white, shaggy cap.

Reed-fringed pond at Manor Farm

Great for including in a walk around Potteric Carr. See our walk route on page 42.

Rabbit

Setting up home

There's something to enjoy all year round at Manor Farm, but nest building season in the spring is a highlight, when swans and little grebes are on the pond, and nuthatches call in the woods.

In late summer and early autumn, the heather on the heath comes into flower, with its blues and purples creating a visual treat. As autumn continues, the leaves on the trees turn warm shades of gold and orange – and once the leaves have fallen it's the ideal time to look for woodland birds. How many can you spot?

★ **Magic** ★
moment

The first appearance of cute, fluffy little grebe chicks on the pond in spring.

Great crested grebe

Seasonal highlights

❈ Spring
Little grebe
Nuthatch
Mute swan
Wild rabbit

❈ Summer
Heather
Common frog
Comma butterfly

❂ Autumn
Shaggy inkcap
Fly agaric

❈ Winter
Grey heron
Blue tit
Great spotted woodpecker
Long-tailed tit
Roe deer

Discover Yorkshire's Wildlife | 125

Parson's Carr

A long, thin reserve of wetland and grassland next to Doncaster's iPort development, Parson's Carr is one of several new sites around the edges of neighbouring Potteric Carr.

The lowdown...

Nearest town: Loversall, near Doncaster (1.6m/2.6km)
Nearest postcode: DN11 9DG / DN11 9DY
Grid ref: SK5825699332 (bridge over M18); SK5864897143 (Carr Lane entrance)
///poets.flashing.elections
Parking: Park at Carr Lodge on Hall Balk Lane and walk over the M18, or park in Wadworth and walk down Carr Lane.
Size: 104ha

A great place for:

☑ Bird watchers
☐ Cyclists
☐ Wildflower enthusiasts
☑ Families
☐ Leisurely stroll
☑ Peace and tranquility
☑ Walkers

Recommended time to make the most of your visit:

☐ Full day
☑ Half day
☐ Just an hour

ℹ Before you go...

Access to the site from the road is on rough track. There are hard-standing paths, including a bridleway and cycleway once on the reserve. Ideally walked or cycled from Potteric Carr.

Everybody needs good neighbours

Parson's Carr is a young nature reserve, but one that's already attracting interesting wildlife, and has great potential.

Part of a network of sites around Potteric Carr, it is a welcome extension of Potteric Carr's wetland habitat, allowing birds including avocets and marsh harriers to move between the two reserves. A colony of black-headed gulls has been quick to move in too, taking advantage of lakes that were created in 2017.

As you move away from the direction of Potteric Carr, there is wet grassland and previously arable land that has been turned to grass, attracting some bird species not found at Potteric Carr, including yellowhammers. Brown hares have also been spotted on some of these grasslands, aided by the mixture of hedgerows, nearby fields and places to feed at night.

Bring some binoculars to watch birds on the lakes and islands, from common nesting species in spring to passage waders in autumn and wildfowl in winter. On calm, sunny days look for butterflies on the flowers besides the paths.

Combine with a visit to Potteric Carr or try our walk on page 42.

Looking over Parson's Carr lake towards the iPort

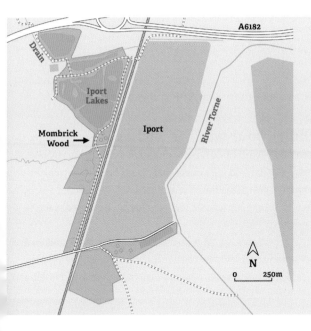

A6182

Drain

Iport
Lakes

Mombrick
Wood

Iport

River Torne

N

0   250m

A6182   A638

Carr
Lodge   Doncaster   Manor
                          Farm

Potteric Carr

M18

Parsons
Carr

River Torne

N

Rossington

Can you help?

We'd love to know what species are using Parson's Carr – please share your sightings by tagging **@yorkswildlife** on Twitter or using iRecord.

One to watch

New ponds with shallow, sloping sides will provide a haven for newts, dragonflies and waders. New hedges will provide additional homes, shelter and food for birds like linnets, reed buntings and yellowhammers, as well as small mammals.

The Trust will introduce grazing by cattle and ponies on the reserve, contained within newly fenced off areas. Grazing will help to manage the drier areas, stop quick-growing willows from taking over and provide attractive open habitat for nesting birds.

Jack snipe

★ Magic ★ moment

Catching sight of a Jack snipe constantly bobbing on the water's edge in the winter.

Seasonal highlights

✿ Spring
Coot
Moorhen
Mute swan
Yellowhammer

❀ Summer
Black headed gull colony
Avocet
Common blue butterfly

◑ Autumn
Marsh harrier
Passage waders

❄ Winter
Wildfowl
Jack snipe
Little egret
Fieldfare
Redwing

Potteric Carr

Leave the grey bustling roads, railways and industrial estates of Doncaster behind and you might feel like Dorothy stepping into a new realm. Welcome to another world...

The lowdown...

Nearest town: Doncaster (2.5m/4km)
Nearest postcode: DN4 8DB
Grid ref: SE 58858 00663
///towers.happily.snuggled
Parking: Car park off Mallard Way, open 9am to 5pm
Size: 220ha

A great place for:

- ☑ Bird watchers
- ☐ Cyclists
- ☑ Wildflower enthusiasts
- ☑ Families
- ☐ Leisurely stroll
- ☑ Peace and tranquility
- ☑ Walkers

Recommended time to make the most of your visit:

- ☑ Full day
- ☐ Half day
- ☐ Just an hour

ⓘ **Before you go...**
Facilities on site include toilets (including accessible toilet and baby changing facilities) and a gift shop and café in the visitor centre. Much of Potteric Carr is accessible for standard wheelchairs and pushchairs. Free entry for members onto the reserve.

Indulge your wildlife wishes

There's no Wizard of Oz here to grant your wishes, but this huge, diverse wonderland for wildlife really does have something for everyone – great facilities, fun activities, space to explore in joyful peace, and so much wildlife you won't know where to start.

Over 230 bird species, 28 butterfly species, 902 moth species and 23 dragonfly species have been recorded here, alongside many other fascinating insects, plants, fungi, mammals and amphibians.

★ Magic ★ moment
When the north of England's first four black-winged stilt chicks fledged here in summer 2022.

Black-winged stilt

"I don't think we're in Doncaster any more..."

The variety of habitats and numbers of wildlife here on the urban fringe of Doncaster might seem remarkable today, but this low-lying landscape is a remnant of a vast fenland that once stretched all the way to the coast.

Potteric's modern life as a nature reserve began in 1968, when it was a comparatively miniscule 13 hectares. A major extension in 2005 provided important habitat for a wealth of species, including breeding 'booming' bitterns and marsh harriers.

Reed-fringed pool at Potteric Carr

Thank you

Your support helps us to maintain and develop this wonderful wetland habitat for both people and wildlife.

Magic in the marshes – and much more

In the expansive marshes and pools, there's a wide range of plants, including greater and lesser spearwort, water soldier, water violet southern marsh-orchid, and old man's beard – Britain's only wild clematis – on the disused railway embankments. In the pools, look for great crested and palmate newts, toads, water voles and water shrews.

An impressive invertebrate list includes purple hairstreak and brown argus butterflies along with many moths, spiders, beetles, bugs and hoverflies.

There's an incredible number variety of birds: wildfowl, warblers, waders, woodpeckers, willow tits... and frequent surprises during spring and autumn migration.

Seasonal highlights

✿ Spring
Avocet
Little ringed plover
Marsh harrier
Black-necked grebe
Primrose

✿ Summer
Purple loosestrife
Southern marsh orchid
Green sandpiper
Brown argus
Banded demoiselle

✿ Autumn
Little egret
Teal
Willow tit
Fungi

✿ Winter
Bittern
Starling murmurations

Water vole

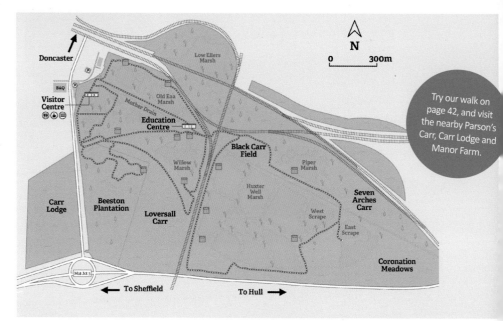

Try our walk on page 42, and visit the nearby Parson's Carr, Carr Lodge and Manor Farm.

For a wild day...

Discover the story trail, try some pond-dipping, and finish with a hot drink and treat at the visitor centre.

Go a little wilder...

Visit late in the afternoon on a winter's day to see a jaw-droppingly spectacular starling murmuration, and maybe spot a bittern emerging from the reedbeds.

Experience Potteric Carr's wildest side...

Enjoy a day full of wildlife experiences the whole year round by exploring the paths throughout the reserve and visit all the hides. You'll need more than a page in your notebook for your species list!

And there's more...

Potteric Carr has a brilliant programme of regular seasonal events for everyone, including Forest Tots, guided walks and an adventurous monthly outdoor play session for pre-school children and toddlers.

Pond-dipping

Showtime with Potteric Carr's spectacular shape-shifters

Witnessing a starling murmuration as dusk approaches on a winter's day is a truly awesome wildlife experience.

The starlings don't arrive all at once – they gather in smaller groups at first, before merging into larger flocks. At its peak, tens of thousands of birds form a shape-shifting cloud that twists and turns against the darkening sky. You can hear their wingbeats whooshing over your head, before the flock drops in one mighty funnel into the reedbeds to roost. The starlings' astonishing display actually gets its name from their chattering – or 'murmuring' – as they settle down to sleep.

It's mesmerising, both for us and for predators like peregrines, sparrowhawks and marsh harriers, which are left bemused as they hunt for their supper.

Starling murmurations appear at dusk

Sprotbrough Flash

No trip to Sprotbrough Flash is ever the same, thanks to the varied wildlife, habitats and choice of walking routes – but you can always count on a sense of peace and connection with nature.

The lowdown...

Nearest town: Doncaster (4m/6.4km)
Nearest postcode: DN5 7LA
Grid ref: Woodland entrance- SE 53627 01339
Tow path entrance- SE 53693 01371
///newspaper.shiny.collects
Parking: 30 metres downstream on Nursery Lane
Site designation: SSSI
Size: 28 ha

  Trans Pennine Trail runs along towpath but no cycling access elsewhere on reserve

A great place for:

☑ Bird watchers
☐ Cyclists
☑ Wildflower enthusiasts
☑ Families
☐ Leisurely stroll
☑ Peace and tranquility
☑ Walkers

Recommended time to make the most of your visit:

☐ Full day
☑ Half day
☐ Just an hour

ⓘ Before you go...

Spring and early summer are best when the wildflowers are blooming, insects are buzzing, and the wetlands are bustling with breeding birds.

Gorgeous river walks and much more

There's so much to enjoy at Sprotbrough Flash: a riverside walk along the Don as it passes through the picturesque Don Gorge; close views of wetland wildlife from hides and viewing screens – perhaps a bittern if you're lucky – taking the trail through the extensive ancient woodland, or enjoying a great diversity of wildflowers.

Sprotbrough Flash stands on magnesian limestone, a distinctive geological feature of the formerly quarried landscape, supporting a rich range of characteristic limestone plants including common spotted-orchid, pyramidal orchid, common twayblade, autumn gentian and cowslip.

There's variety in the woodland too, with native trees such as small leaved lime and an impressive avenue of yews.

Did you know?

Woolly mammoth and woolly rhino lived in the area during the last Ice Age – their bones have been found locally.

Looking across the River Don to the woodland

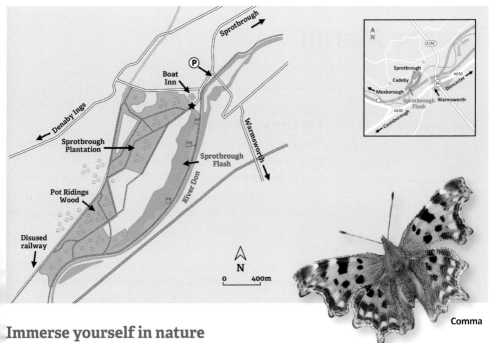

Comma

Immerse yourself in nature

Although it welcomes many visitors, the reserve feels secluded and wild – a place where you can fully immerse yourself in nature and savour the incredible wetland, meadow and woodland wildlife. Don't rush round – take time to linger and explore all that Sprotbrough Flash has to offer.

There are endless possibilities for walkers of most abilities, with many interconnected trails, allowing circular walks on surfaced footpaths or rougher woodland tracks. And you can take in one of the best views anywhere in South Yorkshire.

Seasonal highlights

❂ Spring
Displaying great crested grebe
Early purple orchid
Sanicle
Woodpeckers

❀ Summer
Kingfisher
Ruddy darter
Comma
Common twayblade

❂ Autumn
Osprey
Bittern
Fungi in the woods
Spindle
Small-leaved lime

❀ Winter
Mixed bird flocks
Woodpeckers
Brown hare

Great spotted woodpecker

★ Magic ★ moment

Hearing a drumming woodpecker in early spring.

Thorpe Marsh

The mixture of wetland, woodland and grassland on the east bank of the River Don floodplain means there's always something interesting to see at Thorpe Marsh.

The lowdown...

Nearest town: Barnby Dun (2.5m/4km)
Nearest postcode: DN5 0LN
Grid ref: SE594087
///dairy.doors.chain
Parking: Small layby off Fordstead Lane. Do not park in front of access gate.
Size: 77ha

 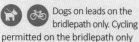 Dogs on leads on the bridlepath only. Cycling permitted on the bridlepath only

A great place for:

☑ Bird watchers
☐ Cyclists
☑ Wildflower enthusiasts
☑ Families
☐ Leisurely stroll
☑ Peace and tranquility
☐ Walkers

Recommended time to make the most of your visit:

☐ Full day
☑ Half day
☐ Just an hour

ⓘ Before you go...
The site is not suitable for wheelchairs or buggies. Cattle graze some parts of the site. Take extra care on the steep stairs and stiles going down the embankment.

Up from the ashes

This reserve's string of habitats owes some of its diversity to how the land was used in the past. While the East Coast Mainline still runs to the west, an older railway embankment runs across the site, with hides and vantage points overlooking the landscape, giving you a different perspective. The embankment also supports many plants, insects and breeding birds.

The land was previously owned by the power station that stood to the east and was purchased by the Central Electricity Generating Board in the 1960s for tipping fly ash, resulting in a great blend of flourishing plants. Ea Beck is to the south, and the island of land between these features was never intensively farmed – you can still see the pattern of ridge and furrow in the fields, dating back to the Middle Ages. These fields are home to adder's-tongue fern, pepper saxifrage, devil's-bit scabious, great burnet and common figwort. They are also a great place to watch moths, butterflies, dragonflies and damselflies, which can be spotted from the paths.

Applehurst pond at Thorpe Marsh

Thank you
We rely on your donations to help us maintain the hide and paths at Thorpe Marsh.

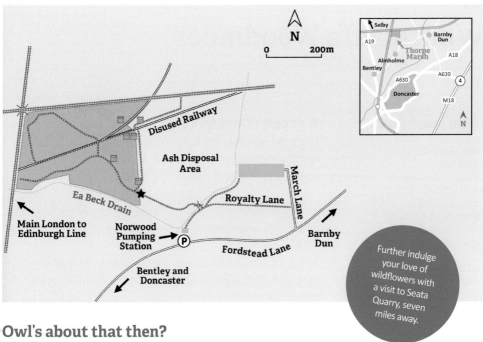

Owl's about that then?

With a thriving population of voles, mice and shrews, there's a banquet for owls, including barn owls, tawny owls, and long-eared owls in winter. Insects, birds, mammals and grass snakes all use the hedgerows, while great spotted woodpeckers, long-tailed and willow tits and treecreepers can be found in the woods.

Thorpe Mere is the largest lake. Waders like oystercatcher, green sandpiper and redshank are regular visitors, and overwintering ducks include wigeon and goosander. Look for little grebe and water rail at the Mere Scrape, and keep an eye out for bitterns. In spring, listen for the familiar call of the cuckoo.

Further indulge your love of wildflowers with a visit to Seata Quarry, seven miles away.

Seasonal highlights

✿ Spring
Cuckoo
Blackcap
Orange-tip
Cuckooflower
Common spotted-orchid

✹ Summer
Kingfisher
Cinnabar moth

◑ Autumn
Bittern
Migrant hawker
Common darter
Comma

✺ Winter
Goosander
Long-eared owl
Wigeon
Lesser redpoll

★ **Magic** ★
moment
A surprise encounter with one of our most secretive birds, the long-eared owl.

Long-eared owl

Wharncliffe Woodmoor

Reclaimed from the old colliery, this expansive grassland with pockets of broadleaved woodland is an ideal green getaway for walkers, runners, horse riders or some time out.

The lowdown...

Nearest town: Barnsley (3m/4.8km)
Nearest postcode: S71 2QG
Grid ref: SE 37330 09102
///rear.basin.hurt
Parking: Small layby off roundabout on West Green Way
Size: 42ha

Cycling permitted on the Trans Pennine Trail only

A great place for:

☐ Bird watchers
☐ Cyclists
☐ Wildflower enthusiasts
☑ Families
☐ Leisurely stroll
☐ Peace and tranquility
☑ Walkers

Recommended time to make the most of your visit:

☐ Full day
☐ Half day
☑ Just an hour

ℹ Before you go...
There is good access from the Trans Pennine Trail, and flat, well-walked routes crossing the site, on grass or gravel.

A green scene in an urban setting

This well-connected site is close to the Trans Pennine Trail and is linked to our neighbouring reserve at Carlton Marsh, so you can enjoy a visit as part of a day or half-day's walking in the area.

It's a quiet, green space in an urban setting, so perfect for a picnic or dog walk, and there are great views of Barnsley along the way.

Spring is the best time to visit. Watch and listen for meadow pipits and skylarks, or perhaps a kestrel or buzzard flying over. Buttercups and other common flowers provide a bright splash of colour around the reserve, and on warm, sunny days, this is a great place to see butterflies and other insects.

Did you know?
Meadow pipits are a cuckoos' favourite host for their chicks. A single egg is laid in the pipit's nest, and the much bigger cuckoo chick forces the young pipits out, to be raised alone and well fed.

Buttercups

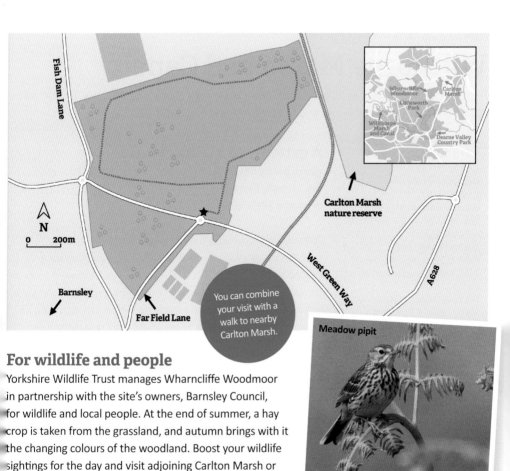

Fish Dam Lane

N

0   200m

Barnsley

Far Field Lane

Carlton Marsh
nature reserve

West Green Way

A628

You can combine your visit with a walk to nearby Carlton Marsh.

Wharncliffe Woodmoor
Carlton Marsh
Littleworth Park
Wilthorpe Marsh and Canal
Dearne Valley Country Park

Meadow pipit

For wildlife and people

Yorkshire Wildlife Trust manages Wharncliffe Woodmoor in partnership with the site's owners, Barnsley Council, for wildlife and local people. At the end of summer, a hay crop is taken from the grassland, and autumn brings with it the changing colours of the woodland. Boost your wildlife sightings for the day and visit adjoining Carlton Marsh or nearby reserves for more habitats and wildlife wonders.

Skylark

★ **Magic** ★
moment

The springtime 'trill' of skylarks as they rise singing into the sky.

Seasonal highlights

❄ **Spring**
Skylark
Meadow pipit
Kestrel
Buzzard

❀ **Summer**
Butterflies

☂ **Autumn**
Autumn colours

❄ **Winter**
Mixed flocks of birds in the wood

Wilthorpe Marsh and Canal

Barnsley Canal closed in 1953, but it's not quite true to say it's no longer in use. Instead of carrying barges laden with coal, you'll find a refuge for wetland wildlife.

The lowdown...

Nearest town: Barnsley (1.3m/2.1km)
Nearest postcode: S71 1QZ
Grid ref: SE 34614 07914 (Car park on Smithies Lane)
///urban.occupy.movie
Parking: Small car park on Smithies Lane. Height restriction barrier applies.
Site designation: Local Wildlife Site
Size: 11ha

A great place for:

☑ Bird watchers
☐ Cyclists
☑ Wildflower enthusiasts
☐ Families
☐ Leisurely stroll
☑ Peace and tranquility
☑ Walkers

Recommended time to make the most of your visit:

☐ Full day
☑ Half day
☐ Just an hour

 Before you go...
Take the footpath alongside Barnsley Canal to join the wider footpath network across the reserve. The path is mostly flat but can get muddy in winter and isn't suitable for wheelchairs. There's a steep incline from the towpath towards the grasslands.

A gateway to a wilder world

You're barely out of Barnsley town centre before you reach this gateway into the Upper Dearne Valley and step out into an extensive wetland oasis.

Following the course of the old canal, you'll get great views over the valley's cut-off meanders, swamps and sprawling reedbeds. The canal bed is dry at first as you head west from the car park, where you'll see crack willow growing. This soon gives way to a wetter marsh, then the water opens up, providing an excellent habitat for amphibians, including great crested newts.

Stop to admire the interesting water plants that grow here, especially the only population of frogbit in the Barnsley area. Frogbit floats on the water's surface, looking like a small water lily, with sweet, three-petalled white flowers that bloom in July and August.

Winter can be a great time to look for some of the more unusual bird species that sometimes visit the marsh, including Jack snipe and water pipit, with raptors like peregrines and merlins hunting for prey.

Did you know?
Why is a crack willow called a crack willow? Because of its habit of splitting with cracks, and the loud noise of its branches when they break.

A wetland wildlife refuge

Stay longer to explore other routes in the immediate area, including the path to Dearne Valley Country Park.

Wilthorpe

Smithies Lane

Honeywell

Huddersfield Road

Frogbit

Life on the hedge

To the south of the site, bee orchids bloom in summer in the open grassland. To the north, the longest continuous hedgerow in Barnsley provides food and shelter for flocks of birds that include rare willow tits, thrushes and bullfinches.

The Trust is working on the site to create a better habitat for willow tits to colonise, by creating an open canopy in the young woodland that grows alongside the canal.

★ **Magic** ★
moment
Spotting a kingfisher perched by the disused canal as you walk along the towpath.

Kingfisher

Seasonal highlights

✿ Spring
Willow tit
Grasshopper warbler
Great crested newt

❀ Summer
Frogbit
Field scabious
Yellow flag iris
Reed bunting

❂ Autumn
Mallard
Teal
Gadwall
Green woodpecker

❀ Winter
Water rail
Bullfinch
Kingfisher
Great spotted woodpecker

Wogden Foot

On the edge of the Peak District, close to South Yorkshire's border with Derbyshire, lies Wogden Foot, a former railway siding that's now a peaceful area of grassland and scrub.

The lowdown...

Nearest town: Dunford Bridge (1m/1.5km)
Nearest postcode: S36 4AF
Grid ref: Car park SE158024
///slang.richly.pacemaker
Parking: Car park at Dunford Bridge. Walk east along the Trans Pennine Trail to the site.
Site designation: Local Wildlife Site
Size: 7ha

  No cycling on site, but easy to cycle here on the Trans Pennine Trail

A great place for:

☐ Bird watchers
☐ Cyclists
☑ Wildflower enthusiasts
☐ Families
☐ Leisurely stroll
☑ Peace and tranquility
☑ Walkers

Recommended time to make the most of your visit:

☐ Full day
☑ Half day
☐ Just an hour

ℹ️ **Before you go...**
The route from the car park is level and flat, but once on the reserve it is uneven and can be muddy, so not suitable for wheelchairs or buggies. There are toilets at Winscar Reservoir near Dunford Bridge.

On track for a countryside stroll

This narrow strip of land sandwiched between the Trans Pennine Trail and the Upper Don river has an interesting mix of grassland types and associated plants, thanks to a combination of acidic soils and limestone ballast deposits from the construction and subsequent closure of the railway in 1981.

Despite being at the foot of the moors, the reserve itself is relatively flat, and is a pleasant countryside spot for a quiet walk and perhaps a picnic.

Visit in spring or summer to enjoy the reserve at its finest – 150 plant species have been recorded here, including the rare Jacob's ladder, found in fewer than six places in the Peak District. Others include wild mignonette, cowslip, bird's-foot trefoil, common-spotted orchid, heath bedstraw, wild marjoram, hairy violet, thyme-leaved sandwort, pignut, wild teasel, wild strawberry, fairy flax and musk mallow. The grassland is grazed by sheep to maintain the habitat for this variety of species.

Common blue and meadow brown are just two of the butterfly species you might see, and frogs are at home in the pond and ditches.

Did you know?
You can run, walk or cycle the 27 miles from Wogden Foot to Sprotbrough Flash on the Trans Pennine Trail – that's our idea of a great marathon!

Former railway siding welcomed new arrival

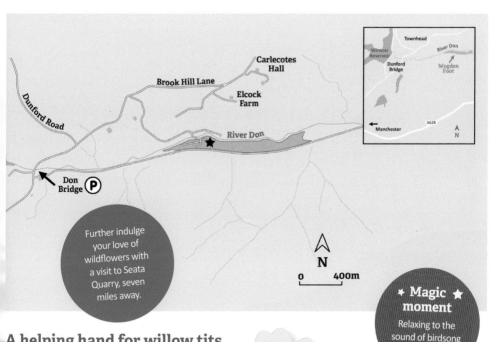

Brook Hill Lane

Carlecotes Hall

Elcock Farm

Dunford Road

River Don

Don Bridge ℗

Townhead

Winscar Reservoir

Dunford Bridge

River Don

Wogden Foot

Manchester

A628

N

Further indulge your love of wildflowers with a visit to Seata Quarry, seven miles away.

N

0   400m

Further indulge your love of wildflowers with a visit to Seata Quarry, seven miles away.

★ **Magic** ★ **moment**

Relaxing to the sound of birdsong in the spring.

A helping hand for willow tits

In 2022, as part of work to replace pylons with underground electricity cables, the National Grid supported improvements to the reserve's ecology, with features including shelters for reptiles and amphibians. Willow tits have bred around Wogden Foot and the habitat has been carefully managed – including leaving more decaying wood – to support their declining population.

Other birds to look for on site include skylark, tree pipit and bullfinch, and keep looking up – a curlew or peregrine might be passing over. In spring and summer listen for the croaky, rasping call of red grouse, and in winter watch for mixed flocks of birds in the woodland.

Cowslip

Seasonal highlights

☼ **Spring**
Jacob's ladder
Cowslip
Hairy violet
Skylark
Tree pipit

❋ **Summer**
Wild mignonette
Musk mallow
Wild strawberry
Common blue
Meadow brown

◉ **Autumn**
Fungi
Autumn colours

❋ **Winter**
Mixed bird flocks

East

Impressive wetlands, heaths, marshy lowlands, and meadows meet the iconic seascapes of Spurn and Flamborough Cliffs. This is a landscape of big skies and diverse wildlife spectacles, where some of our rarest species can be found.

Allerthorpe Common

One of just three remaining pockets of lowland heath in the Vale of York, Allerthorpe Common is rich in wildlife, and one of the best places in the area to see adders.

The lowdown...

Nearest town: Pocklington (3.9m/6.3km)
Nearest postcode: YO42 4DQ
Grid ref: SE752473
///waged.relax.arranges
Parking: Forestry Commission car park on site
Size: 6ha
Site designation: SSSI

  Dogs not allowed on the reserve, but welcome on leads in Allerthorpe Wood, managed by the Forestry Commission.

A great place for:

- ☑ Bird watchers
- ☐ Cyclists
- ☑ Wildflower enthusiasts
- ☐ Families
- ☐ Leisurely stroll
- ☑ Peace and tranquility
- ☑ Walkers

Recommended time to make the most of your visit:

- ☐ Full day
- ☑ Half day
- ☐ Just an hour

ℹ **Before you go...**
To reach the reserve, walk 1km on the track from the car park. Take two stiles onto open access land. Uneven ground with tussocks, hollows and overgrown ditches.

1086 and all that

Allerthorpe Common's history can be traced back to AD 1086, when it was recorded in the Domesday Book. Back then it was known as Aluuarstorp, meaning a village belonging to a man called Alfard. We hope Alfard would like what we've done with the place since we began managing it in 1966. Some of it would be familiar, and some not – the common itself is a smaller patch of land, now surrounded by pine forest managed by the Forestry Commission, rather than the agricultural land that had come to surround it. The common still has the same kind of mix of habitats, though: wet and dry heath, acid grassland, woodland, scrub and open water.

It's full of wildlife all year round. Ling heather, tormentil, sheep's fescue and wavy hair-grass grow in the drier areas, with cross-leaved heath and purple moor grass in damper areas, along with the nationally rare May lily. Patches of gorse provide shelter for birds, and their network of roots supports a healthy population of adders.

Lowland heath at Allerthorpe Common

Did you know?
Allerthorpe Common has been covered with heather, birch and a little pine for the last 2,000 years.

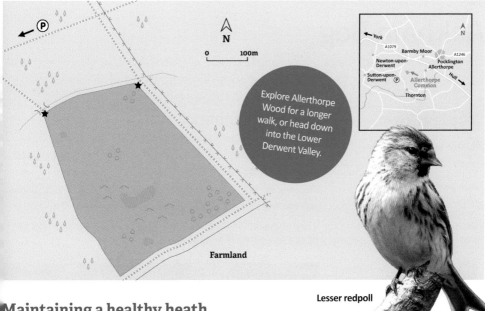

N

0 ——— 100m

Explore Allerthorpe Wood for a longer walk, or head down into the Lower Derwent Valley.

York
A1079
Barmby Moor
Newton-upon-Derwent
A1246
Pocklington
Allerthorpe
Sutton-upon-Derwent
Allerthorpe Common
Hull
Thornton

Farmland

Lesser redpoll

Maintaining a healthy heath

The reserve is visited by badgers, foxes and roe deer, and its mature birch and willow trees attract birds including green and great spotted woodpeckers, and flocks of lesser redpolls in winter. Listen out for crossbills calling as they fly around the surrounding forest. Broad-bodied chasers and blue-tailed damselflies are among the many insects you can find around the pools.

We keep the heath healthy with grazing by rare breeds to reduce tree saplings and some coarse grasses, and volunteers regularly control bramble and bracken and remove any birch saplings that the livestock have missed.

Seasonal highlights

☼ Spring
Adder
May lily
Green woodpecker
Woodlark
Willow warbler

❇ Summer
Tormentil
Ling heather
Marsh cinquefoil
Broad-bodied chaser
Blue-tailed damselfly

◑ Autumn
Woodcock
Siskin
Lesser redpoll

❇ Winter
Jay
Treecreeper
Coal tit

★ **Magic moment** ★

Beautifully patterned adders emerging from hibernation in spring.

Adder

Askham Bog

This precious surviving remnant of Yorkshire's ancient peatland is the birthplace of Yorkshire Wildlife Trust and holds a special place in the hearts of our members and our organisation.

The lowdown...

Nearest town: York city centre (3.5m/5.6km)
Nearest postcode: YO23 2UB
Grid ref: SE 5745 4792
///next.obey.armed
Parking: Onsite car park
Site designation: SSSI
Size: 44ha

  Dogs allowed on a lead on the boardwalk only. Easy to cycle to, and with racks in the car park, but no cycling on the reserve

A great place for:

☑ Bird watchers
☐ Cyclists
☑ Wildflower enthusiasts
☑ Families
☑ Leisurely stroll
☑ Peace and tranquility
☑ Walkers

Recommended time to make the most of your visit:

☐ Full day
☐ Half day
☑ Just an hour

 Before you go...
The wooden boardwalk is accessible for wheelchairs and buggies, with a short, sloped track from the car park. There are no facilities on site, but you'll find accessible toilets at Askham Bar park and ride.

In the beginning...

A "cathedral of nature conservation." That's what the great Sir David Attenborough called Askham Bog when he visited in 2016. He was right, of course – this ecologically important reserve on the edge of York is a wild paradise for visitors of all ages. Yorkshire Wildlife Trust (under our former name of Yorkshire Naturalists' Trust) was originally set up to receive the gift of Askham Bog in 1946 and care for it in perpetuity.

Meadow thistles at Askham Bog

Life on the bog edge

Despite being enclosed by a railway and busy roads, Askham Bog is a remarkably peaceful place. The bog edges have the greatest diversity of plants and insects, including several very rare sedges, as well as beautiful fenland flowers such as meadow-rue, bog myrtle and meadow thistle. Some of the grand old royal ferns are huge and possibly the oldest living things in York. There are rare water beetles, and over 800 species of moths have been recorded here including dentated pug, whose nearest location is in East Anglia. In summer, you'll see dragonflies zipping past, including the spectacular emperor.

★ **Magic** ★
moment

Standing still on the boardwalk when the rest of the Bog is flooded in winter, watching a mixed flock of finches feeding on birch and alder seeds overhead.

Looking from the boardwalk into the bog

Roving birds, bounding deer and hopping froglets

Along with common woodland species, including nuthatch, treecreeper, jay and great spotted woodpecker, you can find marsh and willow tit, and there are often buzzard, red kite, kestrel and sparrowhawk overhead. Spring and summer welcome several species of warbler, particularly around the pond. In winter, roving flocks of siskin, lesser redpoll and goldfinch feed on birch and alder, and you might flush a skulking woodcock from the undergrowth.

Roe deer are often seen, with a flash of their white bottoms as they bound away. Look for frogs and newts in the ponds and ditches, especially when tiny froglets are hopping around in spring.

Goldfinch

Seasonal highlights

✿ Spring
Brimstone butterfly
Large red damselfly
Willow tit
Common frog
Marsh violet

❀ Summer
Yellow flag iris
Marsh thistle
Water violet
Migrant hawker
Sedge warbler

◉ Autumn
Royal fern
Guelder rose
Common darter
Alder beetle
Jay

❅ Winter
Bog myrtle
Woodcock
Lesser redpoll
Roe deer

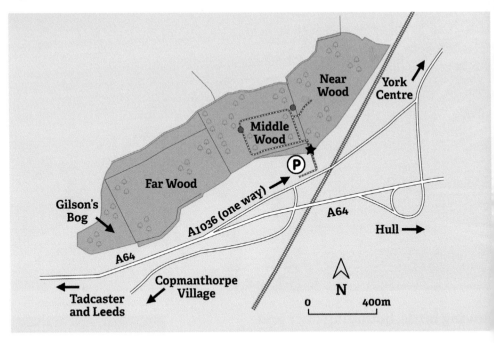

For a wild day...

Enjoy a short walk around the boardwalk, see the woodland birds up close, peek at the livestock carrying out their conservation grazing duties and have a nosy at the pond.

Go a little wilder...

Get up early for the dawn chorus in spring and enjoy the sights and sounds of the wildlife waking up.

Experience Askham Bog's wildest side...

Get your wellies on and step off the boardwalk to explore Far Wood, home to England's largest colony of gingerbread sedge. Be careful when the weather's been wet – this is a bog, after all!

And there's more...

Join a guided walk to discover the bog's famous plantlife and complex history by visiting **ywt.org.uk/our-events**

Thank you!

The amazing support of our members helped us save Askham Bog from a proposed development on neighbouring land, which could have had devastating consequences, following a high-profile legal battle in 2019/20.

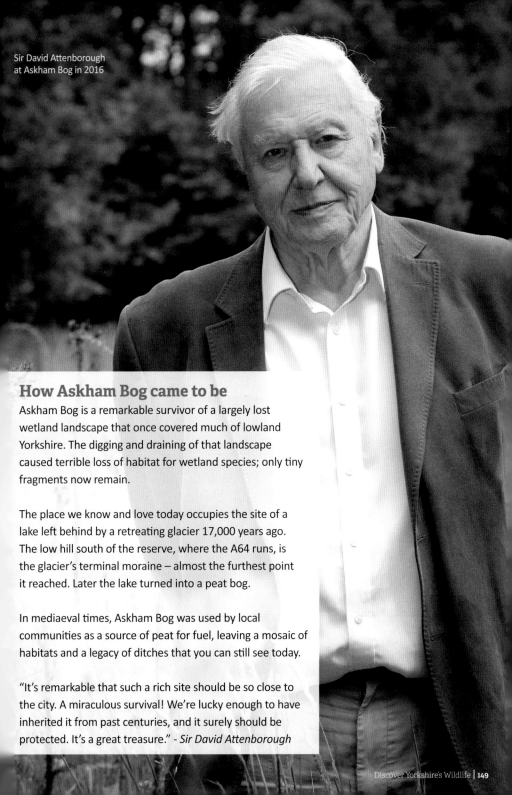

Sir David Attenborough at Askham Bog in 2016

How Askham Bog came to be

Askham Bog is a remarkable survivor of a largely lost wetland landscape that once covered much of lowland Yorkshire. The digging and draining of that landscape caused terrible loss of habitat for wetland species; only tiny fragments now remain.

The place we know and love today occupies the site of a lake left behind by a retreating glacier 17,000 years ago. The low hill south of the reserve, where the A64 runs, is the glacier's terminal moraine – almost the furthest point it reached. Later the lake turned into a peat bog.

In mediaeval times, Askham Bog was used by local communities as a source of peat for fuel, leaving a mosaic of habitats and a legacy of ditches that you can still see today.

"It's remarkable that such a rich site should be so close to the city. A miraculous survival! We're lucky enough to have inherited it from past centuries, and it surely should be protected. It's a great treasure." - *Sir David Attenborough*

Barlow Common

With trails to explore and varied wildlife to discover, Barlow Common is the perfect place for a family outing or peaceful walk. Not bad for a former tip next to a power station!

The lowdown...

Nearest town: Selby (4.2m/6.8km)
Nearest postcode: YO8 8EZ
Grid ref: SE 633 285
///bitters.shakes.repelled
Parking: Car park at main entrance.
Site designation: Local Nature Reserve (LNR)
Size: 37ha

A great place for:

☑ Bird watchers

☐ Cyclists

☑ Wildflower enthusiasts

☑ Families

☐ Leisurely stroll

☑ Peace and tranquility

☑ Walkers

Recommended time to make the most of your visit:

☐ Full day

☑ Half day

☐ Just an hour

ℹ Before you go...

Paths are hard-surfaced and relatively flat, and there are benches around the reserve. The paths can get muddy in winter.

Stoatally awesome!

From the very first wooden waymarker you encounter – featuring a cute stoat – Barlow Common invites visitors of all ages to step out onto its well-marked trails and discover the wildlife that lives in the common's varied habitats.

From the car park, follow the tree-lined path past the main fishing lake and round to the education centre. Take a trail and wander round the woods or wonder at the wildflower meadows and wetland wildlife.

Did you know?

Viper's bugloss may have got its name from its spotted stem, which is thought to resemble a snake's markings. 'Bugloss' is from the Greek for 'ox's tongue', referring to the tongue-shaped leaves.

Viper's bugloss

More trees please

Up until the early 1900s, people grazed cattle, pigs and sheep on the common – and then it was used as a tip! Since British Rail reclaimed the land in 1983 and capped the tip using local soils, Selby District Council and then Yorkshire Wildlife Trust have transformed the site. Now native woodland is naturally regenerating and, in time, this will become an even better home for wildlife.

★ Magic ★ moment

Masses of stripy yellow-and-black cinnabar moth caterpillars feeding on ragwort in summer.

Cinnabar moth caterpillar

Wildflowers at Barlow Common

Summer lovin'

Barlow Common's wildlife and beauty peak between May and July, when the trees are in full leaf and the wildflowers are in bloom, including orchids, viper's bugloss, evening primrose, lady's bedstraw, wild basil and common centaury. In the grasslands, listen for the yaffling call of green woodpeckers – maybe you'll see one too. This is also the time to look for grass snakes basking in the sun and butterflies visiting the flowers.

In spring, intrepid pond dippers might discover newts and dragonfly larvae, and see little grebes on the lakes. Winter brings flocks of finches to feast on teasel seeds.

Seasonal highlights

✿ Spring
Green woodpecker
Kingfisher
Reed bunting
Grey heron

❋ Summer
Common spotted-orchid
Bee orchid
Red admiral
Painted lady
Cuckoo
Grass snake

✦ Autumn
Viper's bugloss
Fox
Great spotted woodpecker

❋ Winter
Roe deer
Long-tailed tit
Siskin

Wild basil

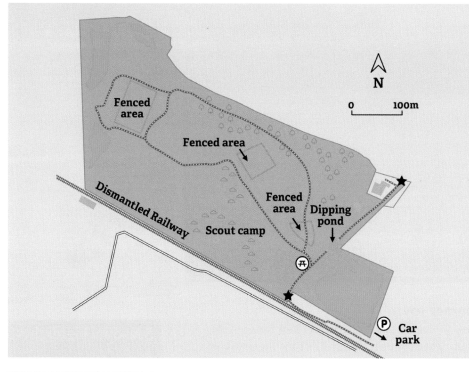

For a wild day...

Head out for a family stroll, with a picnic and some pond-dipping – and see what's on the bird feeders.

Go a little wilder...

Visit in early summer and explore the whole reserve to see its wildlife and wildflowers at their peak.

Experience Barlow Common's wildest side...

Find a quiet woodland corner one morning and listen to the springtime birdsong. How many different songs can you pick out?

And there's more...

Can you find all 25 hand-carved wooden waymarkers, featuring the reserve's wildlife?

A tale of two trails

Exploring Barlow Common is easy, thanks to our wildlife trails, developed with funding from SUEZ.

Starting from the education centre, get set for your wild adventure – but wait… which path will you choose first?

The main trail, which is 1.7km long or 1.4km if you take the short cut, guides you in a loop around the common, with views of wetland, meadows and woodland, and two ponds at the far end of the reserve if you decide to walk the full route.

Or you might want to discover the shorter woodland trail, tucked away in a quiet corner. If you're really lucky, you might spot a great crested newt in the pond.

Bolton Percy Station

Trains no longer stop at the station, which closed in 1965, and nature has moved back in, taking over the site of the old platform, goods shed, yard and track bed.

The lowdown...

Nearest town: Tadcaster (3.4m/5.6km)
Nearest postcode: YO23 7AW
Grid ref: SE 527 416
///expert.digitally.punks
Parking: Small on-site car park, or walk from Bolton Percy village
Size: 2ha

A great place for:

☐ Bird watchers
☐ Cyclists
☑ Wildflower enthusiasts
☐ Families
☐ Leisurely stroll
☑ Peace and tranquility
☐ Walkers

Recommended time to make the most of your visit:

☐ Full day
☐ Half day
☑ Just an hour

ℹ Before you go...
The paths are not suitable for wheelchairs or buggies. There's a tea room in Bolton Percy, and the nearest public toilets are in Tadcaster .

Extend your trip with a visit to Askham Bog, five miles down the road, or, in the opposite direction, to Sherburn Willows and Ledsham Bank.

Nature is never stationary

Where passengers once stood, brambles now scramble, and grassland grows where rail tracks once ran. It's fascinating to see wildlife slowly populating a place that people have abandoned, working to its own timetable.

The scrub that grows on the boundaries provides shelter for butterflies and moths in the summer, with common blues and small heaths among the butterflies drawn to the underlying ballast and chalk, and six-spot burnets and latticed heaths among the moths. This scrubby habitat also provides food and shelter for songbirds, including bullfinches, linnets and the elusive lesser whitethroat.

Spring and summer are the best times to visit the reserve, particularly between May and July to see the small meadow in flower and hear the birds singing. Primroses line the railway banks in spring. Our work on the meadow should be rewarded with a greater spread and variety of wildflowers in the years to come.

Wildflowers by the track through Bolton Percy Station

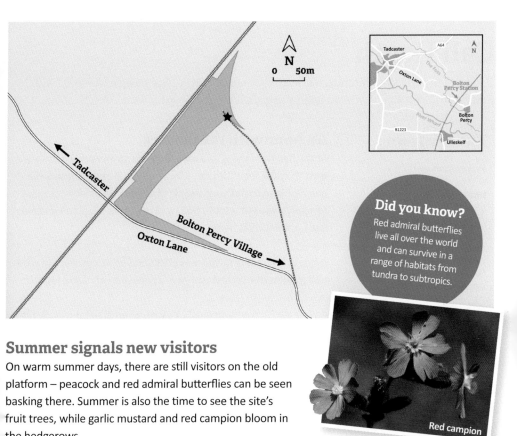

Did you know?
Red admiral butterflies live all over the world and can survive in a range of habitats from tundra to subtropics.

Red campion

Summer signals new visitors

On warm summer days, there are still visitors on the old platform – peacock and red admiral butterflies can be seen basking there. Summer is also the time to see the site's fruit trees, while garlic mustard and red campion bloom in the hedgerows.

There are two linear paths on the reserve, on firm and mostly level surfaces: one has a grassy surface and follows a slight slope from outside the main gate; the other is through the gate and on gravel and cinder.

★ **Magic moment** ★

The attractive orange-and-brown patterning of gatekeepers and wall butterflies, found along the flowering hedgerows in summer.

Seasonal highlights

❀ **Spring**
Primrose
Common blue
Small heath

❀ **Summer**
Red campion
Peacock
Lesser whitethroat

☉ **Autumn**
Red admiral
Linnet

❀ **Winter**
Bullfinch

Gatekeeper

Cali Heath

Taking its name from California, this heath may not obviously have much in common with America's Golden State, but what it lacks in glamour it makes up for with a wealth of insect life.

The lowdown...

Nearest town: Pocklington (3.5m/5.6km)
Nearest postcode: YO41 5PF
Grid ref: SE751496
///recliner.blog.prepared
Parking: Park on the lane behind the restaurant and carefully cross the A1079
Size: 11ha
Site designation: SSSI

A great place for:

☐ Bird watchers
☐ Cyclists
☑ Wildflower enthusiasts
☑ Families
☐ Leisurely stroll
☑ Peace and tranquility
☑ Walkers

Recommended time to make the most of your visit:

☐ Full day
☐ Half day
☑ Just an hour

ℹ️ **Before you go...**
There's a nice circular walk, but be careful of rabbit holes and some uneven areas. There's a small café just up the road. The nearest toilets are in Pocklington.

An hour with the flowers

At the height of the gold rush in America, when people travelled west to make their fortune, a local trust in Yorkshire granted a patch of land to the poor people of Barmby Moor. As the locals similarly travelled west to find work, the area become known as Cali (or California) Heath.

It doesn't have the palm trees of its sunnier namesake, but who needs palm trees when you have a collection of native ferns?

Cali Heath is an area of grassy heath – a rare habitat in Yorkshire. Concealed in the grassland is a marvellous array of tiny flowering plants, including bird's-foot trefoil, dove's-foot cranesbill and common stork's-bill – all typical of these sandy soils. Take a magnifying glass for a more detailed view. Look out for hare's-foot clover and shepherd's cress, recorded in only three other places in Yorkshire.

The rough grassland is valuable for a huge number of insects, including over 370 fly species. One of these – *Hilara gallica* – was thought to be extinct in Britain until it was re-discovered here, and Cali Heath is now its UK stronghold.

★ **Magic** ★
moment
Discovering wild pansies in patches of bare ground.

Wildflowers on Cali Heath

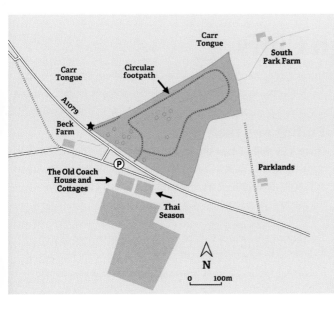

Buzzard

Battling bracken

Cali Heath is a diamond in the rough and still a work in progress. As we introduce more grazing, we hope to battle back against encroaching bracken and encourage more wildflowers, and we're re-digging the ponds to create more wet areas.

As well as the grassy habitat, there are areas of oak woodland, with alders and willows fringing the ditches, and there's a small section of heather. In quiet moments, you may see roe deer sheltering in the woods. Buzzards are a common sight, look out too for red kite, barn owl or green woodpecker.

Did you know?

Hare's-foot clover is named after its fluffy-looking flower heads

Seasonal highlights

✿ Spring
Heath bedstraw
Green woodpecker
Whitethroat
Blackcap

❀ Summer
Lady's bedstraw
Musk mallow
Small copper
Red admiral

◐ Autumn
Buzzard
Hare's-foot clover
Harebell

❀ Winter
Red kite
Barn owl
Roe deer

Hare's-foot clover

Flamborough Cliffs

Yorkshire's 'Great White Cape' is stunning, spectacular... we could go on. But these towering white cliffs are more than merely beautiful. Welcome to one of Europe's most important seabird colonies.

The lowdown...

Nearest town: Bridlington (6.2m/10km)
Nearest postcode: YO15 1BJ
Grid ref: TA 239 720
///section.tabs.libraries
Parking: At North Landing and Thornwick Bay (charges apply)
Size: 36ha
Site designation: SSSI, SAC, SPA, Flamborough Head Heritage Coast

A great place for:

☑ Bird watchers
☐ Cyclists
☑ Wildflower enthusiasts
☑ Families
☐ Leisurely stroll
☐ Peace and tranquility
☑ Walkers

Recommended time to make the most of your visit:

☑ Full day
☐ Half day
☐ Just an hour

ℹ **Before you go...**
The reserve is accessed by the coastal public footpath from North Landing car park, where there are toilets (closed in winter) and a cafe. The path is hilly and steep in places, with some steps. Take extra care if it's windy.

Puffins and their pals

There'll be puffins over the white cliffs of Flamborough... OK, not quite the words to Vera Lynn's famous song, but these charismatic auks will make your heart sing, and this is the best place in mainland Britain to enjoy seeing them up-close.

The puffins are far from alone in this bustling seabird city. From May to July the chalk cliffs host an astounding number of seabirds, including fulmar, kittiwake, guillemot, and razorbill.

Rocky shoreline at Flamborough Cliffs

They too like to be beside the seaside...

Flamborough has buckets (and spades!) of coastal charm and the beaches, caves and rockpools delight us all year round, but it's the breeding birds on the cliffs that really take our breath away ...and we're not just talking about the way they smell!

The headland, jutting out into the North Sea, is a renowned raucous migration hotspot, especially in autumn, with rarities attracting birdwatchers from all over the country. The grassy clifftops and gullies host a wide variety of chalkland plants, butterflies, and songbirds.

Magic moment

When the seabird city is in full swing with tens of thousands of auks, gulls and you spot a seal too.

Breil Nook at Flamborough Cliffs

There's no better place for sea watching

The waters around Flamborough Head are full of food for seabirds and other marine wildlife due to the 'Flamborough Front' – the meeting of cold and warm water creates an upwelling of nutrients and plankton. In spring and summer watch gleaming white gannets plunging into the sea for fish, in late summer and autumn look for passing skuas and shearwaters, and in winter watch for divers and sea ducks.

There's a wealth of marine mammals here too. On a calm day, watch for the playful splashes of bottle-nosed dolphins, the arched back and black fin of a harbour porpoise, the bobbing head of a seal, or even a minke whale.

Razorbill and guillemots

Seasonal highlights

✿ Spring
Puffin
Razorbill
Guillemot
Kittiwake

❋ Summer
Harbour porpoise
House martin
Wall butterfly

❂ Autumn
Minke whale
Grey and common seals
Sooty shearwater
Arctic skua
Wheatear

❋ Winter
Peregrine
Lapland bunting
Snow bunting

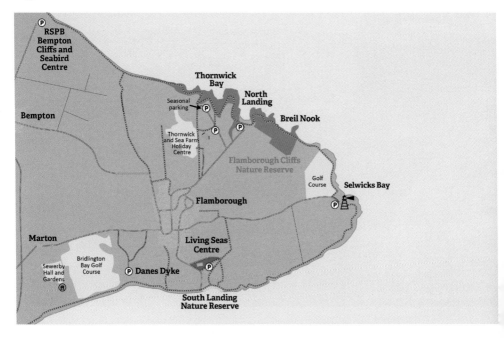

For a wild day...

If you do one thing, go and see the puffins between mid-May and mid-July, when they're on their nests near the clifftops.

Go a little wilder...

Visit in autumn and search for the marvellous migrants in the gullies and along the cliffs.

Experience Flamborough's wildest side...

For an unforgettable coastal walk, follow the King Charles III England Coast Path around Flamborough Head to the Living Seas Centre at South Landing and on to Dane's Dyke, or head north to Bempton Cliffs.

And there's more...

To see the cliffs and wildlife from a different angle, take a summer boat trip from North Landing, or explore the beaches, caves and rockpools – but check tide times first.

Take a full day to explore the reserve's three bays – Breil, Holmes and Thornwick – and its grassy clifftops and steep gullies, or 'guts'.

Connecting and protecting our marine habitats

Puffins are one of our most recognisable and beloved birds. Flamborough Head is a safe haven for these 'clowns of the sea', but their populations globally are declining. A puffin's favourite meal is sand eels; a small, silver, eel-like fish that makes up around 90% of their diet. If something happens to this food source, they will suffer.

Yorkshire Wildlife Trust has welcomed protection for sand eels and other marine wildlife at Dogger Bank Special Area of Conservation in the North Sea, but we urgently need to connect and protect more areas like this. Our ongoing work to save Yorkshire's seas is only possible thanks to the support of our members. Please consider joining us at **ywt.org.uk/membership**

Puffin at Flamborough cliffs

Discover the wildlife beneath Yorkshire's waves

We run marvellous marine events and sessions for all ages at the Living Seas Centre at South Landing. Discover our programme and plan your journey to the bottom of the North Sea, accompanied by a delicious snack from the cafe **ywt.org.uk/living-seas-centre**

Hodgson's Fields

A peaceful oasis of rough grassland and scrub providing shelter and food for wildlife amongst the arable landscape of South Holderness.

The lowdown...

Nearest town: Patrington (4.3m/7km), Hull (21m/34km)
Nearest postcode: HU12 0UU
Grid ref: TA 376 205
///just.arranger.birthing
Parking: Onsite
Size: 45ha

  Dogs on lead but please note grazing cattle and sheep.

A great place for:

- ☑ Bird watchers
- ☐ Cyclists
- ☑ Wildflower enthusiasts
- ☑ Families
- ☐ Leisurely stroll
- ☑ Peace and tranquility
- ☐ Walkers

Recommended time to make the most of your visit:

- ☐ Full day
- ☑ Half day
- ☐ Just an hour

ⓘ Before you go...
There are no formal footpaths and the ground is uneven, so sturdy footwear is recommended. The fields can get muddy in winter months.

Yellowhammer

An oasis of calm

Take a slow wander around the bushy scrub and tussocky grassland of Hodgson's Fields and you'll be rewarded with a heady mix of seasonal sights and sounds, as well as a sense of calm and lungfuls of fresh air. In spring, the chattering song of whitethroats and distinctive trill of grasshopper warblers complement farmland birds including yellowhammers, linnets and tree sparrows. Watch for whimbrel stopping by to feed with their curved bills on their spring and autumn migration. In summer, a vividly colourful covering of marsh orchids blankets the fields, attracting butterflies like small tortoiseshell, large skipper and ringlet.

0   300m

Out Newton

Paddock
Neats Furse
Southfield Farm
Holmpton Byway Close
Newton Gate Close
Gilcross Road Close
Ⓟ Bettywells
Out Newton Road Close   Copse
Skeffling

Easingwold

Hollym
Withernsea
A1033
North Sea
Holmpton
B1445   Hodgson's Fields   Out Newton
Welwick
Weeton
Skeffling   Easington
River Humber

Combine a visit with our other Holderness reserves.

Wildflowers at Hodgson's Fields

★ Magic ★ moment
A ghostly white barn owl silently hunting against a pink and orange sunset.

Jeffry Bog

In the lush, green, rolling countryside of the Howardian Hills, the wet pasture and lowland marsh of this tiny riverside reserve come alive with wildflowers in spring and summer.

Delightful flower displays by the Derwent

Jeffry Bog lies in the tranquil Kirkham Gorge on the river Derwent. Its grasslands and marsh sport an impressive array of wildflowers: cowslip, primrose, early purple orchid and marsh marigold in spring; and betony, common spotted-orchid, ragged robin and yellow flag iris in summer.

It's an ideal habitat for spiders and insects, with abundant damselflies and day-flying moths on warm, sunny days. Barn owls patrol for voles, and look for kingfishers along the river, and handsome goosanders in the winter.

The lowdown...

Nearest town: Malton (6m/9.7km)
Nearest postcode: YO60 7NJ
Grid ref: SE 761 665
///director.pace.chosen
Parking: Limited parking on roadside verge
Size: 3ha

🐕 🚲⃠

A great place for:

☐ Bird watchers
☐ Cyclists
☑ Wildflower enthusiasts
☐ Families
☐ Leisurely stroll
☑ Peace and tranquility
☑ Walkers

Recommended time to make the most of your visit:

☐ Full day
☐ Half day
☑ Just an hour

Extend your trip for a longer circular walk park at Kirkham Abbey and walk back to Jeffry Bog.

ⓘ **Before you go...**
There's just one path through the reserve, but the hillside is steep and grassy with wet flushes dropping to a wetter area and riverside footpath.

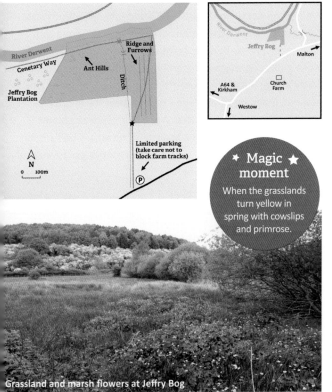

★ **Magic moment** ★
When the grasslands turn yellow in spring with cowslips and primrose.

Grassland and marsh flowers at Jeffry Bog

Kilnsea Wetlands

Created as recently as 2012, it hasn't taken long for Kilnsea Wetlands to establish itself as a birdwatching hotspot and an unmissable part of a visit to the Spurn peninsula.

The lowdown...

Nearest town: Patrington (7.5m/12km), Hull (24m/38.6km)
Nearest postcode: HU12 0UB
Grid ref: TA 405 167
///fondest.fewest.hindered
Parking: Onsite
Size: 35ha

A great place for:

☑ Bird watchers

☐ Cyclists

☑ Wildflower enthusiasts

☐ Families

☑ Leisurely stroll

☑ Peace and tranquility

☐ Walkers

Recommended time to make the most of your visit:

☐ Full day

☑ Half day

☐ Just an hour

Or add on to a trip to Spurn.

ⓘ Before you go...
The grass paths can get muddy in winter but are flat and accessible. There's a hide and viewing screens but no facilities – there is a pub and toilets in Kilnsea. Combine with a visit to Spurn where you'll also find facilities in the Discovery Centre (pg.188).

A refuge for waders

Neatly sandwiched between the coast and Humber Estuary, Kilnsea Wetlands was developed by the Environment Agency as a replacement refuge for wading birds as the Holderness coastline rapidly erodes and habitat is lost.

It provides a place to roost and feed for waders that leave the Humber mudflats at high tide in autumn and winter, including redshank, golden and grey plovers, knot, black- and bar-tailed godwits and dunlin, and passage migrants like curlew sandpiper, greenshank and little stint.

Waders are not the only birds you'll find here. Plentiful ducks, gulls and geese join the waders on the wetlands, along with little egrets and sometimes great white egrets and spoonbills, while pipits and wagtails are among the smaller birds around the water's edge. Anything could drop in, especially in spring and autumn. Listening Dish Hedge – named after the nearby concrete 'sound mirror' built in the First World War – attracts scarce migrants like barred warbler, and the same area is brilliant for short-eared owls. Raptors include marsh harrier, occasional hen harrier, merlin and peregrine.

Waders on the mudflats at Kilnsea Wetlands

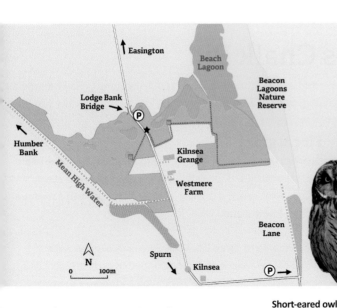

Short-eared owl

Further indulge your love of wildflowers with a visit to Seata Quarry, seven miles away.

Ure going to love the view

Featuring freshwater and saline pools with islands and spits, and wet grassland with seasonal scrapes, Kilnsea Wetlands has great potential to attract more species as these habitats develop, perhaps encouraging birds like oystercatchers, ringed plovers and lapwings to breed.

The reserve is managed sustainably using local livestock, and as the grassland becomes more established, it should attract more farmland birds, including corn bunting and tree sparrow. Wildflowers will attract a variety of insects, including dragonflies. Salt-tolerant plant species such as spiral tassel weed may well find a home here too.

★ **Magic** ★
moment

Spectacular wader roosts at high tide in autumn and winter.

Dunlin

Seasonal highlights

✿ Spring
Avocet
Little ringed plover
Oystercatcher
Tree sparrow

❀ Summer
Little tern
Clouded yellow
Wall butterfly
Oxeye daisy

◊ Autumn
Curlew sandpiper
Little stint
Greenshank
Short-eared owl

❄ Winter
Brent goose
Merlin
Dunlin
Pintail

Kiplingcotes Chalk Pit

A dazzling array of floral colours and scents, hundreds of butterflies, singing yellowhammers, chirruping grasshoppers – a summer walk at Kiplingcotes Chalk Pit is a treat for the senses.

The lowdown...

Nearest town: Market Weighton (1.2m/2km)
Nearest postcode: YO43 3NA
Grid ref: SE91424347
///romance.skillet.loosens (entrance gate); eradicate.outboard.mergers (Hudson Way car park).
Parking: Hudson Way car park
Site designation: SSSI
Size: 4ha

A great place for:

- ☑ Bird watchers
- ☐ Cyclists
- ☑ Wildflower enthusiasts
- ☐ Families
- ☐ Leisurely stroll
- ☑ Peace and tranquility
- ☑ Walkers

Recommended time to make the most of your visit:

- ☐ Full day
- ☐ Half day
- ☑ Just an hour

ⓘ Before you go...
To keep the grassland in good condition for plants species and insects, we graze the reserve with Hebridean sheep, so no dogs please.

Thank you!
Your support helps us to improve access, steps and benches on the reserve.

Floral glory

Quarried until 1902, Kiplingcotes Chalk Pit must once have been noisy and dusty, but today this lovely spot, nestled in a classic rolling Wolds valley, is calming, charming and home to a plethora of chalk-loving plants.

The best time to visit is late spring into early summer, when pyramidal, twayblade and common spotted-orchids bloom and stand to attention, along with common and greater knapweed, field scabious, harebell and lady's bedstraw, all in harmonious contrast to the white of the bedrock. You can find the adder's tongue here too.

Flitting and fluttering its way through this blaze of colour is one of Kiplingcotes' main attractions – the marbled white. Like the glamorous screen legends of Hollywood's golden era, this stunning black-and-white butterfly is a real star. There's a strong supporting cast too, including dingy skipper, gatekeeper and brimstone.

The floral carpet is interrupted by the domed homes of yellow meadow ants, which are covered in the lush green of fragrant wild thyme.

Nestled in a Wolds valley

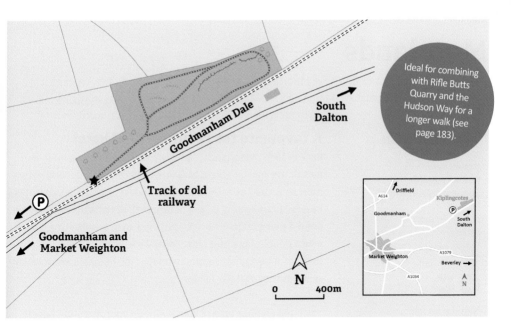

Ideal for combining with Rifle Butts Quarry and the Hudson Way for a longer walk (see page 183).

Goodmanham Dale

South Dalton

Track of old railway

Goodmanham and Market Weighton

N

0   400m

Driffield
A614
Kiplingcotes
Goodmanham
South Dalton
Market Weighton
A1079
Beverley →
A1034
N

Surround sound

A visit to Kiplingcotes is accompanied by a natural soundtrack that's amplified by the chalk walls – the haunting cries of buzzards and red kites, the yaffling of a green woodpecker, the 'little bit of bread and no cheeeeese' wheeze of the yellowhammer, and the chirping of grasshoppers.

It's a gentle and easy stroll through the reserve, but if you're feeling up to a short, steep climb up to the bank top, you'll be rewarded with glorious views back down the valley towards Market Weighton.

★ **Magic** ★ **moment**
The dazzling summer display of wildflowers and butterflies.

Pyramidal orchid

Seasonal highlights

❀ Spring
Cowslip
Willow warbler
Yellowhammer
Brimstone

❀ Summer
Marbled white
Dingy skipper
Common twayblade
Pyramidal orchid
Common spotted-orchid

❀ Autumn
Autumn gentian
Little owl
Fieldfare
Redwing

❀ Winter
Buzzard
Red kite
Brown hare

Moorlands

It might surprise you to find that Moorlands has nothing to do with moors. Instead it's a charming little woodland, with majestic old trees, and colourful flowers in spring.

The lowdown...

Nearest town: York (6.5m/10.5km)
Nearest postcode: YO32 2RE
Grid ref: Roadside parking: SE579587
///control.backhand.rainbow
Parking: Limited spaces in the narrow layby near the entrance gate
Size: 7ha

A great place for:

☐ Bird watchers

☐ Cyclists

☐ Wildflower enthusiasts

☑ Families

☐ Leisurely stroll

☑ Peace and tranquility

☐ Walkers

Recommended time to make the most of your visit:

☐ Full day

☑ Half day

☑ Just an hour

ℹ️ **Before you go...**
The kissing gate at the entrance is accessible to most wheelchairs and the route is open. Paths are flat and mostly even. Nearest toilets are in Haxby Shopping Centre, two miles away.

A favourite for families – and bats!

Back in 1955, Moorlands – an Edwardian woodland garden and part of the ancient Forest of Galtres – became our second nature reserve. As well as being one of our oldest reserves, it's one of our best for a family visit, with a nature trail, opportunities for gentle pond-dipping, wooden sculptures, and an irresistible tree house, which doubles as a bird hide. Enjoy views of a variety of woodland birds, including great spotted woodpecker, nuthatch and a variety of tits as they visit the feeders.

You'll see another type of tree house on your visit – bat boxes! These have been successfully used by common pipistrelle and brown long-eared bats, while soprano pipistrelle, Brandt's and Daubenton's bats have also been recorded here. We also have badgers on site, so please stick to the path to avoid disturbing them. There's a 1km circuit around the wood on a mostly-flat path, with plenty of benches where you can stop and take it all in. Some areas can get waterlogged in winter.

Rhododendron

Thank you!
Your support helps us to maintain the character of Moorlands for everyone to enjoy and to keep improving this habitat for wildlife.

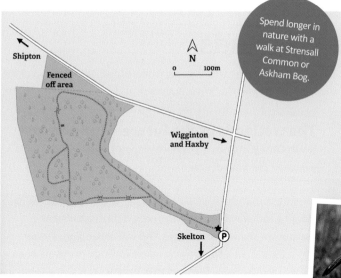

Shipton

Fenced off area

N
0   100m

Spend longer in nature with a walk at Strensall Common or Askham Bog.

Wigginton and Haxby →

Skelton ↓

Thirsk   B1363
Moorlands
Shipton   Wigginton
N   A19   Haxby
River Ouse   Skelton
Harrogate   York
A1237
← A59

Tree time

In autumn, there's a chance of spotting a woodcock, and you can find amazing fungi on a stroll through the leaf litter. It's in spring, though, when Moorlands is at its finest. Along with the spectacular collection of rhododendrons and azaleas, some of which are very old, large and unusual, there's a succession of flowers right through the season – snowdrops, bluebells, primroses and wood sorrel.

And don't forget to admire the trees. Mature native species grow side to side with the more unusual snakebark maple, magnolias and two dawn redwoods.

Woodcock

Seasonal highlights

✿ Spring
Primrose
Cuckooflower
Marsh marigold
Azaleas
Rhododendrons

✸ Summer
Woodland ferns
Foxglove
Brown long-eared bat
Speckled wood
Common blue damselfly

✦ Autumn
Fungi
Maple
Nuthatch

✸ Winter
Great spotted woodpecker
Woodcock

★ **Magic** ★
moment
The trees are the stars!
Pause a moment to
marvel at their age,
structure and beauty.

Mixed woodland at Moorlands

North Cave Wetlands

From quarries and lorries to avocets and bitterns, the ongoing transformation of this working sand and gravel quarry into a shining example of a 21st-century wetland is truly extraordinary.

The lowdown...

Nearest town: Market Weighton (6.3m/10.1km)
Nearest postcode: HU15 2LY
Grid ref: SE 886328
///sage.scoop.limo
Parking: Large car park on Dryham Lane
Size: 56ha but growing to 140ha when restoration is complete

  Dogs allowed on Dryham Lane only

A great place for:

- ☑ Bird watchers
- ☐ Cyclists
- ☑ Wildflower enthusiasts
- ☑ Families
- ☐ Leisurely stroll
- ☑ Peace and tranquility
- ☑ Walkers

Recommended time to make the most of your visit:

- ☐ Full day
- ☑ Half day
- ☐ Just an hour

ℹ Before you go...
The reserve and toilets are open all day all year round, but the car park is open from 7.30am to dusk. The footpaths are all on a flat level. Grass paths can get muddy in winter. All hides except Turret are fully accessible.

The wetlands of the future – and the past

North Cave Wetlands is positively dripping with wildlife, whatever the time of year.

Boasting a mixture of shallow and deep-water lakes with wide margins and islands, reedbeds, grassy banks and meadows, hedgerows and wooded fringes, this still-expanding reserve was once part of a huge marsh called Wallingfen. Having been turned over to agriculture and then quarrying, it's now returning to its former glory – and nature is responding in both numbers and diversity.

Wigeon

★ Magic ★ moment
The whistling of wigeon on a misty winter morning.

Never a dull moment

Easy walking and five perfectly positioned hides (with another due to open in the near future) make this the perfect place to get close to nature.

In summer, the grasslands are alive with butterflies – including the marbled white and brown argus – and the reserve hosts 20 species of dragonflies and damselflies.

Maybe you'll spot a grass snake out in the sun or even having a swim, and look out for stoats skipping along a path. Some lucky visitors even catch a glimpse of an otter.

View across one of the lakes

Birding bonanza

North Cave Wetlands has up to 2% of the national breeding population of avocets, one of Yorkshire's biggest sand martin colonies and up to 2,000 pairs of black-headed gulls – a nationally significant number.

In winter, it's a paradise for wildfowl, welcoming large flocks of ducks and geese. Water rails and bitterns sometimes stray out of the reedbeds to the water's edge. In spring, waders and common terns return for the summer, and the gull colony is in full voice, accompanied by calling reed buntings, sedge warblers and Cetti's warblers.

Autumn is a time of movement, as summer visitors depart, winter visitors arrive and migrants pass through. You never know what might turn up!

Did you know?

The generally accepted view is that the 'Cave' in 'North Cave' derives from the Anglican word "caf", meaning stream or beck.

Seasonal highlights

✿ Spring
Little ringed plover
Sand martin
Avocet
Sedge warbler

☀ Summer
Brown argus
Marbled white
Common tern
Emperor dragonfly

◑ Autumn
Migrant waders
Common darter
Tree sparrow

❄ Winter
Water rail
Snipe
Bittern
Goldeneye

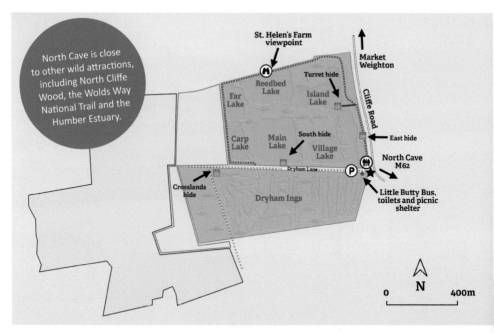

North Cave is close to other wild attractions, including North Cliffe Wood, the Wolds Way National Trail and the Humber Estuary.

St. Helen's Farm viewpoint

Market Weighton

Turret hide

Reedbed Lake

Far Lake

Island Lake

Cliffe Road

Carp Lake

Main Lake

South hide

Village Lake

East hide

North Cave M62

Dryham Lane

Crosslands hide

Dryham Ings

Little Butty Bus, toilets and picnic shelter

N
0   400m

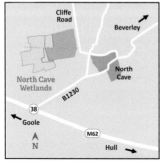

Cliffe Road

Beverley

North Cave

North Cave Wetlands

B1230

38

Goole

M62

Hull

N

Little owl

For a wild day...

Grab a snack and drink at the Little Butty Bus (open six days a week, 8am to 2.30pm), relax and enjoy looking out over Village Lake from the covered platform.

Go a little wilder...

Visit at dusk or dawn to look for one of North Cave's three owl species: barn owls are most likely, but you might encounter little and tawny owls too.

Experience North Cave's wildest side...

Take your time to explore the perimeter path, savour the sights from each hide and count how many different species you can find.

And there's more...

Try searching flocks of birds for something unusual: a green-winged teal amongst its more common relatives; a Mediterranean gull hanging out with black-headed gulls; a white-fronted goose masquerading as a greylag.

North Cave Wetlands – from quarry to one of the north's biggest wetlands

There are a variety of deep and shallow lakes at North Cave Wetlands created for a range of wildlife

The development of North Cave Wetlands could have been a very different story – a rubbish one, in fact. Rather than the thriving reserve you can enjoy exploring today, this site – where there's still a working quarry – was earmarked as a domestic tip.

The local community successfully fought the plan and Yorkshire Wildlife Trust bought the freehold in 2000. We formed a group of reserve managers, environmental consultants, local residents and naturalists, and the transformation began.

Working with the quarrying company, we've restored Dryham Ings alongside the now well-established original reserve. The latest area to return to nature is the north west extension, where we have created new habitats to encourage new species, including wetland birds expanding their ranges north across Europe.

Thank you

Your support makes it possible to create, develop and manage incredible wetlands like North Cave.

 VISITED ☑

North Cliffe Wood

Get yourself down to North Cliffe Wood and gaze in awe at the stunning bluebells and flowering heathland. Listen in wonder to one of the best dawn choruses anywhere.

The lowdown...

Nearest town: Market Weighton (4.1m/6.6km)
Nearest postcode: YO43 4XE
Grid ref: SE859374
///shadow.lunging.facelift
Parking: in roadside lay-by
Size: 33ha

A great place for:

☑ Bird watchers
☐ Cyclists
☑ Wildflower enthusiasts
☑ Families
☐ Leisurely stroll
☑ Peace and tranquility
☐ Walkers

Recommended time to make the most of your visit:

☐ Full day
☑ Half day
☐ Just an hour

ⓘ **Before you go...**
It's a straightforward walk through the wood, with some exposed tree roots and other minor trip hazards. There are no facilities on site.

★ **Magic** ★
moment
Spring's lilac haze of bluebells, and grass snakes basking in sunny glades.

Purple haze all around

A stroll through peaceful North Cliffe Wood on a still spring day – when the sight and scent of the bluebells are at their peak and birdsong carries through the air – is a glorious experience.

Alongside the wet and dry broadleaved woodland, including an area of high oak forest and an old hazel coppice, there's a small reedbed and areas of lowland heath. The heath supports typical plant species like ling heather, heath rush and common cotton grass, while pools in both the woodland and heathland provide homes for damselflies and dragonflies. In summer, the grassy clearings in the wood are bustling with busy butterflies, and on the heath you can see solitary bees and wasps excavating their burrows in the sandy soils.

In autumn the colours change again, bringing the warm hues of autumn leaves, bracken dying off to a rich gold and a smattering of purple from the flowering heather. It's also the season for appreciating North Cliffe's diversity of fungi.

Bluebells at their peak

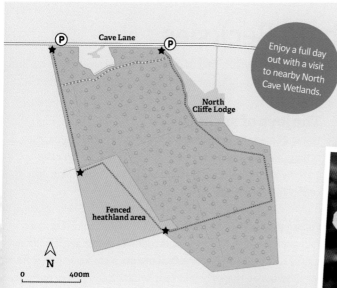

Cave Lane

North Cliffe Lodge

Fenced heathland area

N

0   400m

Enjoy a full day out with a visit to nearby North Cave Wetlands.

York A1079 Driffield

N

A614

Market Weighton

Holme upon Spalding Moor

North Cliffe

A1034

North Cliffe Wood

Hull A63 East
Leeds M62 West

Greater stitchwort

Nature's great sing-song

This is one of the best places in the East Riding for moths, and home to a thriving population of grass snakes, which emerge from hibernation in spring.

As spring approaches summer, the woodland canopy hosts one of nature's great free concerts – a dawn chorus starring migrant willow and garden warblers, chiffchaff and blackcap, along with residents such as treecreeper, great spotted and green woodpeckers. The woodlark is a welcome recent addition to the line-up.

In autumn, flocks of siskins feed on the birch and alder seeds, while winter's a great time to see woodland birds, including marsh tits and nuthatches.

Siskin

Did you know?

The beautiful grass snake is completely harmless to humans, but they emit a really grim smell if handled!

Seasonal highlights

✿ Spring
Bluebells
Greater stitchwort
Primrose
Grass snake
Chiffchaff

✿ Summer
Cotton grass
Garden warbler
Blackcap
Speckled wood

✿ Autumn
Fallow deer
Red deer
Siskin

✿ Winter
Marsh tit
Nuthatch
Green woodpecker
Great spotted woodpecker

North Newbald Becksies

This small wetland reserve in the southern Yorkshire Wolds is fed by several clear chalk springs, with flourishing flowers through the spring and summer months, and snipe in the winter.

The lowdown...

Nearest town: Market Weighton (8.9m/14.3km)
Nearest postcode: YO43 4SQ
Grid ref: SE917371
///charcoal.altering.newlyweds
Parking: In lay-by
Site designation: SSSI
Size: 2 ha

A great place for:

☐ Bird watchers

☐ Cyclists

☑ Wildflower enthusiasts

☐ Families

☐ Leisurely stroll

☑ Peace and tranquility

☐ Walkers

Recommended time to make the most of your visit:

☐ Full day

☑ Half day

☐ Just an hour

ⓘ Before you go...
Wear wellies – it's wet underfoot and there isn't a designated footpath. There's a café and toilets at Drewton's farm shop nearby, or facilities in Market Weighton.

Very close to North Cave Wetlands, North Cliffe Wood and Rifle Butts Quarry if you fancy a longer outing.

The joys of springs

The waters of the Becksies have two stand-out features: the springs have almost never been known to dry up, and the water is a constant 9°C all year. You can see it steaming on cold winter mornings.

Pop on your wellies and see what you can find. In spring, look for cowslip, marsh marigold, cuckooflower, water avens and the locally rare bogbean. Summer's showcase includes honey-scented meadowsweet, marsh orchid, lady's-mantle and yellow rattle. In autumn, search for the purple flowers of devil's-bit scabious.

★ Magic ★ moment
A glimpse of a water vole or water shrew on the stream.

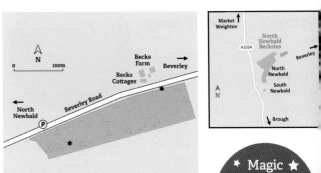

Wetland wildflowers at North Newbald Becksies

Join us at one of our great **wild events!**

From family fun to expert encounters, there's something for everyone in our year-round programme!

Go wild on an adventure near you!

How will you experience Yorkshire's incredible wildlife next? Get planning
ywt.org.uk/our-events

Paull Holme Strays

A vast skyline, raptors stealthily hunting over the saltmarsh, and paradise for wading birds – experience nature's beauty on this stretch of the Humber estuary's north bank.

The lowdown...

Nearest town: Hull (8.7m/14km)
Nearest postcode: HU12 8AX
Grid ref: TA 376 205
///dogs.rotate.save
Parking: onsite car park
Site designation: Adjacent to the Humber Estuary SPA, Ramsar site and SAC
Size: 105 ha

A great place for:

☑ Bird watchers
☐ Cyclists
☑ Wildflower enthusiasts
☑ Families
☐ Leisurely stroll
☑ Peace and tranquility
☑ Walkers

Recommended time to make the most of your visit:

☐ Full day
☑ Half day
☐ Just an hour

ℹ **Before you go...**
For the best chance of witnessing a winter wader spectacle, time your visit a couple of hours before a large incoming tide.

The estuary's alive with the sound of waders

On a quiet spring day, the only sounds you might hear as you cross the reserve are the lonesome call of a cuckoo or the trill of a skylark – but it's a different story on the mudflats later in the year. Thousands of wading birds feed and roost here over the winter. There's a cacophony of calls – curlew, lapwing, redshank, godwits, dunlin, sanderling – and at the turn of the tide the air is filled with a cloud of thousands of golden plovers in a murmuration, moving in unison, their plumage glittering as it catches the winter sunshine.

On the saltmarsh, short-eared owls, marsh harriers, merlins and peregrines hunt, swooping silently in search of rodent prey. Spring and summer are quiet and peaceful. The wingbeats of dragonflies and damselflies are audible on the breeze and butterflies bounce through the air, seeking to gorge themselves on knapweed and ragwort on the flood embankment. Flowering sea aster splashes the saltmarsh with vibrant yellow and purple amidst the faded greens of sea purslane and saltmarsh grass.

A view towards the Humber Bridge from Paull Holme Strays

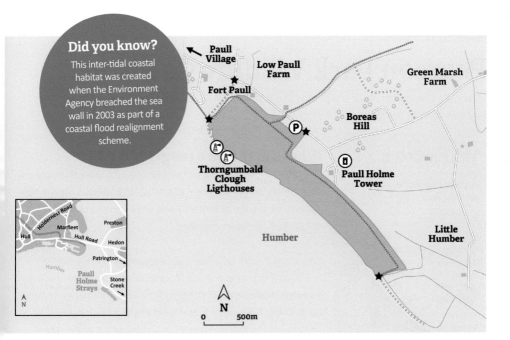

Did you know?
This inter-tidal coastal habitat was created when the Environment Agency breached the sea wall in 2003 as part of a coastal flood realignment scheme.

Paull Village

Low Paull Farm

Green Marsh Farm

Fort Paull

Boreas Hill

Thorngumbald Clough Ligthouses

Paull Holme Tower

Little Humber

Humber

Holderness Road
Marfleet
Preston
Hull
Hull Road
Hedon
Patrington
Humber
Paull Holme Strays
Stone Creek
N

N

0   500m

Photogenic features

The footpath following the flood bank allows excellent views over the estuary. A pair of old lighthouses established in 1870 – Thorgumbald Clough High and Low – are interesting bonus features for photography, and it's worth hanging around for a Humber sunset.

At the end of your walk, the hide is perfect for a nice sit-down and views of avocets in summer and short-eared owl in winter. Don't forget to check the ditches and vegetation for water rails and Cetti's warblers. On the grassland and farmland, watch for brown hares, stoats and roe deer.

★ **Magic** ★
moment
Spectacular, swirling flocks of waders.

Golden plover

Seasonal highlights

✪ **Spring**
Cuckoo
Yellow wagtail
Reed warbler
Sedge warbler
Cetti's warbler

✪ **Summer**
Avocet
Flowering floodbanks
Marsh harrier
Dragonflies

◑ **Autumn**
Whimbrel
Green sandpiper
Common sandpiper
Little stint

✪ **Winter**
Short-eared owl
Merlin
Bar-tailed godwit
Golden plover

Pearson Park Wildlife Garden

Leave the throng of urban traffic and busy pavements and tune in to nature's song in the heart of Hull.

The lowdown...

Nearest postcode: HU5 2TD
Nearest town: Hull (1.8m/3km from station)
Grid ref: TA083430
///grit.glue.pokers
Parking: In Pearson Park
Size: 0.5ha

A great place for:

☐ Bird watchers
☐ Cyclists
☐ Wildflower enthusiasts
☑ Families
☐ Leisurely stroll
☑ Peace and tranquility
☐ Walkers

Recommended time to make the most of your visit:

☐ Full day
☐ Half day
☑ Just an hour

or take longer and visit Pearson Park.

ⓘ Before you go...
The office grounds open Monday to Friday from 9am to 5pm but are closed on bank holidays and over Christmas. Please note gates may be closed when staff are not on site.

Where plants are tangly not tidy!

Despite being tiny and in the middle of a city, our office space is surprisingly rich in wildlife – 10 species of bird have bred in the garden, 14 species of butterfly and 6 species of dragonfly and damselfly have been recorded.

This site is a working office and demonstrates what can be achieved if you view a space for wildlife as a tangle rather than a garden. It shows what happens when nature can get on and do its thing. Vegetation is managed in a wildlife-friendly way and allowed to thrive rather than just being cut back – the space follows the natural cycle of flowering and dying. It tends to be quieter in winter, but creatures are still sheltering and we provide habitat that wildlife needs as it sleeps or hibernates.

The office grounds are a crucial point in a network of habitat corridors, residential gardens and parks that help wildlife to move freely around the city.

Thank you!
Your support and donations have enriched the garden with an urban wildlife sculpture, interactive path games, a day shelter and new interpretation boards.

Pearson Park garden

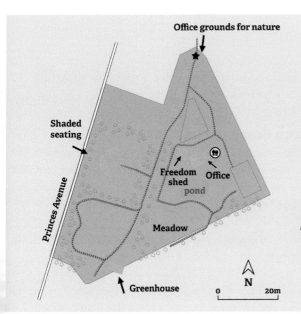

Office grounds for nature

Shaded seating

Freedom shed Office

pond

Meadow

Princes Avenue

Greenhouse

N

0   20m

Bullfinch

Insects and the city

To see the tangle's wildlife at its busiest and best, visit in spring and summer. Why not take a breather, relax on a bench and watch the world go by?

Looking into the densely vegetated pond you'll see newly emerged damselflies in late spring. An array of what many consider flowering weeds attract butterfly species like common blues, small tortoiseshells, brimstones, and orange-tips. Long-tailed tits dance about in the hedgerows and bramble, and in autumn the bramble's seed heads provide food for the striking bullfinch.

★ **Magic** ★
moment

Witnessing the courtship dance of smooth newts in the pond.

Smooth newt

Seasonal highlights

✿ **Spring**
Smooth newt
Blue tit
Goldfinch
Bluebells

❀ **Summer**
Meadow cranesbill
Purple loosestrife
Peacock butterfly
Green shield bug

☉ **Autumn**
Migrant hawker
Pipistrelle bat
Garden spider

❀ **Winter**
Fox
Long-tailed tit
Robin

Pulfin

Bounded on three sides by the river Hull and accessed by a 1.5-mile riverside walk, this spring-fed reserve is a remnant of extensive fens, rich in marsh plants.

The lowdown...

Nearest postcode: HU17 9RX (site), HU17 9RS (parking)
Nearest town: Beverley (2m/3.2km)
Grid ref: TA 04979 41848 (site), TA 04979 41848 (parking)
///refrain.golden.graphic or cadet. cookbooks.heave (gates into Pulfin)
Parking: At Hull Bridge, on Weel Road near the footbridge. Walk north on the footpath for about 1.5 miles to a large lake. Turn left along the bank between the lake and river, then right at the row of trees.
Size: 15ha
Site designation: SSSI

A great place for:

☑ Bird watchers
☐ Cyclists
☐ Wildflower enthusiasts
☐ Families
☐ Leisurely stroll
☑ Peace and tranquility
☑ Walkers

Recommended time to make the most of your visit:

☐ Full day
☑ Half day
☐ Just an hour

ℹ️ **Before you go...**
Often inaccessible and floods in winter. No paths or access to the reedbed or pool because of springs and open water hazards.

March down to the marsh

Plantlife abounds at Pulfin, or 'pool fen' as it was named in a 14th century document: the rare marsh fern and marsh pea, common meadow-rue, common valerian, marsh woundwort, marsh orchid, yellow and purple loosestrifes... all grow here.

16 species of dragonfly have been seen, with large red damselfly and hairy dragonfly two of the first to emerge in spring.

In spring and summer, sedge and reed warblers breed around the pool margins and marsh harriers and hobbies hunt overhead, with kingfishers, water rails and reed buntings throughout the year.

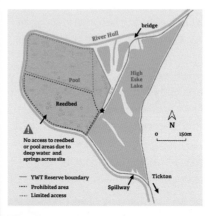

Half a day is enough time to walk along the river to Pulfin and back.

★ **Magic moment** ★
Dashing hobbies hunting dragonflies in summer.

Enjoy Pulfin from the raised bank

Rifle Butts Quarry

It's not every day you come across a Cretaceous unconformity! This nationally important geological feature is the focal point of this fascinating grassland tucked away in the Wolds.

Rock legend!

The exposed rock face in Rifle Butts Quarry is a geological timeline, starting with brown mudrocks from the early Jurassic age. Above this layer is the 'unconformity', revealing a period of 80 million years when sediments deposited on the mudrocks were removed by erosion. This exposure is protected under a shelter to stop it eroding.

Over 150 plants have been recorded here. The site erupts with wildflower colour in spring and summer – cowslip, marjoram, lady's bedstraw, clustered bellflower and many more – attracting butterflies including marbled white.

The lowdown...

Nearest town: Market Weighton (0.9m/1.5km)
Nearest postcode: YO43 3QN
Grid ref: SE 89841 42620
///downturn.presuming.copies
Parking: Roadside or use the car park ¾ mile east, near Kiplingcotes Chalk Pit
Site designation: SSSI
Size: 0.3 ha

A great place for:

- ☐ Bird watchers
- ☐ Cyclists
- ☑ Wildflower enthusiasts
- ☐ Families
- ☐ Leisurely stroll
- ☑ Peace and tranquility
- ☑ Walkers

Recommended time to make the most of your visit:

- ☐ Full day
- ☐ Half day
- ☑ Just an hour

ℹ Before you go...

Spring and summer are the best times to visit Rifle Butts, but the paths are informal and uneven so bring sturdy footwear. Nearest facilities are in Market Weighton.

Geological exposure

N
0   150m

Godmanham

P

Spring Road

Track of old railway

Market Weighton

Driffield

A614

Goodmanham

Rifle Butts Quarry

A1079

Market Weighton

Beverley

A1034

★ **Magic moment** ★
The monochrome magic of marbled whites.

For a longer trip see page 44 for a lovely summer walk combining Rifle Butts with Kiplingcotes Chalk Pit and the Hudson Way.

Cowslip

Saltmarshe Delph

Tucked away by the side of a large bend in the muddy lower Ouse, the wetland and woodland habitats on this small reserve attract some brilliant wildlife all year round.

The lowdown...

Nearest town: Howden (3.4m/5.5km)
Nearest postcode: DN14 7RX
Grid ref: SE 775 248
///alpha.stereos.acrobats
Parking: On grass verge
Size: 5ha

A great place for:

☑ Bird watchers
☐ Cyclists
☑ Wildflower enthusiasts
☐ Families
☐ Leisurely stroll
☑ Peace and tranquility
☐ Walkers

Recommended time to make the most of your visit:

☐ Full day
☐ Half day
☑ Just an hour

ℹ Before you go...
The circular path is narrow and often muddy, with some uneven surfaces. Although there's no wheelchair access on site, you can get good views from the roadside on a quiet country lane.

Extend your day with a trip to North Cave Wetlands.

Here be dragonflies

Saltmarshe Delph is split into two sections by the Hull to Doncaster railway line: the Delph to the east and Willow Garth to the west. The Delph was excavated in 1864 to provide spoil for the approach to the nearby railway bridge, while Willow Garth was used commercially until 1956, providing materials for making agricultural baskets. The pair became a nature reserve in 1972.

At the height of summer, this is an outstanding place to see dragonflies and damselflies, with 19 species recorded. There are other interesting insects to find, including the lesser stag beetle and ringed China-mark moth. Where there's rich insect life, there are other creatures that feed on them, and here those include the Daubenton's bats that skim low over the lake.

Areas of open water and reedbeds contain lesser reedmace, while mature willow, oak and ash grow in the woodland fringe. The area of wet willow carr in the north-east corner is full of birdsong in spring.

Waterfowl on the pool

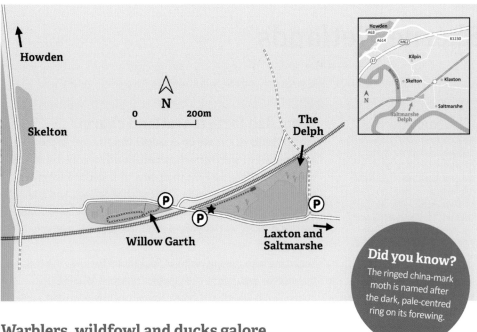

Warblers, wildfowl and ducks galore

This mix of habitats is ideal for a number of birds, from raptors like the marsh harrier and hobby to warblers including reed and sedge warbler, blackcap and chiffchaff.

Some of the other birds to keep an eye out for include cuckoo, sand martin and kingfisher, while in winter, hundreds of ducks return to the water, including gadwall, teal and shoveler. You can watch the birds from an old hide, built on stilts. Another way to enjoy the wildlife is to just sit patiently in the woods and let it come to you.

Water rail

★ Magic ★ moment
Spotting an elusive water rail stepping out from the reedbed.

Seasonal highlights

✜ Spring
Marsh harrier
Cuckoo
Sand martin
Sedge warbler

✸ Summer
Emperor dragonfly
Small red-eyed damselfly
Broad-bodied chaser
Southern hawker
Hobby

☂ Autumn
Ruddy darter
Teal
Wigeon
Gadwall

✸ Winter
Great crested grebe
Water rail
Willow tit

Skerne Wetlands

What is unique about Skerne Wetlands? The answer is clear as crystal: the sparkling waters of the UK's most northerly chalk streams and the wildlife living in and around them.

The lowdown...

Nearest town: Driffield 3.1m/5km (Skerne entrance); 2.5/4km (Snakeholme entrance)
Nearest postcode: YO25 9HU (Cleaves Farm), YO25 8NX (Trout Inn, Wansford)
Grid ref: TA0598 5408 (Skerne); TA0641 5593 (Snakeholme)
///taped.caged.aced (car park); placidly.skate.quest (Skerne entrance; squeaking.sonic.prestige (Snakeholme kissing gate).
Parking: Small car park at Skerne;
Site designation: SSSI
Size: 46ha
No dogs on the reserve.

A great place for:

- ☑ Bird watchers
- ☐ Cyclists
- ☐ Wildflower enthusiasts
- ☐ Families
- ☐ Leisurely stroll
- ☑ Peace and tranquility
- ☑ Walkers

Recommended time to make the most of your visit:

- ☐ Full day
- ☑ Half day
- ☐ Just an hour

ℹ️ **Before you go...**
No direct route from north to south unless you leave the reserve via the footpath through neighbouring farm.

From fish farm to wetland charm

Skerne Wetlands – made up of Snakeholm Pastures to the north, and Skerne Fen and Skerne Reedbeds downstream – is a reserve that's come a long way in a short time. This wetland complex features wet grassland, over a mile of chalk stream, and more than 70 former fish farm ponds, which have been transformed into a mosaic of wet woodland, reedbed, fen and open water.

Beginning with the two fields of Snakeholm Pastures in 2008, the reserve expanded in 2011 when Yorkshire Wildlife Trust bought what was then a large commercial fish farm, and a mile of West Beck. It grew again in 2014 with land on the other side of the stream, when the Copper Hall section of the wetlands was integrated into the reserve.

Every visit to this restored wetland paradise is a chance to discover something new and exciting – a marsh harrier floating above the reedbeds, otters along the stream, green sandpipers on the muddy pool fringes, or dragonflies among the tall purple loosestrife.

Thank you!
With your support, we can maintain the reserve's paths, seating and bird feeding area.

Crystal clear waters of West Beck

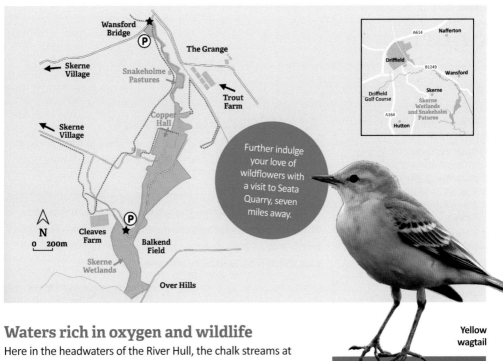

Further indulge your love of wildflowers with a visit to Seata Quarry, seven miles away.

Yellow wagtail

Waters rich in oxygen and wildlife

Here in the headwaters of the River Hull, the chalk streams at Skerne Wetlands are a nationally-important habitat. West Beck's beautifully clear, oxygen-rich waters, lush bankside vegetation and stunning beds of water crowfoot are unmissable in early summer.

The beck is home to wild brown trout, grayling and brook lamprey, as well as water voles and kingfishers. It's rich in insect life too, including mayflies and caddis flies, which attract wagtails and other insect-eating birds.

★ **Magic moment** ★

Watching the crystal-clear waters of the chalk stream and spotting a brown trout or water vole.

Seasonal highlights

❀ **Spring**
Yellow wagtail
Brook lamprey
Orange-tip
Grass snake

❀ **Summer**
Emperor dragonfly
Brown trout
Water vole
Flowering water crowfoot

🍃 **Autumn**
Green sandpiper
Kingfisher
Common darter

❄ **Winter**
Water Rail
Barn owl
Marsh harrier
Otter
Roe deer

Brown trout

Spurn

There's nowhere like Spurn. It's extreme, ever-changing and a magnet for migrating birds, with a human history as captivating as its natural landscape.

The lowdown...

Nearest town: Patrington (9.4m/15.1km), Hull (25.5m/41km)
Nearest postcode: HU12 0UH
Grid ref: TA416154
///rainwater.freely.hill
Parking: Large car park at the visitor centre, with disabled spaces
Site designation: SPA, SAC, NNR, SSSI, RAMSAR
Size: 327 ha

  Dogs allowed on a lead in some areas, please follow signs. Bike hire available at visitor centre.

A great place for:

☑ Bird watchers
☐ Cyclists
☑ Wildflower enthusiasts
☑ Families
☐ Leisurely stroll
☑ Peace and tranquility
☑ Walkers

Recommended time to make the most of your visit:

☑ Full day
☐ Half day
☐ Just an hour

ℹ **Before you go...**
Check the tide times before venturing onto Spurn Point. A tidal surge in 2013 wiped out the road at the narrowest part of the peninsula, and high tides turn it into a temporary island.

An unforgettable experience

Standing at the end of Spurn Point is like being in another world – a remote, breathtaking place with an atmosphere all of its own.

Spurn curves snake-like out into the open water for more than three miles. This is where the mighty Humber joins the North Sea and where Yorkshire's coastline ends with a steeply sloped beach dropping into a deep channel separating this tip of the East Riding from North Lincolnshire.

Spurn Point lighthouse

A kind of magic

Spurn is a magical place at any time of the year, attracting visitors from miles around for many reasons. There's the amazing wildlife, of course – not just birds, but lizards, roe deer, dragonflies, seals and dolphins. Then there's the fascinating military and maritime history. On your way to the point you'll find part-buried bunkers jutting out from sand dunes. Climb to the top of the lighthouse for jaw-dropping views, or simply soak up the sense of peace and solitude.

Aerial view towards the end of Spurn Point

★ Magic ★ moment
Those incredible autumn days when there's a 'fall' of migrant birds.

Legendary for birding

Spurn's iconic status in birding legend inspires a feeling of awe, anticipation and adventure. Spring and in particular autumn migration can be the highlight of the birding year. In autumn, summer visitors depart and the first winter visitors arrive from their Arctic breeding grounds. Thousands of birds not only pass through on their journey south but stay for the winter. Long-distance visitors like sanderling and grey plover join curlew, redshank and dunlin, not to mention knot, which form mesmerising, swirling flocks.

Rarities have included two-barred greenish warbler and Siberian accentor, along with more 'expected' rare migrants like Pallas's warbler and red-flanked bluetail.

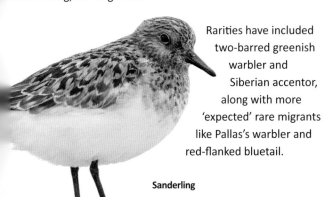

Sanderling

Seasonal highlights

✿ Spring
Swift
Wheatear
Scurvy grass
Whimbrel

✺ Summer
Pyramidal orchid
Little tern
Minke whale

◐ Autumn
Redwing
Wryneck
Yellow-browed warbler
Great grey shrike

✺ Winter
Brent goose
Snow bunting
Merlin
Common seal

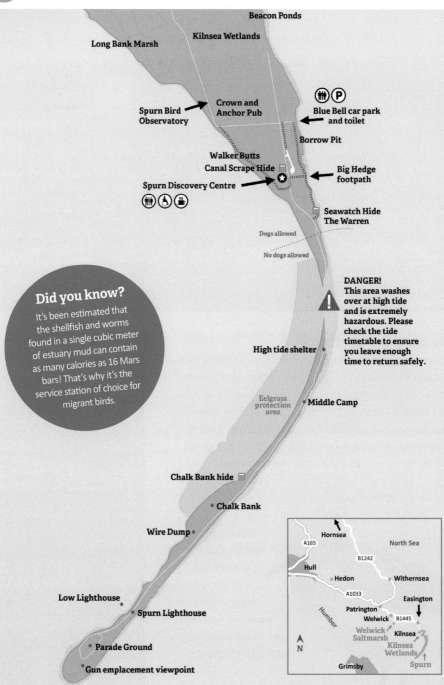

Beacon Ponds

Kilnsea Wetlands

Long Bank Marsh

Crown and
Anchor Pub

Spurn Bird
Observatory

Blue Bell car park
and toilet

Borrow Pit

Walker Butts
Canal Scrape Hide

Big Hedge
footpath

Spurn Discovery Centre

Seawatch Hide
The Warren

Dogs allowed

No dogs allowed

Did you know?

It's been estimated that the shellfish and worms found in a single cubic meter of estuary mud can contain as many calories as 16 Mars bars! That's why it's the service station of choice for migrant birds.

DANGER!
This area washes over at high tide and is extremely hazardous. Please check the tide timetable to ensure you leave enough time to return safely.

High tide shelter

Eelgrass
protection
area

Middle Camp

Chalk Bank hide

Chalk Bank

Wire Dump

Hornsea

North Sea

A165

B1242

Hull

Hedon

Withernsea

A1033

Easington

Low Lighthouse

Humber

Patrington

Welwick

B1445

Spurn Lighthouse

Welwick
Saltmarsh

Kilsea

Parade Ground

N

Kilnsea
Wetlands

Grimsby

Spurn

Gun emplacement viewpoint

Working with nature

Spurn was formed by longshore drift, where sediment eroded by the sea is washed along the coast. It will always be on the move but with your support we can work with nature so wildlife can thrive.

Fenceless grazing: Our cattle, which graze at Spurn and boost the biodiversity of the grasslands, wear collars linked to satellite technology that creates virtual boundaries. This means we don't need fencing, can graze previously inaccessible locations and let wild animals roam freely.

Oyster reintroduction: We've worked with others to successfully reintroduce a native oyster population to the Humber Estuary. These marine molluscs filter and clean the water, and allow more sunlight to reach deeper, encouraging plants to grow.

Seagrass restoration: We've been restoring Spurn's seagrass meadows. Seagrass supports a variety of marine life and stores carbon. Left undisturbed, it acts as a nursery for juvenile fish (great for birds) and helps to stabilise the seabed, protecting the coastline against erosion.

For a wild day...
Enjoy a drink and snack in the visitor centre, pop into the Canal Scrape hide and search for wildlife in the area known as the Triangle.

Go a little wilder...
Join a safari on the Unimog, a former military all-terrain vehicle, down to the point. A short walk through the dunes will take you to Yorkshire's 'Land's End.'

Experience Spurn's wildest side...
Stay for the weekend and get completely absorbed in the Spurn experience in spring or autumn. Almost anything could turn up!

And there's more...
We run events at Spurn throughout the year, including guided birdwatching walks, military history tours uncovering buried bunkers and tunnels, beach cleaning and more: **ywt.org.uk/our-events**

Seashells on the shore

Strensall Common

York's busy ring road seems a million miles away once you're out for a stroll on Strensall Common, savouring its expansive beauty and abundant wildlife.

The lowdown...

Nearest town: Strensall (1.2m/1.9km)
Nearest postcode: YO32 5YB
Grid ref: SE761665
///shook.anthems.harder
Parking: Park in the lay-by at the Common Road level crossing, or near the cattle grid as you enter the common.
Site designation: SSSI, SAC
Size: 42ha

  Dogs on leads on the surrounding paths, but not allowed on the common.

A great place for:

- ☑ Bird watchers
- ☐ Cyclists
- ☐ Wildflower enthusiasts
- ☑ Families
- ☐ Leisurely stroll
- ☑ Peace and tranquility
- ☑ Walkers

Recommended time to make the most of your visit:

- ☐ Full day
- ☐ Half day
- ☑ Just an hour

There are many paths to explore, including a 1.5-mile circuit.

ℹ️ **Before you go...**
Paths are largely footworn through the heathland and follow gravel and tarmacked tracks or the peaty woodland edge, so are uneven and can be very boggy. Take care crossing the railway.

Lizards on a sunny afternoon

Strensall Common is part of a larger area of internationally important lowland heath in the Vale of York. This special environment, featuring wet heath, dry heath, mire, open water, woodland and acid grassland, is home to many insects, birds and reptiles, and over 150 species of plants. In August, ling heather and cross-leave heath turn the heathland purple – quite a sight on a sunny afternoon. Other plants to look out for include marsh cinquefoil, marsh gentian and the carnivorous round-leaved sundew, and, on the drier grassland, the pinky-red flowers of sheep's sorrel and tiny white crosses of heath bedstraw.

This is one of the best places in the area to see reptiles, specifically common lizards – which you might spot basking on tree stumps or scuttling through undergrowth – as well as adders. Stick to the paths to avoid disturbing these beautiful, zigzag-patterned snakes.

The reserve and wider common are great places to find heathland birds – stonechats, woodlarks, tree pipits, green woodpeckers, cuckoos, and maybe a hobby hunting dragonflies.

A rich mix of heath and wetland

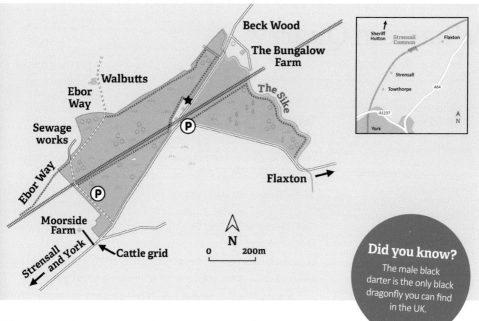

Map labels:
Beck Wood
The Bungalow Farm
Walbutts
The Sike
Ebor Way
Sewage works
Ebor Way
Flaxton
Moorside Farm
Strensall and York
Cattle grid
N
0   200m

Inset map:
Sheriff Hutton   Strensall Common   Flaxton
Strensall
Towthorpe   A64
A1237
York
N

Discover the common's uncommon insects

The common has magnificent insect life, including a nationally important population of dark-bordered beauty moths, southern hawker and black darter dragonflies, green and purple hairstreak butterflies, and bog bush-crickets in the rushy grassland. Yorkshire Wildlife Trust manages the reserve by maintaining the open areas of heath for wildlife.

Grazing livestock help to control birch seedlings, and we remove bracken and invasive coniferous species that are not native to heaths in this part of the UK. We also clear out the ponds occasionally to maintain patches of open water.

★ Magic ★ moment
Spotting a common lizard basking on a silver birch stump.

Common lizard

Seasonal highlights

✱ Spring
Common lizard
Adder
Cuckoo
Woodlark
Four-spotted chaser

✱ Summer
Marsh gentian
Cross-leaved heath
Black darter
Green woodpecker
Hobby

✱ Autumn
Hoof fungus
Fly agaric
Oyster fungus
Siskin

✱ Winter
Stonechat
Brown hare

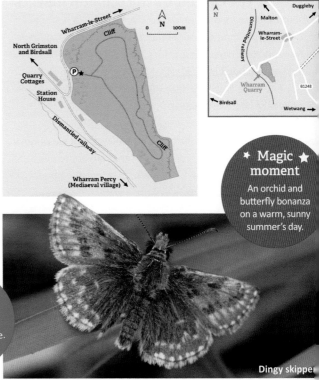

Wharram Quarry

In the 1960s, Wharram Quarry's owner, Lord Middleton, noticed bee orchids growing on the quarry floor and offered the site to the Trust. Today it's a beautiful, species-rich grassland.

The lowdown...

Nearest town: Malton (7.3m/11.7km)
Nearest postcode: YO17 9TW
Grid ref: SE 85836 65364
///proofs.simulates.umbrellas
Parking: Space for two cars by the entrance
Site designation: SSSI
Size: 7 ha

A great place for:

☐ Bird watchers

☐ Cyclists

☑ Wildflower enthusiasts

☐ Families

☐ Leisurely stroll

☑ Peace and tranquility

☐ Walkers

Recommended time to make the most of your visit:

☐ Full day

☐ Half day

☑ Just an hour

ℹ️ **Before you go...**
There's an informal permissive footpath, providing a circular route around the reserve. The nearest toilets and shops are in Malton.

Combine with a visit to Wharram Percy deserted mediaeval village.

Walk that chalk

Chalk, quarried here between 1919 and the 1940s, gives this reserve its thin soil and characteristic flowering plants, in turn attracting butterflies including marbled white, dingy skipper and small heath.

The glorious wildflower display includes the yellows of cowslip, rough hawkbit, mouse-ear hawkweed and bird's-foot trefoil; purple wild thyme and clustered bellflower; pink restharrow and blue common milkwort. Look for common spotted, pyramidal and bee orchids in June and July. This is also one of the few Wolds sites for thistle broomrape.

★ **Magic moment** ★
An orchid and butterfly bonanza on a warm, sunny summer's day.

Dingy skipper

Yorkshire Wildlife Trust

Wheldrake Ings

The Lower Derwent Valley National Nature Reserve, just a few miles south-east of York, is or of Yorkshire's premier wildlife destinations – and Wheldrake Ings is the jewel in its crown.

The lowdown...

Nearest town: Wheldrake village (1.4m/2.3km)
Nearest postcode: YO19 6AX
Grid ref: SE 69413 44416
///soulful.access.commoners
Parking: Site car park, but often floods in late autumn and winter. Alternative parking at Natural England's neighbouring Bank Island reserve.
Site designation: SPA, SAC, RAMSAR, SSSI, NNR
Size: 157ha

A great place for:

- ☑ Bird watchers
- ☐ Cyclists
- ☑ Wildflower enthusiasts
- ☑ Families
- ☐ Leisurely stroll
- ☑ Peace and tranquility
- ☐ Walkers

Recommended time to make the most of your visit:

- ☐ Full day
- ☑ Half day
- ☐ Just an hour

ℹ️ **Before you go...**
Radar key for toilet at Bank Island with an unsurfaced path between the two reserves. Paths can be muddy after floods. Natural England 01904 449589 or check Twitter @ldv_nnr for updates.

A world of wonder, wildfowl, waders and warblers

A walk at Wheldrake Ings is a chance to press pause on daily life, breathe, and take in the stunning wildlife spectacles that change dramatically across the seasons.

In winter, the River Derwent floods, often turning the valley into a huge lake. The water attracts colossal numbers of ducks, geese, swans, gulls and waders – an incredible sight to behold in its own right, but also an enjoyable challenge for keen birders looking for something unusual among the masses of birds. It could be a smew, scaup, or even something rarer, like an American wigeon or green-winged teal. Suddenly hundreds of ducks and waders rise noisily up from the water and chaos briefly ensues, as a hunting peregrine or marsh harrier scatters the flock.

Spring is very different. The reserve is alive with the songs of warblers, the meadow is drying out and wildflowers emerge in abundance, bustling with insects. Listen for the call of cuckoos and watch in awe as hobbies dash over the grassland and wetland.

Winter flooding transforms Wheldrake Ings

Thank you!
Your support helps us to manage this invaluable landscape for wildlife using traditional methods.

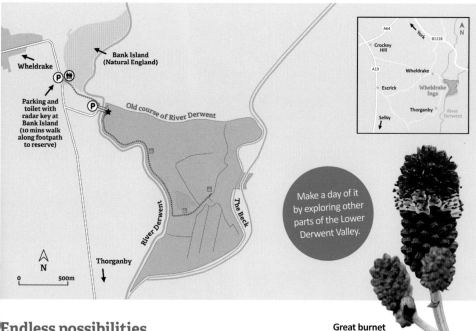

Great burnet

Endless possibilities

There's so much to discover here – the calls of curlews, snipe and skylarks in the spring, a glimpse of an otter or kingfisher along the river, rare plants in the meadow... To see the flowers at their best, join a guided event in summer, as there's no access into the meadow.

Bring binoculars or a telescope to get the best views of the birds on the water from the three hides, and keep an eye out for elusive species like spotted crake and water rail, as well as breeding willow tits. Spring and autumn are best times to check for rare migrants.

Curlew

★ **Magic** ★
moment
The distinctive call of a curlew in the grassland or flying overhead.

Seasonal highlights

✿ Spring
Marsh marigold
Curlew
Whimbrel
Hobby
Brown hare

✿ Summer
Great burnet
Meadowsweet
Banded demoiselle

◑ Autumn
Barn owl
Willow tit
Roe deer
Marsh harrier

✿ Winter
Peregrine
Whooper swan
Pintail
Thousands of wildfowl and waders

West

On the doorstep of our biggest urban region, it's
incredible how much wildlife you can find – from the
wildflowers and butterflies of magnesian limestone
grasslands to the amazing variety of birds and
insects in wetlands and ancient woodlands.

Adel Dam

An inviting blend of woodland and wetland, Adel Dam offers tranquility and close encounters with wildlife on the north-west fringe of Leeds.

The lowdown...

Nearest town: Leeds (5.6m/9.3km)
Nearest postcode: LS16 8AG
Grid ref: SE 2712 4144
///suffer.herds.shell
Parking: Use the main Golden Acre car park on Otley Road – a short, flat walk to the reserve.
Size: 8ha

A great place for:

☑ Bird watchers
☐ Cyclists
☐ Wildflower enthusiasts
☑ Families
☐ Leisurely stroll
☑ Peace and tranquility
☐ Walkers

Recommended time to make the most of your visit:

☐ Full day
☐ Half day
☑ Just an hour

ⓘ Before you go...

There's a circular route of around 1 mile or a shorter 'there and back' path to the hides. The path to Marsh hide is suitable for standard wheelchairs and pushchairs, while the rest of the route is more uneven. Wheelchair users can access the reserve through the gate- no Radar key necessary!

Perfect for peace and pictures

It's been an operational dam, and a central feature of a Victorian garden (there are no fewer than 36 species of high, majestic trees here), but today this reserve is one of the best places in Yorkshire to see kingfishers, enjoy some peaceful downtime, and capture some stunning wildlife photography.

Kingfishers are Adel Dam's star species but there are many other birds to look for from two hides, a viewing screen, and the paths around the reserve. From Lake Hide you can see tufted ducks, grebes, coots and moorhens, which all raise their families on the pool in summer. At Marsh Hide, the feeding station attracts woodland birds including great spotted woodpeckers, nuthatches, jays, finches and tits. Away from the feeding areas, with luck, you might even spot the tiny lesser spotted woodpecker or an elusive water rail. And don't forget to look up for birds of prey, as red kites are a common sight, along with sparrowhawks and buzzards.

The lake at Adel Dam

Thank you!
Your donations help us to maintain the hides and stock up the bird feeding station at Marsh Hide, to help ensure great views of the birds.

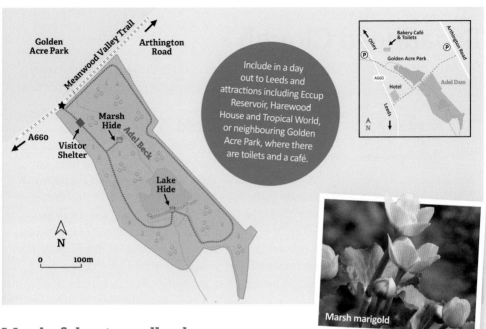

Include in a day out to Leeds and attractions including Eccup Reservoir, Harewood House and Tropical World, or neighbouring Golden Acre Park, where there are toilets and a café.

Marsh marigold

Wonderful wet woodland

Unusually, the reserve combines both dry and wet woodland. Adel Dam is a fantastic example of a wet woodland and the entire habitat acts as a big sponge – the mosses, plants and trees soak up and hold lots of water. This increasingly rare habitat is brilliant for beetles, moths, snails, spiders, frogs and toads. The fungi in autumn is worth a visit all by itself, with a mix of colours and shapes, including the bright scarlet elfcup and yellow sulphur tuft. Last but not least, you might also encounter roe deer, tawny owls, foxes or even a badger.

Kingfisher

★ Magic moment ★

The first time a child (or even a grown-up) sets eyes on a kingfisher or woodpecker – unforgettable!

Seasonal highlights

✿ Spring
Bluebell
Marsh marigold
Blackcap
Chiffchaff

❋ Summer
Foxglove
Mandarin Duck
Dragonflies
Bats

🍂 Autumn
Yellow sulphur tuft
Scarlet elfcup
Siskin
Lesser redpoll

❋ Winter
Goosander
Little grebe
Kingfisher
Nuthatch

Broadhead Clough

The steep, invigorating climb from the deep valley floor through the woods will ultimately reward you with beautifully rugged Pennine views, though there's plenty to savour on the way.

The lowdown...

Nearest town: Mytholmroyd (1.4m/2.3km)
Nearest postcode: HX7 5HB
Grid ref: SE 0002 2502
///meaty.landlords.starter
Parking: Roadside on Cragg Road. Walk 0.6m/1km up the steepish access track to the reserve.
Site designation: SSSI
Size: 23ha

  Dogs are allowed on leads on the footpath only

A great place for:

- ☑ Bird watchers
- ☐ Cyclists
- ☑ Wildflower enthusiasts
- ☐ Families
- ☐ Leisurely stroll
- ☑ Peace and tranquility
- ☑ Walkers

Recommended time to make the most of your visit:

- ☐ Full day
- ☑ Half day
- ☐ Just an hour

ℹ **Before you go...**
Stick to the paths – we don't want you sinking in the bog! The paths are steep, uneven and there are many steps, so it's not suitable here for a buggy or wheelchair.

On top of the world

In the 18th century, Broadhead Clough was home to the notorious Cragg Vale Coiners, who produced fake coins, but the real value of this site is in its rare wet woodland mires and Pennine fringe habitat. The peat mires support an abundance of moss and liverwort, including sphagnum and star mosses, with tufts of rush and other plants, including marsh orchid, and fungi, such as bog beacon. In turn, these conditions are ideal for invertebrate larvae, providing food for birds including curlew, cuckoo, woodpeckers, and finches.

Roe deer

★ **Magic moment** ★
Watching roe deer fawns in the woods in May whilst listening to the beautiful dawn chorus.

Yorkshire's wildlife is in crisis – together we can take action!

#TeamWilder is a rapidly growing movement of people who care about our environment and want to help wildlife thrive, empowering Yorkshire's communities to act for a wilder future.

Scientists tell us that, if we can get 1 in 4 people take visible action for nature, we'll create the social tipping point required to reverse nature's devastating decline, bringing everyone into new, healthier and more sustainable ways of thinking and living.

Now that's a challenge we can all get behind!

We'd love you to sign up and be a part of #TeamWilder – find out how you can get involved and help bring about the change we all need at **ywt.org.uk/team-wilder**

Brockadale

You'll return again and again to this captivating, nationally important reserve where ancient woodland, wildflower and water meadows host an incredible diversity of wildlife.

The lowdown...

Nearest town: Pontefract (6.4m/10.3km)
Nearest postcode: WF8 3LJ
Grid ref: SE 512 173
///rashers.crank.insulated
Parking: Car park on Leys Lane, accessed from the eastern end of New Road. Please note there's a height restriction barrier (maximum clearance 2.1m). If full, try the small layby on Wentedge Road.
Site designation: NNR, SSSI
Size: 59ha

A great place for:

☐ Bird watchers
☐ Cyclists
☑ Wildflower enthusiasts
☐ Families
☐ Leisurely stroll
☑ Peace and tranquility
☐ Walkers

Recommended time to make the most of your visit:

☐ Full day
☑ Half day
☐ Just an hour

ℹ️ **Before you go...**
There are many paths to enjoy exploring, but some are steep and narrow in places and can get muddy. There are grazing animals in the meadows at various times throughout the year.

Flower power!

With more than 320 species of plant, 450 species of moth, 30 species of butterfly and 40 species of breeding bird recorded here, one visit to this much-loved reserve is never enough. There's a wealth of wild experiences for everyone from nature novices to wildlife experts, and a range of terrain from steep magnesian limestone crags to a gentle woodland wander or invigorating riverside ramble.

Brockadale's steep slopes have never been ploughed or fertilised, resulting in a rare grass and woodland habitat that's a wildflower lover's dream in summer: pyramidal orchids, clustered bellflower and subtly beautiful hellibores are just a few of the many species here to delight you, with rarities including daphne, purple milk vetch and spring cinquefoil. The strikingly patterned marbled white, dark green fritillary and silver-washed fritillary are just three of the butterfly species attracted to the abundant wildflowers.

Other than flower power:

Not all wildlife is quite so bright and showy, but with time and patience you might be lucky enough to see common lizards and grass snakes on the woodpiles, purseweb spiders and clearwing moths. For an even trickier challenge, search for a *truncatellina*

Brockadale's meadows are spectacular in summer

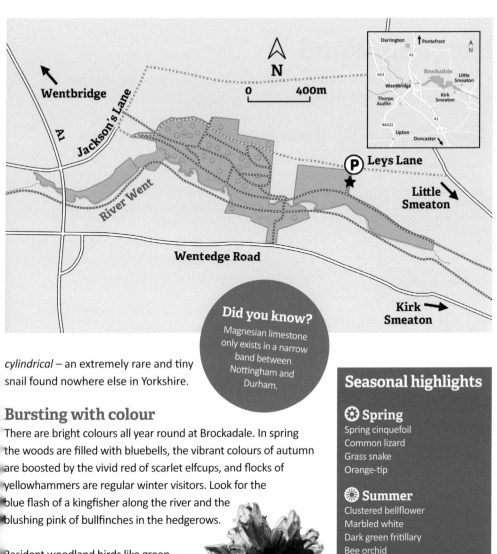

Map labels: Wentbridge, Jackson's Lane, A1, River Went, Leys Lane, Little Smeaton, Wentedge Road, Kirk Smeaton, N, 0 400m

Inset map labels: Darrington, Pontefract, A1, N, A63, Brockadale, Little Smeaton, Wentbridge, Kirk Smeaton, Thorpe Audlin, A1, B6422, Upton, Doncaster

Did you know?
Magnesian limestone only exists in a narrow band between Nottingham and Durham.

cylindrical – an extremely rare and tiny snail found nowhere else in Yorkshire.

Bursting with colour

There are bright colours all year round at Brockadale. In spring the woods are filled with bluebells, the vibrant colours of autumn are boosted by the vivid red of scarlet elfcups, and flocks of yellowhammers are regular winter visitors. Look for the blue flash of a kingfisher along the river and the blushing pink of bullfinches in the hedgerows.

Resident woodland birds like green and great spotted woodpecker, tawny owl, nuthatch and long-tailed tit are joined by breeding chiffchaff, willow warbler, blackcap and whitethroat in spring.

★ Magic ★ moment
The breathtaking spectacle of swathes of tall, vivid purple clustered bellflowers.

Clustered bellflower

Seasonal highlights

❊ Spring
Spring cinquefoil
Common lizard
Grass snake
Orange-tip

❉ Summer
Clustered bellflower
Marbled white
Dark green fritillary
Bee orchid

❉ Autumn
Scarlet elfcup
Redwing
Fieldfare

❉ Winter
Yellowhammer
Corn bunting
Nuthatch
Stinking hellebore

Hetchell Wood

A wild woodland wonderland where childhood memories are made, with activities and adventures to enjoy all year round, wildlife and an especially weird wildflower to discover.

The lowdown...

Nearest town: Wetherby (5.5m/8.9km)
Nearest postcode: LS14 6NA
Grid ref: SE 3798 4228
///milky.prom.shame
Parking: Small laybys for parking off Milner Lane with space for 8-12 cars. No parking available across gate/access track, please.
Site designation: NNR, SSSI
Size: 12ha

A great place for:

☑ Bird watchers
☐ Cyclists
☑ Wildflower enthusiasts
☑ Families
☐ Leisurely stroll
☑ Peace and tranquility
☐ Walkers

Recommended time to make the most of your visit:

☐ Full day
☑ Half day
☐ Just an hour

ℹ **Before you go...**
There's something to enjoy all year round at Hetchell Wood, but wear sturdy footwear if you're visiting in winter or wet weather.

If you go down to the woods today...

Full of zigzagging paths to discover, nooks to explore, and sounds and smells all around... a visit to Hetchell Wood is huge fun. This magnificent ancient woodland is also a soothing retreat, with the soft trickle of the bubbling Bardsey Beck in the background.

A circular walk takes you through a variety of habitats on this undulating reserve, with towering rocky crags, secret pools, and spectacular views of the valley from the top.

In spring, the woodland floor is graced by a beautiful sea of fragrant wild garlic, along with bluebells and yellow archangel, alongside a grassland area filled with flowers that gives the woods a beautiful pop of colour and light, and attracts a variety of insects. In autumn, it's a festival of fungi and foliage as the leaves change colour and fall, and winter brings a chance to spot birds and animals as they emerge from the undergrowth.

Did you know?
Hetchell Wood is close to Harewood House Estate, where red kites were released in 1999. Keep looking up for these impressive birds.

Oak and beech trees

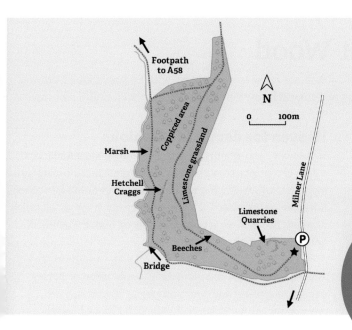

For a full day out, visit the intriguing earthworks of Pompocali, next to Hetchell Wood, and the market town of Wetherby. Explore Ox Close Wood, managed by East Keswick Wildlife Trust.

... You're sure of a big surprise!

Hetchell Wood is home to a very strange and special plant that only occurs in Yorkshire at a handful of sites – the thistle broomrape. It has no leaves or chlorophyll and is a parasite that mostly relies on creeping thistle for nutrients. And if you look closely at the base of hazel trees, you might find the unusual toothwort, another parasitic plant.

There's something for everyone to enjoy here, no matter what your interest or knowledge!

★ Magic ★ moment

Discovering the lilac-blue nodding heads of devil's-bit scabious sprinkled across the meadow.

Devil's-bit scabious

Seasonal highlights

☼ Spring
Wild garlic
Bluebells
Cowslip
Wood anemone
Toothwort

☀ Summer
Thistle broomrape
Blackcap
Dyer's greenweed

☍ Autumn
Fungi
Beautiful autumn colours
Devil's-bit scabious

❄ Winter
Tawny owl
Nuthatch
Roe deer
Treecreeper

Hollinhurst Wood

The woodland and grassland habitats are home to a wonderful array of plants, which grow in the undulating 'ridge and furrows' created by medieval farmers using oxen-pulled ploughs.

The lowdown...

Nearest town: Castleford (3.4m/5.5km)
Nearest postcode: LS26 8AW
Grid ref: SE 40150 28980
///blurred.cafe.waltz
Parking: Small informal lay-by on Wood Lane, then a short walk down the road to the reserve entrance
Site designation: Local Wildlife Site
Size: 11ha

A great place for:

☑ Bird watchers
☐ Cyclists
☑ Wildflower enthusiasts
☑ Families
☐ Leisurely stroll
☑ Peace and tranquility
☑ Walkers

Recommended time to make the most of your visit:

☐ Full day
☐ Half day
☑ Just an hour

ℹ **Before you go...**
There are paths through the woods and across the meadow, but these can get muddy and aren't accessible for wheelchairs or buggies.

Heaven for devil's-bit scabious

September – the month that bridges summer and autumn, and a time of changing colours. Purple is the predominant colour this month at Hollinhurst Wood as vast amounts of devil's-bit scabious flower in the meadow. There's purple aplenty in spring too, when bluebells flower in the woods, following on from the yellow of daffodils and white of snowdrops.

The meadow area is important for its combination of marshy, damp-loving plants and drier acid grassland species, more typically seen in our uplands. It's home to a range of plant species that are still influenced by 'ridge and furrow' marks left by medieval farmers, who grew food here and ploughed using an oxen-pulled plough. The damper soils in the furrows (troughs) support meadowsweet, wild angelica, common fleabane and sneezewort, while the drier conditions along the ridges attract sheep's sorrel, sheep's fescue, harebell and tormentil, among others. As well as the undulating pattern left by ploughing, small craters are evidence of the area's more recent coal-mining past.

Bluebells in the wood

Did you know?
The name Hollinhurst Wood comes from the word 'hollin', which refers to the abundance of holly trees in the area. Hollies were often planted to supply winter feed for livestock.

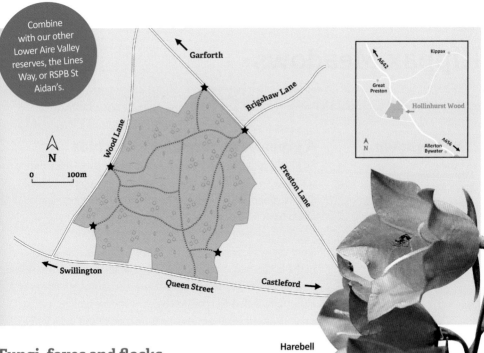

Combine with our other Lower Aire Valley reserves, the Lines Way, or RSPB St Aidan's.

Garforth

Brigshaw Lane

Wood Lane

Preston Lane

Swillington

Queen Street

Castleford

0 100m

N

A642

Great Preston

Kippax

Hollinhurst Wood

Allerton Bywater

A656

N

Harebell

Fungi, foxes and flocks

Hollinhurst Wood is part of the Lower Aire Valley green corridor, where animals move between the different reserves and surrounding fields. Take an early morning stroll to look for foxes and deer passing through. In autumn, look for skeins of migrating pink footed geese flying in a 'V' shape overhead.

In the woodland, tree species include oak, birch, wych elm, hazel, crab apple, guelder rose and field maple, with willows in the damper areas. In autumn, the wood is an excellent place to spot fungi, including clouded funnel and wood blewit mushrooms.

Seasonal highlights

✿ Spring
Wood anemone
Bluebells
Chiffchaff
Blackcap

❀ Summer
Devil's-bit scabious
Sneezewort
Harebells

❀ Autumn
Guelder rose
Crab apple

❀ Winter
Wood mouse
Great spotted woodpecker
Treecreeper

★ Magic ★ moment
Sitting under the large oak tree in summer to listen to the hum of insects in the meadow.

Guelder rose

Kippax Meadows

If you're out walking in the Lower Aire Valley, pay a visit to Kippax Meadows, an accessible reserve with great potential and already home to a number of uncommon plants.

The lowdown...

Nearest town: Castleford (4m/6.4km)
Nearest postcode: LS25 7QQ
Grid ref: SE 41519 29870
///myself.topic.superbly
Parking: Car park on Brigshaw Lane for the tennis courts, which is then a short walk down a bridleway to the reserve
Site designation: None
Size: 3ha

A great place for:

☐ Bird watchers

☐ Cyclists

☐ Wildflower enthusiasts

☑ Families

☑ Leisurely stroll

☐ Peace and tranquility

☐ Walkers

Recommended time to make the most of your visit:

☐ Full day

☐ Half day

☑ Just an hour

 Before you go...
There's a good network of paths around the site, and some are suitable for buggies and wheelchairs. There are benches dotted around the reserve.

A green oasis for kids and orchids

An ideal spot for some fresh air and exercise, or a family outing with a picnic, Kippax Meadows is tucked away on the edge of Kippax village, with a network of accessible paths opening up this green oasis for visitors to get close to nature.

From the sensory gardens beds by the Cromwell Rise entrance to the botanically diverse grasslands that grow on sandstone and magnesian limestone, colourful flowers attract bumblebees and butterflies, including common blues, meadow browns, peacocks, small skippers, small tortoiseshells, and small and large whites.

Smooth tare, greater knapweed, common spotted-orchid, meadow cranesbill and bee orchid are among the many flowers that light up the meadow in summer, and work continues around the site to encourage a greater diversity of species.

Keep your eyes peeled for small mammals, and remember to keep looking up – red kites, buzzards and kestrels can often be spotted flying overhead, and sometimes perch on trees or bushes.

Did you know?
Bullfinches were once considered a pest in orchards. Henry VIII condemned their 'criminal attacks' on new buds. An Act of Parliament said one penny would be paid for every bird killed.

Enjoy a walk through Kippax meadows

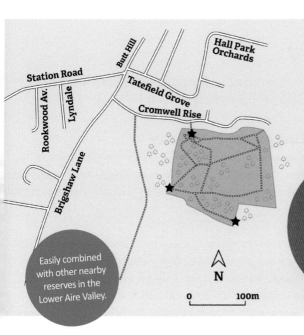

Hall Park Orchards

Station Road
Butt Hill
Tatefield Grove
Cromwell Rise
Rookwood Av.
Lyndale
Brigshaw Lane

> Easily combined with other nearby reserves in the Lower Aire Valley.

N

0   100m

> ★ **Magic** ★
> **moment**
> When the tiny small skipper pauses from one of its darting flights, allowing a quick view of its bright orange-and-brown wings.

Small skipper

Savour a seasonal saunter

Spring and summer are the best seasons for a saunter around Kippax Meadows. In spring, listen for the calls of returning chiffchaffs, and yellowhammers, linnets and bullfinches singing for a mate from scattered hawthorn bushes.

During the summer months, take time to wander through the meadows, enjoy the buzzing of bumblebees, and see which species of flowers and butterflies you can discover. To broaden out your wildlife experience, carry on to one of our other reserves – Owl Wood and Pit Plantation, Townclose Hills and Ledston Luck are all within a mile or two's walk.

Bee

Seasonal highlights

✿ **Spring**
Chiffchaff
Yellowhammer
Blackthorn blossom

❀ **Summer**
Common blue
Small skipper
Bumblebees

✾ **Autumn**
Fieldfare
Redwing
Sloes

❅ **Winter**
Bullfinch
Linnet

Kirkstall Valley

As you stroll through the orchard, woods and grassland of peaceful Kirkstall Valley, you'll completely forget that you're close to the urban heart of one of the UK's biggest cities.

The lowdown...

Nearest town: Leeds (2.0m/3.2km)
Nearest postcode: LS4 2AW
Grid ref: SE 2684 3447
///throw.layers.mass
Parking: Roadside parking on Redcote Lane, with a pleasant short walk up the access track.
Size: 10ha

A great place for:

- ☑ Bird watchers
- ☐ Cyclists
- ☑ Wildflower enthusiasts
- ☐ Families
- ☐ Leisurely stroll
- ☑ Peace and tranquility
- ☐ Walkers

Recommended time to make the most of your visit:

- ☐ Full day
- ☐ Half day
- ☑ Just an hour

Before you go...
The access track can be muddy in winter. Please keep to the paths and follow signage. You'll find lots of shops and cafes nearby on Kirkstall Road.

Thank you!
Your donations and membership mean we can restore and maintain wild places and create homes for wildlife in post-industrial settings like Kirkstall Valley.

Sitting pretty in the city

Birds, mammals, amphibians, flowers and insects are within touching distance of roads, railways, businesses and housing here on the edge of urban Leeds – but the joy of this reserve is that the city feels much further away.

Kirkstall Valley hasn't always been the attractive green landscape you see today. Where there's now a young woodland and wildflower meadow, there was previously a power station and then a landfill site. The variety of wildlife is impressive: over 130 plant species, 65 birds including kingfishers, 16 butterflies including small coppers and commas, and six species of dragonfly have been recorded. Mammals include otters, foxes, and pipistrelle, noctule and Daubenton's bats.

The grassland area is home to a mixture of toads, frogs, voles and common shrews, and buzzards fly overhead. This area was noted for orchards in medieval times and, thanks to recent planting, the fruit trees are back! The orchard is full of fruit in autumn – apples, quince, pear, cherry, plum, greengage and medlar. It's a lovely spot in the springtime, full of greenery and blossom.

A tranquil oasis in urban Leeds

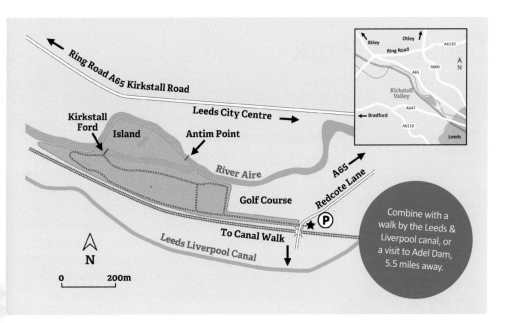

Combine with a walk by the Leeds & Liverpool canal, or a visit to Adel Dam, 5.5 miles away.

N

0   200m

Building a desirable residence for wildlife

Maintaining the reserve for wildlife is a year-round task. We cut and rake the meadows in late summer and lightly coppice the woodland in winter to create good growing conditions for wildflowers. The coppice habitat is also ideal for fritillary butterflies and birds such as garden warblers and robins. Log piles from cut trees are left on site to support the growth of fungi as they decay.

★ **Magic ★ moment**

Stopping by the river to see a kingfisher flit by and a heron standing like a statue.

Grey heron

Seasonal highlights

✿ **Spring**
Cowslip
Primrose
Orchard in bloom

❀ **Summer**
Kingfisher
Small copper
Meadow vetchling
Oxeye daisy

✤ **Autumn**
Autumn colours
Apple
Pear
Guelder rose
Quince
Medlar

❁ **Winter**
Grey heron
Goosander
Bullfinch
Reed bunting
Red kite

Ledsham Bank

It doesn't have to be the Summer of Love to enjoy an explosion of flower power.
Let Ledsham Bank's vivid wildflower display blow your mind this June and July!

The lowdown

Nearest town: Castleford (5.1m/8.2km)
Nearest postcode: LS25 5LL
Grid ref: SE 4596 2977
///tracks.tidal.storming
Parking: Lay-by opposite the reserve on Holyrood Lane. The entrance is hidden behind a bank of trees, across the road and slightly to the left up a small incline.
Size: 5ha

A great place for:

☐ Bird watchers
☐ Cyclists
☑ Wildflower enthusiasts
☐ Families
☐ Leisurely stroll
☑ Peace and tranquility
☐ Walkers

Recommended time to make the most of your visit:

☐ Full day
☐ Half day
☑ Just an hour

ℹ Before you go...

Conservation cattle and sheep graze this fragile habitat at certain times of year, please be careful not to disturb them.

Tie in with our Aire Valley reserves and Lines Way for a longer trip.

Magical meadows

Tucked away in a magnesian limestone valley, Ledsham Bank supports incredible plantlife, including pyramidal and common-spotted orchids, autumn lady's tresses, hoary plantain, yellow-wort, and Dyer's greenweed – rare in Yorkshire. You might be lucky enough to see the extremely rare pasque flower at Easter time. The reserve is fabulous for butterflies, such as marbled white, small and large skipper, comma, and common and holly blue. A mature hedgerow provides food and shelter for winter finches and thrushes – and keep an eye out for little owls.

Red kite

View over the wildflower fields

★ **Magic moment** ★
Lifting your eyes from the incredible flowers to see a red kite soaring over.

Give **volunteering** a try!

All across Yorkshire, people give us their spare minutes, hours and days on beaches, under trees, amongst meadows and in communities, schools and offices. Over 800 volunteers are already working together to create a Yorkshire rich in wildlife for everyone – but our iconic wildlife and wild places still need more support. However much time you have and whatever skills and experience you bring, there are many ways you could support us by volunteering.

100% of our volunteers feel healthier because of their volunteering!

Get involved at: **ywt.org.uk/get-involved/volunteer**

Ledston Luck

When hundreds of orchids are in bloom, the birds are singing, and the ponds are alive with dragonflies and damselflies, it's a far cry from Ledston Luck's industrial past.

The lowdown...

Nearest town: Castleford (3.5m/5.6km)
Nearest postcode: LS25 7BF
Grid ref: SE 42943 31157
///bins.situation.sung
Parking: Parking is available in the Ledston Luck Enterprise Park car park, just a short walk to the reserve
Size: 18ha

A great place for:

☑ Bird watchers
☐ Cyclists
☑ Wildflower enthusiasts
☑ Families
☐ Leisurely stroll
☑ Peace and tranquility
☑ Walkers

Recommended time to make the most of your visit:

☐ Full day
☐ Half day
☑ Just an hour

ℹ Before you go...
If you're walking around the area, use the OS Explorer 289 map. There's a marked trail on the site but paths can be muddy and aren't suitable for wheelchairs or buggies.

A lucky find

It's very easy to drive straight past the reserve, as it's tucked away behind the A656 and local businesses, but this is a hidden gem that's well worth seeking out.

The sights and sounds of this gorgeous site could not be more different to its mining past. Since the pit closed in 1986, a lovely range of wildlife habitats have taken over – some naturally, without much help, including the woodlands and ponds – while some areas of meadow have had a helping hand.

During the summer, the grassland is truly a sight to behold, as it erupts with wildflowers, including hundreds of orchids. These include common-spotted and southern marsh orchids and hybrids between the two, and northern marsh, bee and pyramidal orchids. Grazing gives these beautiful flowers space to thrive.

Did you know?
Ledston Luck coal pit was linked to other pits in a 'super pit' around Selby. It's now part of a super wildlife corridor in the Lower Aire Valley!

A mix of habitat at Ledston Luck

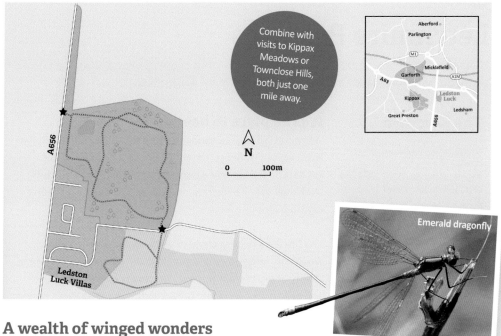

Combine with visits to Kippax Meadows or Townclose Hills, both just one mile away.

Emerald dragonfly

A wealth of winged wonders

There's a great variety of birds here and it would be easy to spend half a day getting absorbed in watching them. Keep your eyes peeled for willow tits and green woodpeckers, and listen for the distinctive calls of nesting blackcaps and yellowhammers. There are herons, coots and moorhens on the lake, while little egrets occassionally fly over.

This is a great place for dragonflies, and they've been helped by clearance work on some of the ponds and ditches. The main pond attracts emerald and large red damselflies, emperor dragonfly and four-spotted chasers, to name just a few.

★ **Magic moment** ★
The incredible June spectacle of the orchids in bloom.

Southern marsh orchid

Seasonal highlights

✿ **Spring**
Brimstone butterfly
Large red damselfly
Broad-bodied chaser
Willow warbler

✺ **Summer**
Common spotted-orchid
Bee orchid
Four-spotted chaser
Grasshopper warbler

☔ **Autumn**
Fieldfare
Redwing

❄ **Winter**
Grey heron
Yellowhammer
Willow tit

Letchmire Pastures

Mining bees now use the exposed coal bank of this former colliery, bee orchids bloom in the meadow, and the lagoons are a magnet for dragonflies!

The lowdown...

Nearest town: Castleford (1.6m/2.5km)
Nearest postcode: WF10 2BW
Grid ref: SE42373 27609
///master.raft.sings
Parking: Small layby in front of the reserve entrance.
Site designation: LNR
Size: 12ha

A great place for:

☑ Bird watchers
☐ Cyclists
☑ Wildflower enthusiasts
☑ Families
☐ Leisurely stroll
☑ Peace and tranquility
☑ Walkers

Recommended time to make the most of your visit:

☐ Full day
☐ Half day
☑ Just an hour

ℹ Before you go...

There are paths around the site, but they can be muddy, and aren't suitable for wheelchairs.

It's the place to bee

When the last days of spring merge into early summer, Letchmire Pastures is at its finest. The meadow — one of a number of habitats on the reserve — bursts into colour, with bee orchids, stork's bill, lady's bedstraw, oxeye daisies, meadowsweet and ragged robin.

The site is a low-lying blend of wetland, bare earth, young woodland, hedgerows and grassland. It's a great place to see a variety of insects, but the star performers are the dragonflies and damselflies, including brown and common hawkers, darters, skimmers and chasers. You can see them in large numbers, and they're relatively obliging for photographs — ruddy darters might even stay still for a while as they sun themselves on the fences around the lagoons.

Take a gentle, quiet amble around the site and see what you can find. The dark, bare earth warms up in the summer, creating special conditions for unusual plants and burrowing insects such as beetles, wasps and bees, like the mining bee — very aptly named for this site!

Did you know?

With the appearance, texture and even scent of a female bee, bee orchids are perfectly designed to attract passing male bees. But our British bee orchids self-pollinate so they don't really need this incredible mimicry!

Letchmire lagoon

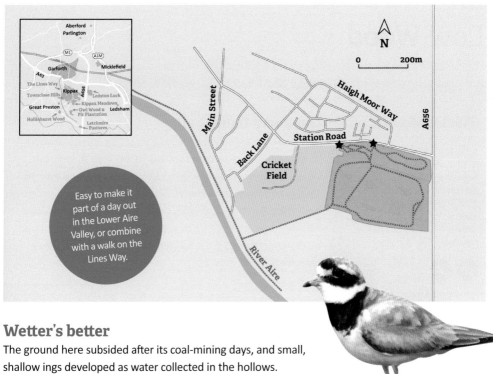

Wetter's better

The ground here subsided after its coal-mining days, and small, shallow ings developed as water collected in the hollows. Landscaping has enhanced these wetland features to create a number of ponds of different sizes and depths, which take on a glistening, wintry appearance in ice and snow, and we're encouraging reed-beds to grow.

The insect life, damp grassland and muddy pond margins attract birds. If you visit at a quiet time you might spot lapwings, common snipes and ringed plovers, but they're easily disturbed by dogs. You might also see little egrets circling overhead.

Ringed plover

Easy to make it part of a day out in the Lower Aire Valley, or combine with a walk on the Lines Way.

★ **Magic** ★
moment
A row of ruddy darters sunning themselves on the fencing around the lagoons.

Seasonal highlights

☼ Spring
Broad-bodied chaser
Grey heron

☀ Summer
Bee orchid
Grass vetchling
Meadow cranesbill
Wood small-reed
Devil's-bit scabious

❂ Autumn
Reed bunting
Fox

❄ Winter
Snipe

Ruddy darter

Low Wood

This secluded canal-side spot offers a tranquil escape from the bustle of urban Keighley and Bradford, while the cliffs above it provide cracking glimpses of the Aire valley.

The lowdown...

Nearest town: Riddlesden (1.4m/2.3km)
Nearest postcode: BD20 5QL
Grid ref: SE 058 437
///mini.puts.wiring
Parking: Small car park by the canal at the end of Elam Wood Road.
Size: 3ha

A great place for:

☑ Bird watchers
☐ Cyclists
☐ Wildflower enthusiasts
☑ Families
☐ Leisurely stroll
☑ Peace and tranquility
☑ Walkers

Recommended time to make the most of your visit:

☐ Full day
☐ Half day
☑ Just an hour

ℹ Before you go...
Public access is limited. There's a circular path around the woods. The path to the crags is steep and rocky.

Badger

Get away from it all

This attractive broadleaved woodland, set on a steep slope, is an enjoyable place to spend an hour at any time of year, but especially worth a visit for the bluebells in spring, and over 36 species of fungi in the autumn. Glades in the woodland encourage butterflies like speckled wood, and there's a small pond where common frogs congregate to spawn in the spring. Birds include blackcap, green and great spotted woodpeckers, tawny owl, treecreeper and nuthatch.

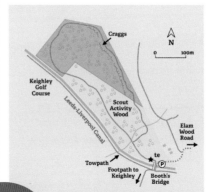

★ Magic moment ★
A visit at dusk to look for bats – and maybe a badger too!

Include as part of a walk along the Leeds and Liverpool Canal.

Bluebells in the woodland

Treecreeper

Owl Wood and Pit Plantation

Owl Wood is perhaps misnamed. Although there are owls, it's a different kind of flying creature that's really at home here and in neighbouring Pit Plantation – bats.

The lowdown...

Nearest town: Castleford (3m/4.8km)
Nearest postcode: WF10 2AQ
Grid ref: Roadside parking: SE 41353 28727
///vowel.presides.ambition
Parking: Small informal lay-by on the road into the woods. Large wagons use this road so please do not block.
Size: 8ha

A great place for:

☑ Bird watchers
☐ Cyclists
☐ Wildflower enthusiasts
☑ Families
☐ Leisurely stroll
☑ Peace and tranquility
☑ Walkers

Recommended time to make the most of your visit:

☐ Full day
☐ Half day
☑ Just an hour

ℹ Before you go...

There are interconnected paths throughout both woodlands but these can be muddy and are not accessible for wheelchairs or buggies. There are no facilities on site.

Hang around for the bats

Owl Wood and Pit Plantation are two connected woodlands, linked to a network of reserves by the Lines Way. Owl Wood is believed to have been wooded since the late 18th century and today it's dominated by sycamore, oak and silver birch. Pit Plantation is younger but still more than 100 years old, having been documented in a 1913 map of Allerton Bywater.

The woods offer a sheltered retreat for wildlife. If you visit during the day, look out for treecreepers climbing the gnarly old trees to find insects. You'll also notice bat boxes high in the trees, which are surveyed by Leeds City Council. At dawn or dusk in spring and summer, it's a bat bonanza: Leisler's, common and soprano pipistrelle, noctule and Daubenton's bats have all been recorded here. The best way to tell the difference is through their calls, using a bat detector. Learn how to use one on one of our guided walks.

Did you know?

Bats can fly in the dark by using echolocation – sound waves to work out where things are – and each species has a different frequency.

The wonderful spring woodland

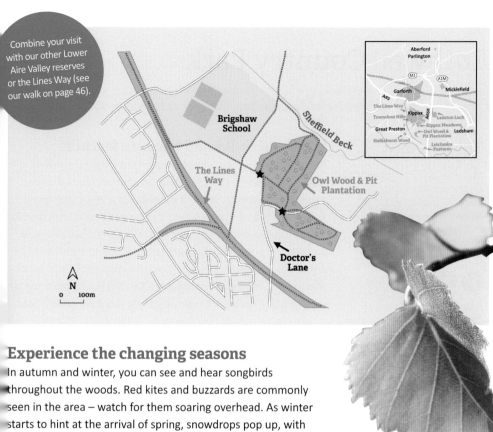

Combine your visit with our other Lower Aire Valley reserves or the Lines Way (see our walk on page 46).

Aberford
Parlington

M1

A1M

Garforth

Micklefield

A63

The Lines Way

Townclose Hills

Kippax

Aire

Ledston Luck

Kippax Meadows

Great Preston

Owl Wood & Pit Plantation

Ledsham

Hollinhurst Wood

Letchmire Pastures

Brigshaw School

Sheffield Beck

The Lines Way

Owl Wood & Pit Plantation

Doctor's Lane

N

0   100m

Experience the changing seasons

In autumn and winter, you can see and hear songbirds throughout the woods. Red kites and buzzards are commonly seen in the area – watch for them soaring overhead. As winter starts to hint at the arrival of spring, snowdrops pop up, with a beautiful display of bluebells following them as the season gets underway. Sheffield Beck passes through the edge of the reserve – one of many local waterways in the once-industrial but now wildlife-rich Lower Aire Valley.

This is also a good place simply to pause, take a breath and enjoy being surrounded by trees.

Silver birch

Liesler's bat

★ **Magic** ★
moment
Seeing bats flying through and around the woodland.

Seasonal highlights

✲ **Spring**
Bluebells

✲ **Summer**
Leisler's bat
Common and soprano pistrelles
Hedgehog

◉ **Autumn**
Yew
Treecreeper
Great spotted woodpecker

✲ **Winter**
Tawny owl

Rothwell Country Park

From a post-industrial wasteland to a family-friendly nature reserve with woodland, ponds and grassland, the transformation of this site benefits both wildlife and people.

The lowdown...

Nearest town: Leeds (6.1m/9.8km)
Nearest postcode: LS26 0JY
Grid ref: SE 34872 29531
///goats.damage.dice
Parking: Roadside parking on Bullough Lane
Size: 54ha

A great place for:

☑ Bird watchers
☐ Cyclists
☐ Wildflower enthusiasts
☑ Families
☐ Leisurely stroll
☑ Peace and tranquility
☑ Walkers

Recommended time to make the most of your visit:

☐ Full day
☑ Half day
☐ Just an hour

ℹ Before you go...

Some parts of the site are suitable for wheelchair users and pushchairs. Take the quieter paths for the best chance of a wildlife encounter.

Weekend walks and creature features

Rothwell Country Park is an ideal spot for a peaceful weekend walk close to urban West Yorkshire, and for families to discover a variety of wildlife. It's part of a corridor of green spaces in the Lower Aire Valley – a very different picture to its medieval days as a royal hunting ground and later as a busy colliery, which closed in 1983. It lay derelict until it was brought back to life in the mid-1990s by a partnership between local people, Leeds City Council and Groundwork Leeds, opening in 2000. The park is managed by the Friends of Rothwell Country Park and Yorkshire Wildlife Trust.

There's an extensive network of paths including a sculpture trail and pond trail. Come along to one of our pond-dipping events to discover creatures including common frogs and toads, smooth newts, and lots of dragonfly nymphs. The sculpture trail features a special work called 'Breaking the Mould' by Andrew McKeown - a giant seed emerging from an industrial mould - installed to celebrate the changing places programme, which transformed post-industrial land into parks and open spaces.

Walk to the summit of the old spoil heap for one of the best views in Leeds!

Tranquility in the Lower Aire Valley

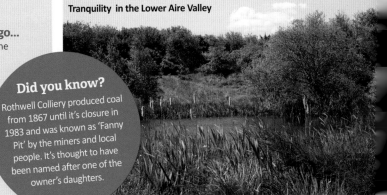

Did you know?
Rothwell Colliery produced coal from 1867 until it's closure in 1983 and was known as 'Fanny Pit' by the miners and local people. It's thought to have been named after one of the owner's daughters.

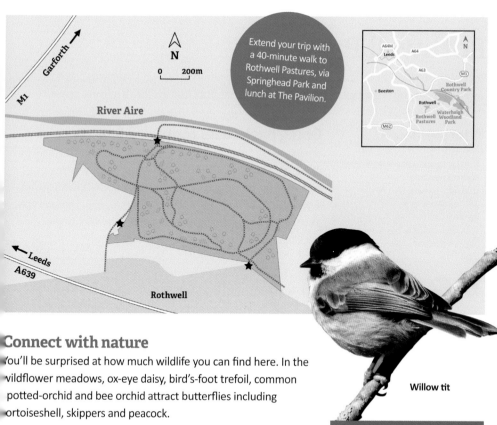

Extend your trip with a 40-minute walk to Rothwell Pastures, via Springhead Park and lunch at The Pavilion.

Willow tit

Connect with nature

You'll be surprised at how much wildlife you can find here. In the wildflower meadows, ox-eye daisy, bird's-foot trefoil, common spotted-orchid and bee orchid attract butterflies including tortoiseshell, skippers and peacock.

The woodlands are home to hedgehogs, rabbits, bats and roe deer. Look for the classic 'fairy toadstool', fly agaric, amongst the variety of fungi in autumn. Many birds have been recorded, including tree sparrow, skylark, linnet, cuckoo, yellowhammer, reed bunting and willow tit. If you'd like to volunteer to help manage the site, please contact us at **volunteering@ywt.org.uk**

Smooth newt

★ **Magic** ★
moment
Finding wiggly newts on a pond dip in spring.

Seasonal highlights

✿ Spring
Common toad
Willow warbler
Whitethroat

❋ Summer
Purple loosestrife
Bird's-foot trefoil
Emperor dragonfly

❂ Autumn
Fly agaric
Skylark
Tree sparrow

❄ Winter
Green woodpecker
Willow tit

Rothwell Pastures

Rothwell Pastures is branching out! As part of a woodland creation scheme in Leeds, new tree-planting is giving the reserve's existing habitats and wildlife a natural boost.

The lowdown...

Nearest town: Leeds (6.1m/9.8km)
Nearest postcode: LS26 0QL
Grid ref: SE 34312 28217
///drop.sweep.guilty
Parking: Church Street Car Park, Rothwell, LS26 0QL
Site designation: Leeds Nature Area
Size: 13ha

  Cycling allowed on the greenway

A great place for:

☑ Bird watchers
☐ Cyclists
☐ Wildflower enthusiasts
☑ Families
☐ Leisurely stroll
☑ Peace and tranquility
☑ Walkers

Recommended time to make the most of your visit:

☐ Full day
☑ Half day
☐ Just an hour

ⓘ Before you go...

The Rothwell Greenway runs for 3 miles from Long Thorpe Lane in Lofthouse to Haigh Road in Rothwell, right through Rothwell Pastures. This wide, surfaced route is suitable for bikes, buggies and walkers. There is a mix of surfaced and unsurfaced paths across the nature reserve.

Going back to its roots

Woodland isn't new to Rothwell Pastures. The land was granted to Ilbert de Lacy by William the Conqueror in 1069, when a vast woodland covered the district. This then became a hunting park, where wild boar and deer were hunted until 1339. The land was also the site of grand mansions, but all that remains of those is a stack of stones, known locally as Rothwell Castle.

With a history of royal visitors including King John and Edward II, Rothwell Pastures now welcomes royal visitors of a different kind. You might be lucky enough to see a kingfisher on one of the ponds or becks, where you may also glimpse a rare water vole, along with frogs, toads, mallards and moorhens.

The disused railway connects a variety of smaller habitats, providing an important corridor for wildlife. Butterflies including common blues, speckled woods and meadow browns, and the day-flying cinnabar moth, are attracted to wildflowers in the large meadow.

Did you know?
The collective noun for a group of goldfinches is a 'charm' – seems appropriate for these delicate little birds.

Step into Rothwell Pastures

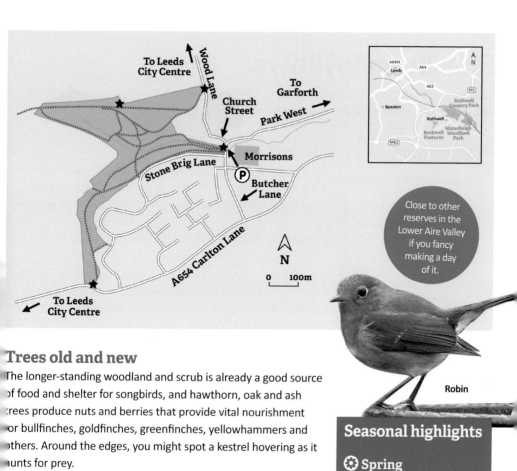

Trees old and new

The longer-standing woodland and scrub is already a good source of food and shelter for songbirds, and hawthorn, oak and ash trees produce nuts and berries that provide vital nourishment for bullfinches, goldfinches, greenfinches, yellowhammers and others. Around the edges, you might spot a kestrel hovering as it hunts for prey.

The younger trees are part of Leeds City Council's woodland creation scheme, which aims to plant 5.8 million trees over 25 years at sites around the area, helping Leeds to become carbon neutral.

Robin

Close to other reserves in the Lower Aire Valley if you fancy making a day of it.

★ Magic ★ moment

A cinnabar moth stretching out its wings to reveal its striking red-and-black pattern.

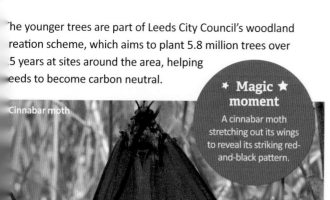

Cinnabar moth

Seasonal highlights

✿ Spring
Common toad
Blackcap
Whitethroat
Willow warbler

☀ Summer
Bird's-foot trefoil
Bladder campion
Purple loosestrife
Cinnabar moth

◌ Autumn
Hawthorn
Jelly ear fungi
Elder berries

❄ Winter
Robin
Bullfinch

Discover Yorkshire's Wildlife | **227**

Sherburn Willows

With singing birds, feeding butterflies and wildflowers in bloom, a walk around this small reserve is a very pleasant way to spend a lazy hour in spring or summer.

The lowdown...

Nearest town: Sherburn in Elmet (0.9m/1.4km)
Nearest postcode: LS25 6AG
Grid ref: Roadside parking: SE 4867 3261
///laminate.apply.reversed
Parking: Roadside parking on New Lane
Size: 3ha

A great place for:

- ☐ Bird watchers
- ☐ Cyclists
- ☑ Wildflower enthusiasts
- ☐ Families
- ☐ Leisurely stroll
- ☑ Peace and tranquility
- ☑ Walkers

Recommended time to make the most of your visit:

- ☐ Full day
- ☐ Half day
- ☑ Just an hour

 Before you go...
Please stick to the permissive paths to avoid squishing plants and other wildlife or disturbing grazing animals.

Did you know?
The lovely yellow cowslip is named after 'cow-slop' (cowpat!) because of its choice of meadow habitat.

The joys of spring

With flower-filled magnesian grasslands sloping steeply down to a wet area of fen and willow carr woodland, Sherburn Willows provides excellent habitats for breeding birds and feeding insects.

It comes alive in spring and into summer, when the vivid colours of the grassland change with the months. The flowers are at their best in June and July, but you can enjoy the colours from May to August. Cowslips, oxeye daisy, hairy violet and greater knapweed paint a pretty picture, along with good displays of common spotted- orchids, agrimony, restharrow, and the locally rare sainfoin, with its pointy pink flowers irresistible to pollinating insects.

Other locally rare plants recorded here include purple milk-vetch and pale St John's-wort. There are many butterflies, moths and other insects to look for, including marbled white and orange-tip butterflies as well as elephant hawk-moths.

Wildflower grassland

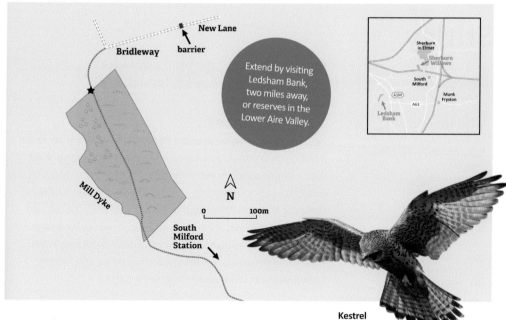

New Lane

Bridleway   barrier

Extend by visiting Ledsham Bank, two miles away, or reserves in the Lower Aire Valley.

Sherburn in Elmet
Sherburn Willows
South Milford
A1M
A63
Monk Fryston
Ledsham Bank

Mill Dyke

N

0   100m

South Milford Station

Kestrel

The birds are back in town

Another welcome sign of spring is the return of migrant songbirds, including whitethroat, lesser whitethroat, chiffchaff, blackcap and reed warbler. Bullfinches are resident on site, and red kites are a common sight overhead, while redwings and fieldfares can be seen during the autumn and winter.

We maintain the grassland by removing scrub and grazing with rare breed livestock, and we coppice the willow in the areas of wet woodland to keep the structure varied and rich in wildlife.

★ **Magic moment** ★
Finding the elusive and attractive sainfoin among the wildflowers.

Rabbits and foxes make their home here, and look out for the distinctive 'hills' created by yellow meadow ants!

Sainfoin

Seasonal highlights

✿ Spring
Violets
Cowslip
Chiffchaff

❀ Summer
Sainfoin
Agrimony
Oxeye daisy
Knapweed
Willow warbler

❧ Autumn
Crab apple
Redwing
Fieldfare

❀ Winter
Red kite
Reed bunting
Buzzard
Kestrel
Bullfinch

Stirley

Once an intensively grazed dairy farm, Stirley is now an inspiring showcase for conservation grazing methods and a place to enjoy nature's sights and sounds.

The lowdown...

Nearest town: Huddersfield (2.8m/4.5km)
Nearest postcode: HD4 6FA
Grid ref: SE 1459 1354
///intent.origin.body
Parking: The onsite car park is reserved for event attendees only. Visitors to the reserve are encouraged to park at Castle Hill (bright.places.tulip or HD4 6TA).
Size: 94 ha

A great place for:

- ☐ Bird watchers
- ☐ Cyclists
- ☐ Wildflower enthusiasts
- ☑ Families
- ☐ Leisurely stroll
- ☑ Peace and tranquility
- ☑ Walkers

Recommended time to make the most of your visit:

- ☐ Full day
- ☑ Half day
- ☐ Just an hour

ℹ **Before you go...**
Take your walking boots and an OS map (Explorer 288) to explore Stirley and the surrounding area. Don't miss a walk up to Castle Hill to see the incredible view of Huddersfield below and the Pennines in the distance.

Views and moos

Here on a hill on the edge of the Pennines, your senses are in for a treat. The first thing you notice is the quietness, interspersed with a few peaceful sounds – the buzz of bees or the chatter of our fantastic volunteers working in the vegetable patches. And then there are the views: the hills, the ancient folly of Castle Hill, and lush green meadows, where you might spot our roving traditional-breed cows. The wildflowers growing outside the barns, in the verges and hedgerows create a beautiful aroma, and 'wildest' visitors might enjoy a foraged fruit or herbal tea.

Yorkshire Wildlife Trust bought the site in 2011 and since then has restored an old barn into an excellent education facility (the Cre8 Barn Education Centre), developed a thriving food garden, planted an orchard, and provided conservation training to a host of young people. It demonstrates how wildlife-friendly grazing methods can benefit the landscape and involve the community – a healthy environment for wildlife supporting healthy living for people.

Did you know?
You can hire the Cre8 eco-barn for your own meetings and events, with seating for up to 30 people.

Enjoy peaceful Pennine views

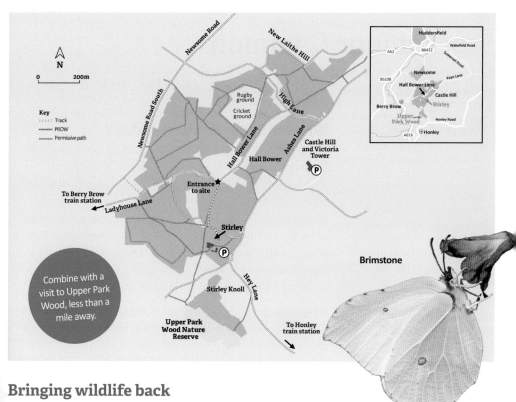

Key
:::::: Track
━━━ PROW
━━━ Permissive path

Combine with a visit to Upper Park Wood, less than a mile away.

Brimstone

Bringing wildlife back

Stirley is a patchwork of habitats, designed to increase the number and diversity of flowers, insects, birds and mammals. We are re-seeding large areas of grassland with wildflower seed, planting and managing hedgerows and scrub, encouraging rough grassland as a hunting ground for birds of prey, and creating ponds, which will be full of life.

From deer galloping across the fields to kestrels hovering above, Stirley just goes to show how wildlife can thrive on the edge of a big town. If you wait until dusk, maybe you'll spot a barn owl swooping across the horizon.

Sparrow hawk

★ Magic ★ moment
A magnificent sparrowhawk gliding overhead.

Seasonal highlights

✿ **Spring**
Harebells
Brimstone butterfly
Barn owl

☀ **Summer**
Weasel
Swallow
Pied wagtail
Kestrel

🍂 **Autumn**
Meadow waxcaps

❄ **Winter**
Roe deer

Stocksmoor Common

Stocksmoor Common is a reserve of two halves – one part rough grassland with marshy areas and one part woodland and wet flushes – the whole of which attracts a diverse mix of wildlife.

The lowdown...

Nearest town: Wakefield (6.0m/9.7km)
Nearest postcode: WF4 4JQ
Grid ref: SE 2735 1496
///mastering.stops.mornings
Parking: Layby on South Lane
Size: 12ha

A great place for:

☑ Bird watchers
☐ Cyclists
☑ Wildflower enthusiasts
☐ Families
☐ Leisurely stroll
☑ Peace and tranquility
☑ Walkers

Recommended time to make the most of your visit:

☐ Full day
☐ Half day
☑ Just an hour

ⓘ **Before you go...**
There's one public right of way through the woodland, along with permissive footpaths. The fenced grassland area grazed by cattle has a stile and kissing gates. Visit in autumn to see impressive displays of shaggy inkcaps.

Combine with nearby Stoneycliffe Wood for a longer outing.

What will you discover today?

You can find adder's tongue fern, common spotted-orchid and common fleabane in the more grassy areas, and mat grass, wavy hair-grass and tufted hair-grass in the damper parts. The woodland is home to a range of birds, including coal tit, song thrush, spotted flycatcher and long-tailed tit. The ponds are an integral part of the ecosystem too. They're home to great crested, smooth and palmate newts, frogs and toads, and numerous invertebrates that provide food for bank voles and wood mice, which are themselves food for foxes and tawny owls.

Tree pipit

Grassland hides gems including adder's tongue fern

★ **Magic moment** ★
A tree pipit singing proudly in the treetops.

Yorkshire
Wildlife Trust

This spring, Terence helped us to create wild places for lapwing and oystercatcher chicks.

This summer, he helped us safeguard wildflowers on floodplain meadows.

This autumn, he is helping us to survey for water voles.

This winter, it will be two years since Terence passed away.

Leave a **lasting legacy** for Yorkshire's wildlife with a gift in your Will

Stoneycliffe Wood

A gorgeously green place to stop in spring, enjoy the fragrance of wild garlic, and listen to the trickling stream and songs of woodland birds.

The lowdown...

Nearest town: Wakefield (5.3m/8.5km)
Nearest postcode: WF4 4NF
Grid ref: SE 2751 1603
///placidly.gather.expose
Parking: Lay-by on Coxley View
Size: 40ha

A great place for:

☐ Bird watchers
☐ Cyclists
☐ Wildflower enthusiasts
☑ Families
☐ Leisurely stroll
☑ Peace and tranquility
☑ Walkers

Recommended time to make the most of your visit:

☐ Full day
☑ Half day
☐ Just an hour

ⓘ Before you go...
Access is generally good but steep in places and can get very muddy in winter – wear wellies after heavy rain!

Calming and charming

This stunning woodland, with its meandering beck, charms visitors with bluebells and wild garlic in spring, breeding birds in summer, and fungi in autumn. Stoneycliffe Wood's trees are mostly oak and birch, with some amazing veteran sweet chestnuts, and areas of wet woodland with alder and willow. Listen for the high-pitched call of treecreepers, which you might see climbing up the trees in search of food. There's a chance of seeing all three species of woodpecker here. They feed on the many insects in the dead wood, which provides an important habitat. Several rare spiders have been recorded too. You might also encounter mammals including stoats, voles, shrews, and foxes.

This is a great place to spot interesting fungi in autumn, including fly agaric, jelly ears, puffballs, and chicken of the woods, which gets its name from the texture and taste of its flesh, said to resemble cooked chicken.

After the glorious springtime displays of bluebells and wild garlic, summer flowers include the lovely yellow archangel. By the stream, look for wood club-rush, hemlock water dropwort and Sprengel's bramble.

Wild garlic

★ Magic ★ moment
The late summer sun streaming through the still-green leaves onto the woodland floor by the rippling beck.

Did you know?
Leaves and flowers from the wild garlic plant – also known as ramsons – can be eaten. It smells and tastes like the garlic we are more familiar with.

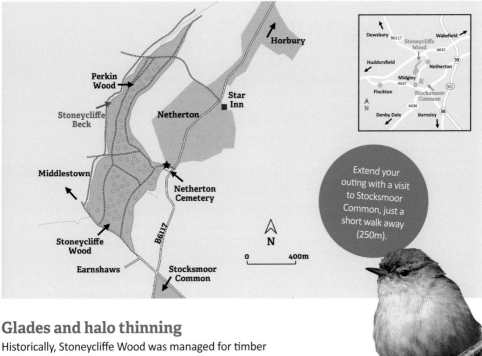

Extend your outing with a visit to Stocksmoor Common, just a short walk away (250m).

Glades and halo thinning

Historically, Stoneycliffe Wood was managed for timber production, but we now manage it to protect the older trees by halo thinning – removing newer trees from around the mature ones to prevent overcrowding and improve the structural diversity of the woodland. Creating glades helps too by allowing for more scrub cover on the woodland floor, which is ideal for birds including chiffchaffs. Felled timber is now left on site and, in summer, spotted flycatchers are among the birds that benefit from the insect life that thrives on the decaying wood.

We control Himalayan balsam and bracken to make sure they don't swamp the woodland flowers.

Chiffchaff

Seasonal highlights

✿ Spring
Bluebells
Wild garlic
Chiffchaff
Willow warbler

❋ Summer
Yellow archangel
Spotted flycatcher
Stoat

◉ Autumn
Fungi

❄ Winter
Lesser spotted woodpecker

Stoat

Townclose Hills

Townclose Hills has spectacular views, fabulous flowers and beautiful butterflies, but it's a small beetle that's the twinkling star attraction.

The lowdown...

Nearest town: Castleford (4.1m/6.6km)
Nearest postcode: LS25 7LQ
Grid ref: SE 40943 30020
///shopping.zoos.steadily
Parking: Available in the Kippax Leisure Centre Car Park
Site designation: SSSI, Local Nature Reserve
Size: 26ha

A great place for:

- ☑ Bird watchers
- ☐ Cyclists
- ☑ Wildflower enthusiasts
- ☑ Families
- ☐ Leisurely stroll
- ☑ Peace and tranquility
- ☑ Walkers

Recommended time to make the most of your visit:

- ☐ Full day
- ☑ Half day
- ☐ Just an hour

ⓘ Before you go...

There are several footpaths into the site, but the main one runs up from Kippax Leisure Centre car park on Station Road. This reserve is accessible by public transport. There's some wheelchair access but this is limited due to steep slopes and muddy paths.

Time to shine

If you've ever read Roald Dahl's *James and the Giant Peach*, you'll have heard of glow-worms. But have you ever seen one? Townclose Hills, also known as Billy Wood, is the perfect place for an illuminating encounter with these fascinating but often elusive creatures, which are actually beetles! Join one of our summer guided walks for the best chances of seeing them and learning more. Stick to the Lines Way to avoid slipping or tripping in the dark if you venture out, when you might also spot a fox or owl.

The magnesian limestone grassland at the top of the site becomes a sea of wildflower colours in the summer: cowslips give way to orchids, knapweeds, clustered bellflowers and others. This encourages huge numbers of butterflies, including marbled whites, dark green fritillaries and gatekeepers. Yearly coppicing of the woodland helps the flowers by increasing the amount of daylight reaching the ground.

The grassland was designated as a Site of Special Scientific Interest (SSSI) in 1984 for being the largest example of a magnesian limestone grassland in the county.

Step into Townclose Hills

Did you know?

The green light comes from the female glow-worm's bottom. She glows to attract males, with their big, photosensitive eyes. The larvae and eggs can also glow.

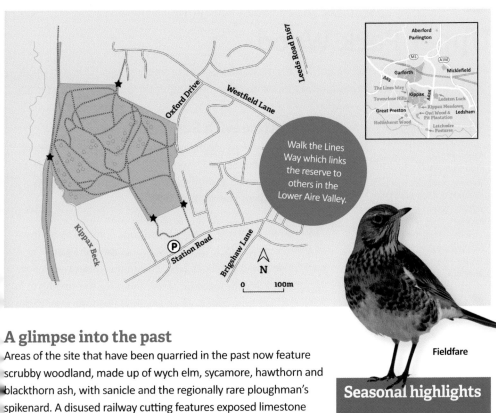

A glimpse into the past

Areas of the site that have been quarried in the past now feature scrubby woodland, made up of wych elm, sycamore, hawthorn and blackthorn ash, with sanicle and the regionally rare ploughman's spikenard. A disused railway cutting features exposed limestone and shallow pools fed by springs.

Very lucky visitors might be fortunate enough to see the increasingly rare and small lesser spotted woodpecker, which is occasionally found here. Listen for its repetitive, high-pitched call in early spring. Other birds you might see include yellowhammers, and, overhead, buzzards, red kites and kestrels.

★ Magic ★ moment
Glow-worms shining like fairy lights on a summer's night.

Glow-worm

Fieldfare

Seasonal highlights

✿ Spring
Lesser spotted woodpecker
Cuckoo
Cowslips
Bluebells

✺ Summer
Glow-worm
Gatekeeper
Marbled white
Dark green fritillary

☽ Autumn
Clustered bellflower
Yellowhammer

✸ Winter
Buzzard
Red kite
Fieldfare
Bullfinch

Upper Park Wood

Where else can you appreciate nature while reminiscing over a classic sitcom? Come to Upper Park Wood for woodland wildlife and spectacular views of 'Last of the Summer Wine' country.

The lowdown...

Nearest town: Huddersfield (2.8m/4.5km)
Nearest postcode: HD9 6QN
Grid ref: SE 1480 1286
///best.notion.track
Parking: Lay-by on Northgate, a short walk from the reserve
Site designation: SSSI, Local Nature Reserve
Size: 5ha

A great place for:

- ☑ Bird watchers
- ☐ Cyclists
- ☐ Wildflower enthusiasts
- ☐ Families
- ☐ Leisurely stroll
- ☑ Peace and tranquility
- ☑ Walkers

Recommended time to make the most of your visit:

- ☐ Full day
- ☐ Half day
- ☑ Just an hour

ℹ️ **Before you go...**
Paths can be muddy and the site is inaccessible for wheelchairs and buggies.

Springtime with Summer Wine

As you gaze out over the Holme Valley from Upper Park Wood, you can imagine seeing Compo, Clegg, Foggy and friends up to their madcap antics in this beautiful, hilly landscape, with its moors, meadows and drystone walls.

The reserve is a young, planted wood surrounding a small area of ancient woodland. It was probably once part of a game park for deer and wild boar, belonging to the ancient Manor of Almondbury. Mostly made up of oak and holly, the wood is at its most enchanting in spring, when bluebells flood the floor of the hazel coppice and the woodland birds are in fine voice.

Encounter a variety of habitats and enjoy views as you explore the network of paths. Look for the different wildlife that inhabits the woodland edge, the field and path margins, pond, wet areas, hedges and dry-stone walls. A small pond, created by damming a stream, is an important refuge for insects and amphibians.

Views across Holme Valley

Did you know?
You can learn more about the local landscape on the geology trail that starts from Castle Hill and passes through the reserve.

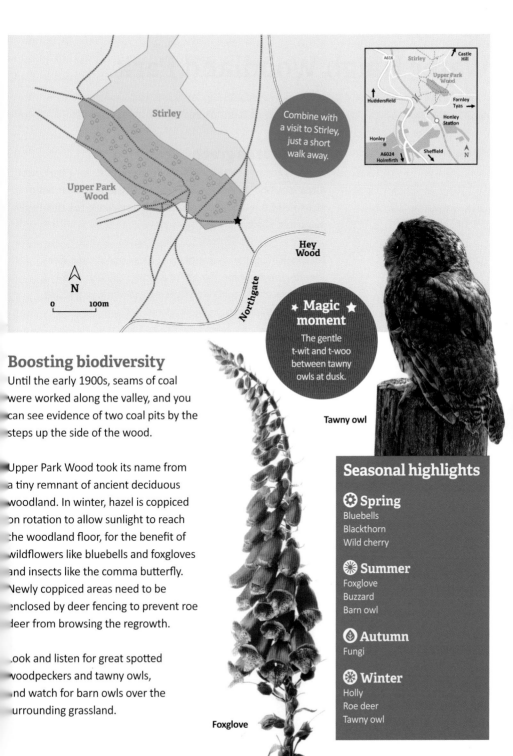

Combine with a visit to Stirley, just a short walk away.

★ **Magic** ★
moment

The gentle t-wit and t-woo between tawny owls at dusk.

Tawny owl

Boosting biodiversity

Until the early 1900s, seams of coal were worked along the valley, and you can see evidence of two coal pits by the steps up the side of the wood.

Upper Park Wood took its name from a tiny remnant of ancient deciduous woodland. In winter, hazel is coppiced on rotation to allow sunlight to reach the woodland floor, for the benefit of wildflowers like bluebells and foxgloves and insects like the comma butterfly. Newly coppiced areas need to be enclosed by deer fencing to prevent roe deer from browsing the regrowth.

Look and listen for great spotted woodpeckers and tawny owls, and watch for barn owls over the surrounding grassland.

Foxglove

Seasonal highlights

✿ **Spring**
Bluebells
Blackthorn
Wild cherry

❃ **Summer**
Foxglove
Buzzard
Barn owl

◉ **Autumn**
Fungi

❄ **Winter**
Holly
Roe deer
Tawny owl

Water Haigh Woodland Park

A varied and developing site straddling the Aire and Calder Navigation and railway, Water Haigh Woodland Park sports an array of habitats and a growing species list.

The lowdown...

Nearest town: Castleford (6.8m/10km)
Nearest postcode: LS26 8AE
Grid ref: SE 37936 28531 (1. Canal end, Fleet Lane car park), SE 37837 28219 (2. Fleet Bridge car park), SE 36814 28484 (3. Eshald Lane Amenity grassland and woodlands), SE 36879 28501 (4. Eshald Wood and wood pasture)
///polite.erase.lands (1), patching.salutes.simple (2), shop.part.carbon (3), curve.energetic.jobs(4)
Parking: 3 car parks on Fleet Lane
Size: 97ha

A great place for:

- ☑ Bird watchers
- ☐ Cyclists
- ☐ Wildflower enthusiasts
- ☑ Families
- ☐ Leisurely stroll
- ☐ Peace and tranquility
- ☑ Walkers

Recommended time to make the most of your visit:

- ☐ Full day
- ☑ Half day
- ☑ Just an hour

ⓘ Before you go...
Surfaced walk along the way marked canal tow path. Reserve is a short walk from Woodlesford Station.

The future's green

The park is part of the important green corridor along the Lower Aire Valley and, as with many other local reserves, it has been reclaimed from industry for nature – a transformation that began in the late 1970s.

Managed in partnership with Leeds City Council, who own the site, the reserve – the site of a former colliery – offers a patchwork of different habitats to explore, including young woodland, meadows, hedgerows and wetland.

The Coronation and Eshald Lane Meadows are rewilding rapidly, with the latter now able to boast 31 species of wildflower. Taking the trail through the Eshald Lane Wood brings you out behind football pitches onto a grassy pasture with growing trees, where you may see deer, willow tits and jays. It's a great place to see bats if you're there at dusk. Keep an eye out for hunting tawny owls and kestrels.

Between the canal and railway, a flood alleviation scheme to help protect nearby homes features wet woodland. Walking along the riverside, you can see orange-tip butterflies and banded demoiselle damselflies fluttering around, with kingfishers and cormorants on the river itself.

Did you know?
The Aire and Calder Navigation is 34 miles long, and this stretch of the canal runs between Leeds city centre and the tidal river Ouse at Goole.

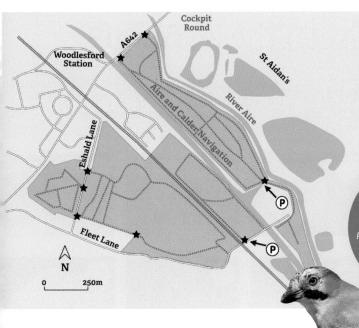

For a full day out, visit some of the other reserves in the Lower Aire Valley, such as Rothwell Pastures, Rothwell Country Park and RSPB St Aidan's.

Jay

Meeting the wildlife on your doorstep

As well as providing great habitats for wildlife, this is a valuable recreational space, where people can experience and enjoy nature close to home. In spring and summer, the wildflowers are beautiful, and there are birds to see all year round, such as long-tailed, great, blue and willow tits in the woodlands, and birds of prey including red kites, buzzards and even marsh harriers. There's a chance of happening across an otter on the canal and perhaps a field vole moving in the meadows.

Seasonal highlights

✿ Spring
Siskin
Skylark
Song thrush
Willow tit

☀ Summer
Kingfisher
Otter

◐ Autumn
Roe deer
Marsh harrier
Jay

❄ Winter
Lesser redpoll
Buzzard
Tawny owl

Roe deer

★ Magic ★ moment
Seeing roe deer grazing in the long grass of Eshald Woods on an early spring morning walk.

Have you seen these...**fungi?**

We've picked out a small selection of fungi for you to look out for in different habitats and seasons around Yorkshire. There are, of course, many more to see! For more help with identifying them, visit **ywt.org.uk/wildlife-explorer/fungi or first-nature.com**

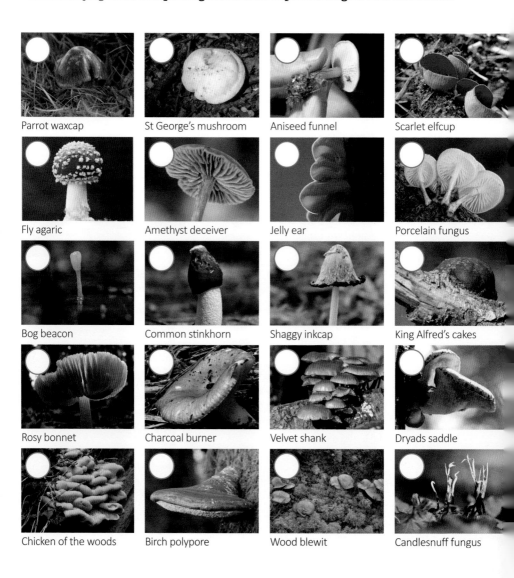

Parrot waxcap

St George's mushroom

Aniseed funnel

Scarlet elfcup

Fly agaric

Amethyst deceiver

Jelly ear

Porcelain fungus

Bog beacon

Common stinkhorn

Shaggy inkcap

King Alfred's cakes

Rosy bonnet

Charcoal burner

Velvet shank

Dryads saddle

Chicken of the woods

Birch polypore

Wood blewit

Candlesnuff fungus

Have you seen these...**wildflowers?**

We've picked out a small selection of wildflowers for you to look out for in different habitats around Yorkshire. There are, of course, many more to see! For more help with identifying them, visit **ywt.org.uk/wildlife-explorer**

Sneezewort

Wild garlic

Harebell

Clustered bellflower

Cowslip

Bee orchid

Oxeye daisy

Yellow rattle

Common knapweed

Teasel

Vipers bugloss

Wood anemone

Yellow archangel

Water avens

Purple loosestrife

Meadowsweet

Marsh marigold

Bird's-foot trefoil

Ragged robin

Cow parsley

Have you seen these... **birds?**

We've picked out a small selection of birds for you to look out for in different habitats around Yorkshire. There are, of course, many more to see! For more help with identifying them, visit **ywt.org.uk/wildlife-explorer/birds**

Coast

Guillemot

Razorbill

Fulmar

Gannet

Oystercatcher

Kittiwake

Puffin

Herring gull

Wetland

Grey heron

Reed bunting

Kingfisher

Little egret

Black-headed gull

Snipe

Dunlin

Redshank

Avocet

Shelduck

Teal

Bittern

Woodland

Long-tailed tit

Great spotted woodpecker

Nuthatch

Treecreeper

Goldcrest

Jay

Fields and moors

Skylark

Yellowhammer

Curlew

Swallow

Barn owl

Meadow pipit

Parks and gardens

Blue tit

Great tit

Dunnock

House sparrow

Chaffinch

Bullfinch

Chiffchaff

Starling

Song thrush

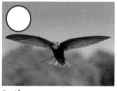
Swift

Sparrowhawk

Wren

Have you seen these...**mammals?**

We've picked out a small selection of mammals for you to look out for in different habitats around Yorkshire. There are, of course, many more to see! For more help with identifying them, visit **ywt.org.uk/wildlife-explorer**

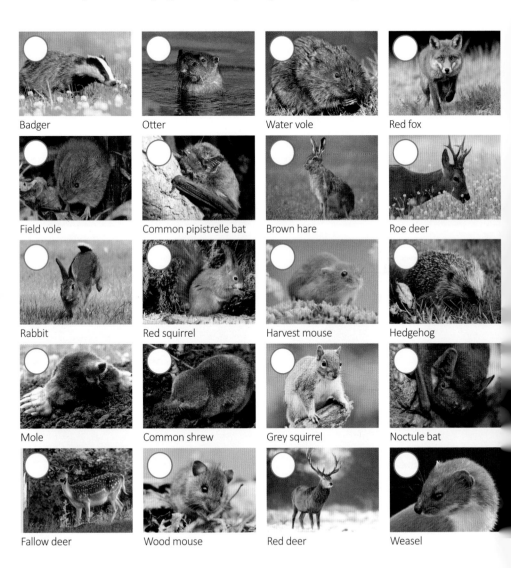

Badger

Otter

Water vole

Red fox

Field vole

Common pipistrelle bat

Brown hare

Roe deer

Rabbit

Red squirrel

Harvest mouse

Hedgehog

Mole

Common shrew

Grey squirrel

Noctule bat

Fallow deer

Wood mouse

Red deer

Weasel

Have you seen these...**marine marvels?**

We've picked out a small selection of weird and wonderful creatures for you to look out for on the Yorkshire coast. There are, of course, many more to see! For more help with identifying them, visit **ywt.org.uk/wildlife-explorer**

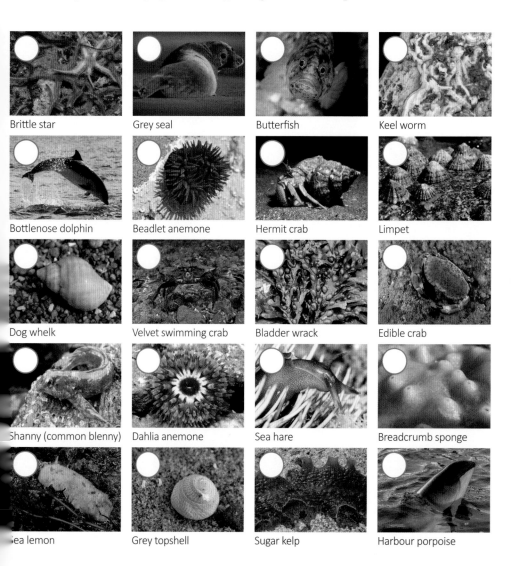

Brittle star

Grey seal

Butterfish

Keel worm

Bottlenose dolphin

Beadlet anemone

Hermit crab

Limpet

Dog whelk

Velvet swimming crab

Bladder wrack

Edible crab

Shanny (common blenny)

Dahlia anemone

Sea hare

Breadcrumb sponge

Sea lemon

Grey topshell

Sugar kelp

Harbour porpoise

Have you seen these...**minibeasts?**

We've picked out a small selection of invertebrates for you to look out for in different habitats around Yorkshire. There are, of course, many more to see! For more help with identifying them, visit **ywt.org.uk/wildlife-explorer**

Green shieldbug

Brown-lipped snail

Nursery web spider

Meadow grasshopper

Scorpion fly

Buff-tailed bumblebee

Hornet

Crane fly

Emperor dragonfly

Common cockchafer

Seven-spot ladybird

Garden spider

Pill woodlouse

Tansy beetle

Lacewing

Common froghopper

Azure damselfly

Lesser stag beetle

Early bumblebee

Glow-worm

Have you seen these...**butterflies?**

We've picked out a small selection of butterflies for you to look out for in different habitats around Yorkshire. There are, of course, many more to see! For more help with identifying them, visit **butterfly-conservation.org**

Holly blue

Speckled wood

Orange-tip

Small white

Large white

Peacock

Green-veined white

Red admiral

Brimstone

Comma

Painted lady

Ringlet

Meadow brown

Marbled white

Dingy skipper

Gatekeeper

Small tortoiseshell

White-letter hairstreak

Green hairstreak

Dark green fritillary

Photo Credits

Acknowledgements

Thank you for reading *Discover Yorkshire's Wildlife*, which was first published in 2012 and comprehensively revised in 2017.

It's amazing that we've had to fully revise and publish a third edition just six years later – a real testament to the growth of the Trust and the rapid rate of change we've achieved across the wild places in our care. With thanks to the tireless support and enthusiasm of our members, volunteers, donors, partners and staff.

Writing new and revised copy for so many nature reserves is no small task and we thank the incredibly talented Paul Brook for his expertise, and methodical and commited approach. It was a joy to bring him on board.

This book was beautifully designed and laid out thanks to Sally Gregory and Sarah Shipley, the Trust's talented creative team, whose visual flair has brought the content to life.

Pulling together the book's contents, from the overall concept to the smallest details, has been an epic labour of love, driven by the commitment and expertise of Lauren Perthen and Emma Lusby.

Huge thanks too to our reserve and regional managers for sharing their expert knowledge – built up over many years of hard outdoor graft – and their magical wildlife moments with such inspiring passion.

Special thanks to all our contributors from our wider Trust family including Professor Sir John Lawton and Professor Alastair Fitter.

Thank you to Laura Atkinson of the University of York for carrying out and meticulously managing the extensive research, and to Clea Grady for helping us with the almighty task of proofing.

We hope our words and images inspire you to plan some wild visits and enjoy the best of Yorkshire's wildlife.

Comprehensively updated by:
Paul Brook, Laura Atkinson, Emma Lusby and Lauren Perthen, 2023.

First researched, edited and written by:
Jono Leadley and Joanna Richards 2012.

Designed by:
Sally Gregory and Sarah Shipley, 2023.